A GREAT AND GLORIOUS ADVENTURE

A GREAT
AND GLORIOUS
ADVENTURE

A History of the Hundred Years War
and the Birth of Renaissance England

GORDON CORRIGAN

PEGASUS BOOKS
NEW YORK LONDON

A GREAT AND GLORIOUS ADVENTURE

Pegasus Books LLC
80 Broad Street, 5th Floor
New York, NY 10004

First Pegasus Books cloth edition 2014

ISBN: 978-1-60598-579-4

10 9 8 7 6 5 4 3 2 1

Printed in the United States of America
Distributed by W. W. Norton & Company, Inc.

CONTENTS

ILLUSTRATIONS

MAPS

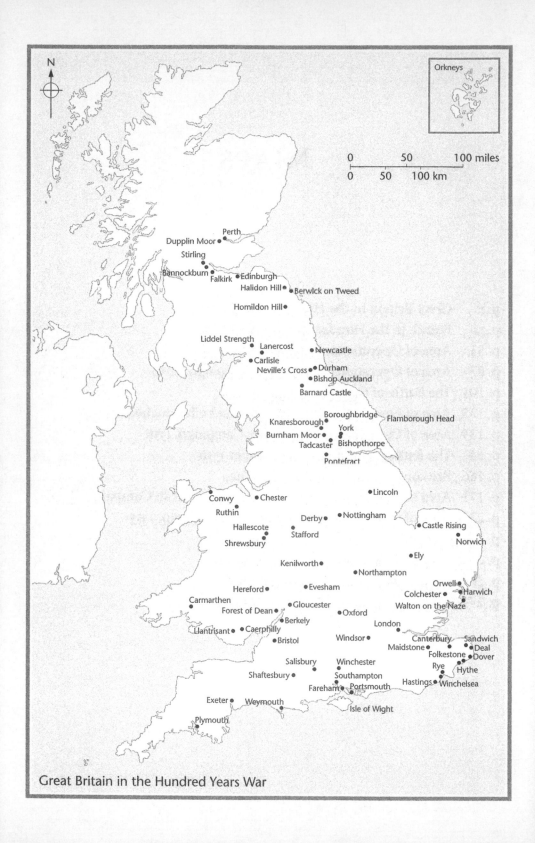

N

Orkneys

| 0 | 50 | 100 miles |
| 0 | 50 | 100 km |

Perth
Dupplin Moor
Stirling
Bannockburn
Falkirk
Edinburgh
Halidon Hill
Berwick on Tweed
Homildon Hill

Liddel Strength
Lanercost
Carlisle
Newcastle
Neville's Cross
Durham
Bishop Auckland
Barnard Castle

Boroughbridge
Flamborough Head
Knaresborough
York
Burnham Moor
Bishopthorpe
Tadcaster
Pontefract

Conwy
Chester
Lincoln
Ruthin
Derby
Nottingham
Hallescote
Castle Rising
Shrewsbury
Stafford
Norwich
Kenilworth
Ely
Northampton
Hereford
Evesham
Orwell
Colchester
Harwich
Carmarthen
Forest of Dean
Gloucester
Walton on the Naze
Berkely
Oxford
Llantrisant
Caerphilly
London
Bristol
Windsor
Canterbury
Sandwich
Maidstone
Deal
Folkestone
Dover
Salisbury
Winchester
Rye
Hythe
Shaftesbury
Southampton
Hastings
Winchelsea
Fareham
Portsmouth
Exeter
Weymouth
Plymouth
Isle of Wight

Great Britain in the Hundred Years War

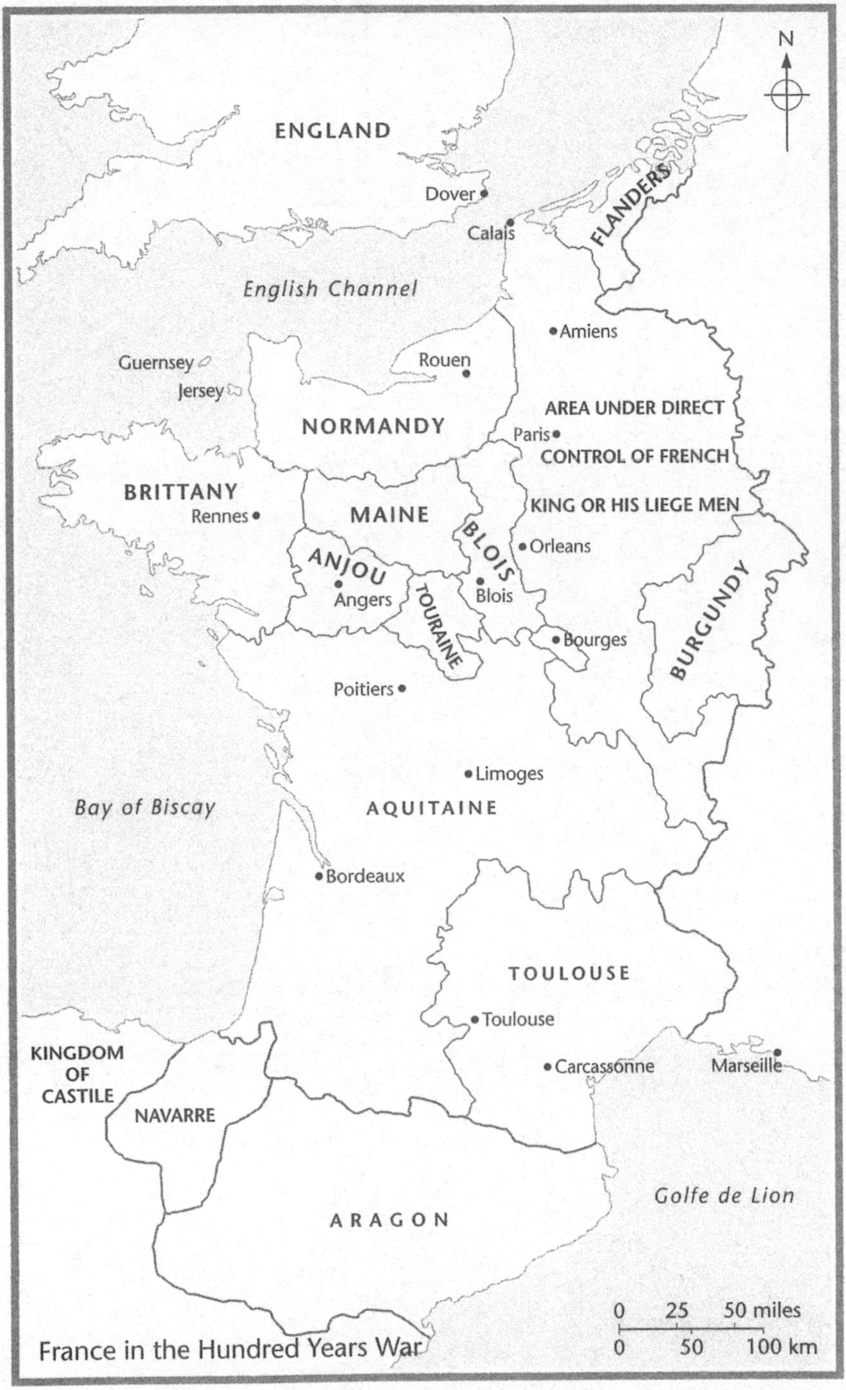
ENGLAND
Dover
Calais
FLANDERS
N
English Channel
Amiens
Guernsey
Jersey
Rouen
NORMANDY
AREA UNDER DIRECT
CONTROL OF FRENCH
KING OR HIS LIEGE MEN
Paris
BRITTANY
Rennes
MAINE
BLOIS
Orleans
ANJOU
Angers
TOURAINE
Blois
Bourges
BURGUNDY
Poitiers
Limoges
Bay of Biscay
AQUITAINE
Bordeaux
TOULOUSE
Toulouse
Carcassonne
Marseille
KINGDOM
OF
CASTILE
NAVARRE
Golfe de Lion
ARAGON
0 25 50 miles
0 50 100 km

France in the Hundred Years War

INTRODUCTION

In 1801, George III, by the Grace of God king of Great Britain, France and Ireland, dropped the English claim to the throne of France. For 460 years, since the time of the great king Edward III, all nineteen of German George's predecessors had borne the fleur-de-lys of France on the royal coat of arms along with the lions (or leopards*) of England and latterly the lion of Scotland and the Irish harp. The withdrawal of the claim, which had been prosecuted with varying degrees of enthusiasm, was purely pragmatic: France and England had been at war since 1793, and, if England opposed the French Republic and supported a restoration of the Bourbon monarchy, then she could not also claim the throne for herself. A year later, in the Treaty of Amiens, which ushered in a short break in the war with France, England recognized the French Republic, and in so doing negated her own claims. It was the end, at least in theory, of England's, and then Britain's, claim to be a European power by right of inheritance.

It was not, of course, the end of Anglo-French rivalry. For two great powers occupying opposite sides of a narrow sea, both looking outwards, both concerned with trade and trade routes, and both with imperial ambitions will inevitably clash. And if in the twenty-first century that rivalry is concerned more with the interpretation of regulations emanating from the European Union rather than the ownership of sugar

---

* Technically, the lions are *passant gardant* (walking with a paw raised) and are sometimes in English heraldry, and always in French heraldry, known as 'Leopards'.

islands, and if the weapons are words rather than swords and gunpowder, the inescapable fact is that on average England and then Britain has spent one year in every five since the Norman Conquest at war with France. One can, of course, twist statistics to suit one's purpose, but the alliances with France in both the Crimean War and the First World War, pre-Vichy France's brief participation in the Second World War, de Gaulle's Free French activities, and more recent French participation in NATO operations are very much the exception, and many old soldiers cannot forget that the armed forces of Vichy France fought British troops in the Middle East, Madagascar and North Africa between 1940 and 1943. The relationship between the Common Agricultural Policy and Crécy is not as distant as might appear, and some of the effects of that centuries-old enmity are with us still: when president of France, General Charles de Gaulle had a standing order that while travelling around the country he was never to be within thirty kilometres of Agincourt.

While the English claim to the French throne was the major cause of what came to be called the Hundred Years War, there were other factors too: the sovereignty of parts of France that had become English by inheritance, the annoying habit of the Scots to ally themselves with France, and English mercantile activities and ambitions in Flanders. It was not, of course, a sustained period of fighting, nor was it called the Hundred Years War at the time or for many years afterwards. Rather, it was a series of campaigns punctuated by truces, some of them lasting many years. And if we take the beginning of the war as Edward III's claim to the French throne in 1337, and its end as the withdrawal of all English troops from Europe except for Calais in 1453, then it lasted for rather more than a hundred years. No one who stood on the docks at Orwell and cheered as the soldiers of the first English expeditionary force of the war sailed for France under Edward III was alive to welcome the men returning from the last campaign, and anyone living at the end of the war who could remember the great battle of Agincourt would have been well into middle age. The period might more accurately be described as the series of events which transformed the English from being Anglo-French into pure Anglo. But in as much as the causes of the war and the English war aims remained more or less constant, even if alliances did not, it is reasonable – and convenient – to consider the series of struggles as one war.

It was a good time to be a soldier. If a billet under Edward III or Henry V or commanders such as Bedford or Talbot was not available because of yet another truce, then there were always the Wars of the Breton Succession, where experienced soldiers could be sure of employment. And if a warmer or more exotic clime was an attraction, then the armies of John of Gaunt and the Black Prince campaigning in Spain were always looking for good men. It was not, however, a good time to be a civilian, or at least a civilian in what is now northern France. Ever-increasing taxation to pay for the war; conscription into the armies; marauding soldiery trampling over crops; looting and plundering; atrocities by both sides; the deflowering of daughters and the commandeering of food and wine: all combined to ensure that the lot of the European commoner was not a happy one. No sooner had the rural population recovered from one period of hostilities than the whole dreadful cycle would be repeated all over again. Disease stalked medieval armies, and, if dysentery or typhus spread by the movement of troops did not bring down the hapless peasant, then a visit from the plague probably would.

The Hundred Years War was hugely significant in the political and military development of Europe, of Britain and of France. Politically, it implanted the notion of a French national identity that replaced more local loyalties – and in this sense one could argue that, for all the destruction and devastation, France came out of the war in a far better state than she entered it. The war reinforced English identity and implanted a dislike and suspicion of foreigners that have not yet entirely gone from our national psyche. Militarily, it saw a real revolution in the way of waging war, initially in England and then, belatedly and partially, in France. In England came the growth of military professionalism, with the beginnings of all the consequences that flow from having a professional – and thus expensive – army; the rejection of war as a form of knightly combat in favour of deploying trained foot-soldiers supported by a missile weapon; and the beginnings of military law and a command structure that depended more on ability than on noble birth.

To most of us, the war means three great battles – Crécy, Poitiers and Agincourt – and some of the finest prose in the English language, put into the mouth of Henry V by Shakespeare. And while Henry may not actually have said, 'Once more unto the breach, dear friends...' he will have said something, like any commander on the eve of battle, and his 1415 campaign is a study in leadership that is still relevant today. But the war was far more than three battles, and in the latter stages the English were pushed back and eventually, with the exception of Calais, abandoned Europe altogether. While the withdrawal of English troops by 1453 was as much to do with a shortage of money and political instability at home as it was with military factors, winning battles without the numbers to hold the ground thus captured could not guarantee success, and this too is a lesson as relevant now as it was then.

In this book I have tried to stick to what I know best and to look at the war from the military perspective. But no subclass of history can stand alone – social, political, economic and military history all impinge upon each other – and it is impossible to comprehend why things happened, as opposed to what happened, without understanding the way people lived at the time: their ambitions, their lifestyles and their beliefs, and the motivating factors of religion on the one hand and acquisitive greed on the other. While some medieval kings might have planned for the long term, the vast bulk of their subjects could think only of the immediate future, at least in this world: for the farmer was but one visitation of murrain from ruination, the magnate or pauper one flea jump from the Black Death.

Historians must, of course, present both sides of the argument, but they do not have to be neutral. I hope that I have treated the facts, as far as they can be determined with accuracy, as sacred, but I cannot hide my conviction that England's demands on France were lawful and justified, and, even where they were not, I feel pride in the achievements of Edward III, the Black Prince and Henry V. For all the cruelty and bloodthirstiness exhibited by many English soldiers of the time, I would far rather have marched with Henry V, Calveley, Knollys, Dagworth et al than with Bertrand du Guesclin, the best-known French commander, or Joan of Arc.

Sources for the period exist in great number, but not all are reliable, often being after-the-event propaganda, an exercise in *post hoc ergo propter hoc* logic (or lack of it) or, particularly in tapestry and painting, fanciful flights of the imagination. Battle paintings are many, some painted not long after the event, but they are sanitized and stylized, not the trampled and horse manure-covered fields of blood, gore, agony, sweat and death of unwashed, unhealthy men that a medieval battlefield must have been. Instead, we see nice neat lines of opposing soldiers, armour all brightly polished, everyone shaved, horses beautifully groomed, and always the sun shining against an impossibly blue sky. It cannot have been like that.

Whatever their limitations, original sources have to be considered, partly because their authors were there or talked to people who were there, so at least some of what they describe will have a grain, or more, of truth in it, and partly because, even if not historically accurate, they at least reflect what some people thought at the time. Jean Froissart is generally accepted as being one of the best contemporary sources for the early part of the war. A contemporary of Chaucer, Froissart was born in Valenciennes and was a minor official in the court of Edward III's queen and also in that of Richard II. He was born around 1337, so his account of the preparations for and conduct of the Crécy campaign can only have been hearsay, but for all that he did approach the happenings of his time in a manner that would stand up to at least a cursory assessment of his methodology today. He had an inside seat for much of what he describes, he interviewed people who were present where he was absent, he contrasted differing reports, and he gives due credit to other chroniclers from whose work he has borrowed. That said, there is a discernible French bias in his later writings which has to be balanced against the equally biased work of some English authors. There are numerous other reporters whose works have survived – the Paston letters are particularly valuable as a social comment on the time, albeit written rather later. The chronicles of Le Bel, Lanercost, Le Baker, Brut, Meaux, Knighton, Walsingham, Chandos and the anonymous author of the *Gesta Henrici Quinti* have also all been helpful, albeit that they are often very broad-brush indeed.

My own modern French is passable, and Norman French, the language of the English court for much of the period, is not that different. As my school Latin lessons were spent in the surreptitious study of racing form books and doodling on the corners of *Kennedy's Latin Primer*, my understanding of that tongue, the diplomatic and ecclesiastical language of the time, is rudimentary, but I had assured myself that, armed with a decent dictionary, I could cope. That pious hope was shattered when I discovered that Medieval Latin uses many abbreviations not taught to English schoolboys, but fortunately modern translations exist.

Indeed, one of the major changes that took place in England over the period was linguistic: the shift from Norman French for the rulers and Old (moving to Middle) English for the ruled, to the use of English by all. Edward III learned English as part of his education, and it was in his reign, in 1362, that the official language of the courts became English rather than Norman French. The generation of his grandsons, Richard II and Henry IV, was probably the first to use English equally with French, and, by the time Henry V came to the throne, he wrote and spoke in English by preference, as did the English nobility – a change prompted by nationalism as much as by convenience.

English itself evolved over time. The English of the middle or late 1200s would be difficult to the modern ear, as one can see from these lines, written around 1250 by Saint Godric:

Sainte Marye Virgine
Moder Jesu Christes Nazarene
Onfo, schild, help thin Godric,
Onfang, bring heyilich with thee in Godes Riche.

The reference to St Mary the Virgin, mother of Jesus Christ the Nazarene, is straightforward enough, after which we would be stumped. 'Onfo' means 'receive', 'schild' is 'defend' (modern 'shield'), 'thin' is 'your' ('thine'), hence the second line reads, 'Receive, defend and help your Godric'. In the last line, 'onfang' is the past participle of 'onfo', thus 'having received'; 'heyilich' means 'on high'; and 'Riche' means 'kingdom' (as in the German *Reich*), so the line reads: 'Having received, bring (him) on high with you in God's kingdom'.

Compare this with a similar verse written a hundred years later by Richard Rolle, concerning the holy sacrament:

Jesu, Lord, welcome thou be
In form of bred as I thee see
Jesu for thine holy name
Shild me today from sinne and shame.

Apart from the spelling, we would have little difficulty, and by the end of the war, around 1450, John Lydgate in a prayer to Mary says:

> Blessed Mary moder virginal
> Integrate maiden, sterre of the see
> Have remembraunce at the day final
> On thy poore servaunt now praying to thee.[1]

By this time, Chaucer's English was spoken by all Englishmen, and, while the accent would seem strange and we in the twenty-first century would have to listen carefully, we would understand most of what was said, even if the emphases, the intonation, the stresses, the slang and the nuances would be quite different. The spelling is of course quaint and not consistent, even in the same document, but I have found that if Middle English is read quickly, without reference to the spelling, it is relatively easily understood. The original sources for the war are therefore a mix of Norman French, French French, Latin and Middle English. Most have, of course, been translated into modern English by eminent scholars, to whom I am grateful.

If the primary sources cannot be relied upon in their entirety, particularly when it comes to the minutiae of a particular battle, then other methods must be employed. The great Colonel Alfred Burne's Theory of Inherent Military Probability may seem a little simplistic, stating as it does that, when the student of warfare has no idea what actually happened, he should put himself in the shoes of the commander at the time and decide what he would have done. In fact, an understanding of the assets available (equipment, weapon ranges, accepted tactics, methods of supply), allied to a thorough examination of the ground, can very often provide a good insight into how a particular engagement probably developed. Vital ground – that is, ground that must be taken by the attacker to achieve his aim, and ground that must be held by the defender to achieve his – is vital ground in any era, and, while marshes are drained, rivers change their courses and roads get built, the contours of the land generally do not change very much. Medieval man's brain was the same size as ours. He was just as intelligent, or unintelligent, as we are, and just as capable of producing a sound military appreciation. The Black Prince would not have been out of place in Wellington's army; John of Gaunt would have been just as capable (or incapable) of dealing with the wily Pathan (or Taliban) as he was with the obdurate Spaniard; Henry V could size up a situation just as well and probably as quickly as Bill Slim, Britain's best general of the Second World War; and Sir John Hawkwood would doubtless have made as short work of the Irish as he did of squabbling Italians. There are no new military problems: only the means to tackle them have changed.

I have used New Style dating throughout, the conversion to which can be confusing. Until 1582, England and most of Europe used the Julian calendar – the Old Style – until Pope Gregory XIII introduced the far more accurate Gregorian version – the New Style – which was Julian plus eleven days. This was duly adopted in Europe, but, as Elizabeth I's England had no intention of kow-towing to some foreigner in the Vatican, she stayed on the Julian calendar until 1752. It gets more complicated. Under both Old and New Styles the year started on Lady Day, 25 March, and did not switch to 1 January until 1752 – except in Scotland, which also retained the Julian calendar until 1752 but had switched New Year's Day to January in 1600, just to be awkward. A difference of eleven days might not matter very much, but the date on which the year begins does, and, whereas we might describe an event as happening on 20 March 1377, people who recorded it at the time or before 1752 would date the same event as happening on 9 March 1376.

It is almost impossible to translate medieval prices into their modern-day equivalent, if only because things that were expensive then are not necessarily so now, and vice versa, and occupations that today would attract a living wage (like commander of an army) might then only receive an allowance towards expenses. Even comparing like with as near as possible like does not help very much. The medieval English pound sterling was divided into twenty shillings, each shilling into twelve pennies, a system expressed in writing as £sd; this lasted until decimalization in 1971, when the same pound became 100 (new) pence, so the old shilling equated to five new pence and the penny to 0.416 new pence. We know that in the year 1400 an ounce of gold was equivalent to £0.75, while if we take the average price of gold for the five years between 2000 and 2004 inclusive, before recession began to skew the market, the same amount of gold would cost £212, giving an inflation factor of 283 (for the five years between 2006 and 2010 the factor is 722). The same exercise for silver (£0.04 an ounce then, £3.30 now) gives a factor of 82.5. If we take wages, then a foot archer under Edward III, paid three pence (3d or 1.23p) a day, earned £4.48 per year, whereas today's equivalent, the infantry private, is paid £17,500 per year, an inflation factor of 3,906. Admittedly, today's soldier has to pay for his food and accommodation, but even so the two factors are not in the least comparable. One more example: a knight banneret of Edward III's, who acted as a junior officer, was paid four shillings (£0.20) per day, £73.00 per year. A modern lieutenant earns £30,000, giving an inflation factor of 329. However, this is further complicated by a banneret's pay being twelve times that of a foot archer, whereas today's lieutenant gets but 1.7 times that of a private.

A possibly more helpful comparison could be taken from the tax rolls of 1436, where the tax was levied on all with an income of more than £20 per annum. These show that the average income of a nobleman (duke, earl or baron) was £865, that of a knight £208, of a lesser knight (possibly one risen by military service) £60, and of an esquire £24.[2] If we translate that into chief executive of a FTSE 100 company, senior fund manager, upper-middle-class professional and white-collar worker, then we might arrive at an inflation factor of 1,000. Farther down the scale, a ploughman, say, might earn £4 per year in 1436, but this figure is skewed by the effects of the Black Death, which enabled those skilled labourers who survived to put a much higher price on their services (before 1348, he might only have earned an eighth of that). In conclusion, where I have translated prices into modern values, I have used the silver standard, as that appears to have been less volatile than any other comparator. But I would accept that it is probably impossible to arrive at any overall comparison of wages and prices that is more than a very rough approximation.

In the army, any army, it is the commander who gets the acclaim when things go well, although he could not have achieved anything at all without the willing cooperation of his soldiers, the often unnamed and usually unsung heroes of any war. So it is with writing a book. The author's task is a relatively easy one, and once he has committed his scribbling to paper or disk, the real work begins: by the editor, copy-editor, graphics design team, indexer, cartographer and a whole myriad of humpers and dumpers, pushers and pullers, publicists and sales people all working towards the common goal of getting the book on the shelf. It is the author who will attend the book-signing, but he could not do it without all those people behind the scenes, and I am, as always, eternally grateful to them. My wife is also an historian, of the Anglo-Saxon and medieval persuasion, and so far our paths have not crossed: I steeped in blood and slaughter from the seventeenth to the twenty-first centuries, she in dynasties, art, society and culture from before the Conquest to Bosworth Field. In this book I have strayed into her territory, and I am grateful for her constructive comments, which have prevented me from going down divers blind alleys that would have led me to completely irrelevant conclusions. Any remaining errors are of course entirely mine.

A GREAT AND GLORIOUS ADVENTURE

From top to bottom: The coat of
arms of Edward III adopted on
claiming the French throne in 1337;
the coat of arms of King George III
prior to and after the abandonment
of the claim to the French throne
in 1801.

1

WHERE IT ALL BEGAN

The English ownership of lands in what is now France began with Stamping Billy, William the Conqueror, duke of Normandy and king of England, whose claim to the English throne by inheritance may have been thin – he was a distant cousin of Edward the Confessor – but was a lot stronger than that of Harold Godwinson, who had no blood claim at all but was merely a brother-in-law of the late king. William the Norman's conquest of England was a lot easier than he may have expected: in one great battle, Hastings in 1066, Harold was killed and with him died Anglo-Saxon England. William was faced with opposition all over the country, particularly in the north and in East Anglia, but all these revolts were local and uncoordinated, and William was able to put them down, stripping the ringleaders of their lands and awarding them to his Norman vassals. By the 1070s, the old English aristocracy had been virtually wiped out, English churchmen were being replaced by Normans, castles had been built all over the country and, secure within their walls, French-speaking Normans ruled over Old English-speaking Saxons. By the time of the completion of the Domesday Book in 1086,* only two Anglo-Saxons are named as having holdings of any significance. It was the greatest upheaval in English society, law and religion since the Roman withdrawal.

Now the ruling classes held lands on both sides of the Channel, which was fine as long as their feudal overlord was the same person in England as he was in Normandy, as was the case until William I's death in 1087. Then his

---

* The word comes from Old English and means reckoning or accounting day; the day when who owes what in taxes is reckoned.

eldest son Robert became duke of Normandy, while his third son – the second had been killed in a hunting accident – became king of England as William II.* Now the great magnates had a problem, for when William and Robert were opposed, as they often were, cleaving to one lord meant alienating the other, a situation not resolved until Robert went crusading financed by money advanced by William against the stewardship of Normandy. William Rufus never married and nowhere in the chronicles is there any mention of mistresses or bastard children, but by the time he died in 1100, to be succeeded by his brother, the Conqueror's fourth son, Henry I, he had added Maine and much of the Vexin – that area between Rouen and Paris – to his territories.†

Henry was no great soldier, but he did manage to take Normandy from his brother Robert, now returned from crusade, and he did manage to govern England and Normandy for thirty-five years, avoiding revolt by a judicious mixture of terror, reward and shrewd financial management. Although Henry had numerous illegitimate children, he failed to produce a male heir to survive him,‡ and attempts to persuade the barons to accept his daughter Matilda as his successor as queen regnant failed spectacularly. The great men of the kingdom might have accepted Matilda, who was the widow of the Holy Roman Emperor and hence usually referred to as 'the Empress', but they were not going to accept her second husband, Geoffrey of Anjou. Instead, they awarded the throne to Stephen of Blois, duke of Normandy, a nephew of Henry I and grandson of the Conqueror through his daughter Adela – and confusingly also married to a Matilda, this time of Boulogne. The result was a prolonged period of instability and civil war, only resolved when it was agreed in the Treaty of Westminster in 1153 that Stephen should be succeeded on his death by Henry, the son of the empress Matilda and Geoffrey of Anjou.

---

* Called Rufus either because of red hair or a ruddy countenance – we do not know.
† William's death was probably a genuine accident, killed by an arrow while out hunting. Conspiracy theories then and now that allege an assassination plot involving William's brother Henry (who succeeded to the throne) and William's attendant, the courtier Walter Tirel or Tyrrel, count of Poix, are not supported by the evidence.
‡ His legitimate son and heir apparent, William, was drowned in 1120 when the ship on which he was travelling back to England – the 'white ship' – hit a rock and sank in the Channel off Normandy. Theories about the cause at the time ranged from drunkenness among the crew and passengers (possible) to the entire crew being homosexuals (unlikely). The truth almost certainly is that the Channel was, and still is, an extremely dangerous stretch of water.

Henry II came to the English throne in 1154 and is mostly remembered for his disputes with Thomas Becket, one-time chancellor of England and subsequently archbishop of Canterbury. These disputes included the question of 'criminous clerks', or persons in holy orders who committed civil offences and could only be tried by an ecclesiastical court which could not impose the death penalty (Henry thought they should be defrocked and handed over for trial by the civil administration); the appointment of bishops; Becket's feudal duty to provide men-at-arms or cash in lieu for the king's military adventures; and Becket's objections to the crowning of Henry's son and heir, also a Henry, during his father's lifetime, the only such occurrence in English history. Although Becket may well have deserved all he got, and certainly seems to have gone out of his way to provoke his own assassination, it was probably not at the king's instigation but due to the killers' misunderstanding of the latter's wishes – although to this day Canterbury Cathedral continues to attract tourists happy to view the site of the murder.

Henry was, in fact, already enormously rich and a great landowner when he came to the throne. Duke of Normandy from 1150 and count of Anjou from his father's death in 1151, he married in 1152 the fabulously wealthy Eleanor, duchess of Aquitaine and countess of Poitiers, who had inherited both lands and titles in her own right from her father, who had no sons. Eleanor had married the future king Louis VII of France when she was fifteen, but after fifteen years the marriage was annulled on the grounds of consanguinity, although the real reason was presumably because she had produced only two daughters and no sons.* Henry married her a mere two months after the annulment, which cannot have pleased the king of France, who nevertheless must have considered the chances of remarrying and bearing sons worth the loss of Aquitaine and Poitiers to the English.†

---

* There are many societies which did or do regard the failure to produce sons as grounds for dissolution of a marriage. The production of daughters rather than sons is, of course, a factor more of the male sperm than of the female ovum.

† Much confusion is caused to those not familiar with medieval European geography by reference to Aquitaine, Guienne and Gascony. Aquitaine, with its capital of Bordeaux, consisted of an old, smaller county of that name plus Gascony, while Guienne was simply the French name for Aquitaine. This book will refer to Aquitaine except where the person referred to is a native of the original Gascony, in which case he is a Gascon. Reference is also made to the county of Agenais, which was part of Aquitaine and the strip between the Garonne and Dordogne rivers.

By the time of Henry II's death in 1189, he had added Brittany to Normandy and Aquitaine as his domains in France, was the accepted overlord of Scotland and Ireland, and ruled a vast area of lands that stretched from John O'Groats to the Pyrenees. France was little more than the area around what is now the Île-de-France, with the virtually independent duchies of Burgundy to the south and Artois to the north. Henry said himself that he ruled by 'force of will and hard riding', for in an age without instant communications and mass media, medieval kings had to be seen and had to move around their lands to enforce the law and keep over-mighty subjects in check. In the thirty-five years of his reign, Henry spent twenty-one of them in his continental possessions, for it was there that he was threatened, rather than in a united England which was now mainly a source of revenue. A mere twenty years later, nearly all of Henry's empire would be lost, and it was the memory of that empire that would provide one of the provocations for the Hundred Years War.

Henry II's intention was that his eldest son, also Henry, would become king of England, while his second surviving son, Richard, would inherit his mother's lands and titles in Aquitaine and Poitiers. When Prince Henry died in 1183, the king assumed that, as Richard was now the heir apparent, Aquitaine would pass to his third son, John. But Richard, having learnt his trade as a soldier subduing rebellious barons there, had no intention of giving up Aquitaine, and family quarrels, culminating in an invasion of England by Richard supported by the French king, Philip II, in 1189, forced Henry to make a humiliating peace shortly before he died, to be succeeded as king by the thirty-two-year-old Richard.

Every little boy playing with his wooden sword storming imaginary castles sees himself as Richard the Lionheart, the great warrior king of England and chivalrous knight par excellence. His slaughter of prisoners taken at Acre in 1191 did not detract from the contemporary view of him as the epitome of knightly conduct – after all, the prisoners were not Christians. Certainly, Richard was personally brave and a competent general, well educated by the standards of the time, a patron of the arts and especially of musicians, and a reasonable composer and singer of songs himself. He spent little time in England, however, concentrating on putting down rebellion – including that of his brother John – and embarking on a crusade which, while it failed to capture Jerusalem, did take the whole of the coastal strip from Tyre in Lebanon to Jaffa (in modern Israel) and captured Cyprus, which was to prove very useful as a mounting base for military operations both then and since.* Coming back from his crusade, he was captured by Duke Leopold of Austria, sold on to the Holy Roman Emperor, and held prisoner for a year while a 'king's ransom' of 100,000 marks was raised to free him. A mark was eight ounces of silver, so the ransom was roughly equivalent to around £2.6 million today (using the silver standard), raised in the main by a 25 per cent tax on all rents and on the value of all moveable property, both in England and in Normandy – and that from a total population of around three million.

Richard showed little interest in the administration of his empire, but was fortunate in his choice of men to run it for him, particularly in Hubert Walter, King's Justiciar and archbishop of Canterbury, who was not only a thorough and highly competent administrator but, unusually for the time, no more than moderately corrupt. Walter had accompanied the crusading army to Acre when bishop of Salisbury and found conditions in the camp of the army execrable, with a complete lack of sanitation and a breakdown in the commissariat leading to soldiers and officers dying of disease or starvation. He swiftly got a grip of the situation, organized a proper administrative machinery to provide rations and clean water, and insisted on such measures as dug latrines and the prevention of the pollution of wells, paying for sentries on water sources out of his own pocket. When King Richard arrived at Acre, the morale and efficiency of the army had improved markedly, and Walter was marked out in the king's eyes as a man who could get things done.

During Richard's absence on crusade and then in prison, the French had made considerable inroads into the English domains on the continent, and from 1194 Richard spent most of his time in Europe recovering the lost lands and castles, and building new defence works – notably Château Gaillard, which still looms 300 feet above the River Seine – to protect them. Then, at a militarily insignificant skirmish at Châlus, twenty miles southwest of Limoges, Richard sustained a wound from a crossbow bolt which went septic and from which he died on 6 April 1199, aged forty-two. As his

---

* Which is why the United Kingdom, when granting Cyprus independence in 1960, retained and still retains two military bases as sovereign British territory on the island.

marriage to Berengaria of Navarre was childless, he was succeeded by his brother John.

John has not been treated kindly by history, but it is difficult to see how this could have been otherwise: he was a younger son who rebelled against his father; sided with the French in an invasion of England; was a spectacular failure as governor of Ireland, where he managed to alienate both the native Irish and the Anglo-Norman lords who were carving out lands for themselves in England's Wild West; attempted to usurp his brother's throne; and spent a large part of his reign in opposition to his barons. His succession was accepted in England and Normandy, but not in Anjou, Maine or Touraine, where the local lords announced that they recognized John's nephew, Arthur, duke of Brittany, as their overlord. As Arthur was twelve years old in 1199, he would be unlikely to interfere with the magnates' governance of their fiefs as they wished, and, as the only legitimate grandson of Henry II in the male line, he was inevitably going to find himself cast as a pawn. He had been a ward of Richard I's, had spent time at the French court, and had done homage to the French king, and to John, for Anjou, Maine and Brittany.

Then, in what seemed a shrewd and advantageous move, John put aside his first wife, Isabella of Gloucester, and married another Isabella, this time of Angoulême.* The second Isabella had lands that lay between Normandy and Aquitaine which would be a useful addition to English France. There was, however, a snag. The lady had previously been engaged to marry one Hugh of Lusignan, who objected to being deprived of his fiancée (and, presumably, of the lands that she would bring with her) and appealed to King Philip of France. Philip, seizing the chance to discommode the English king, summoned John to appear before him, and, when John refused, in April 1200 he declared all John's continental fiefs forfeit.

In what was to be his only successful military campaign, John recovered the disputed territories and captured Arthur. The young duke disappeared into an English prison in Falaise, may or may not have been mutilated on the orders of John, was transferred to Rouen, and was never seen again, although the legends vary: some say he was killed by John personally and

---

* Like her namesake, the queen of Edward II over a century later, Isabella was reputed to take lovers. It is said that John had them hanged from the frame of her four-poster bed.

his body thrown in the Seine, others that he escaped and stood ready to reappear in Brittany when the time was ripe. This, anyway, was John's last chance to retain his lands in France, for in 1204 the French king declared the dukedom of Normandy forfeit and subsumed into the crown lands of France, the exception being the Channel Islands, which remain British to this day.*

The tide of war now turned against the English and John lost all his French territories except Poitou – and that was on the verge of surrender, only rescued by an expedition in 1206. From now on, John – his nickname now 'Softsword' because of his military reverses rather than 'Lackland' from his lack of patrimony as a younger son – put all his energies into raising the wherewithal to recover his lost lands. This meant that he spent longer in England than any previous ruler since the Norman Conquest, and also meant increased and increasing taxation, leading to more trouble with his barons, a breakdown in relations between church and state, a papal interdict on England and the excommunication of John personally,† civil war, the signing of Magna Carta,‡ invasion and civil war again.

When John died in 1216, his infant son, Henry III, inherited a kingdom divided by war, with rebellious barons in the north and the French dauphin – later Louis VIII of France, who had landed in England in May 1216 and was touted by some as king rather than John – in the south. History has been harsh to Henry III too, but with rather less cause than to his father. Fortunately, with the death of John, much of the impetus of the barons' revolt was defused, and Louis was viewed as a foreign usurper rather than as an alternative king. There were sufficient good men in the Midlands to back young Henry, and, after the Battle of Lincoln and a sea battle off

---

* The Channel Islands are not part of the United Kingdom but a crown dependency. The loyal toast is 'The Duke of Normandy – our Queen'.

† The interdict meant that no 'sacrament' could be carried out – baptism, confirmation, mass, confession, ordination of clergy, marriage and the last rites for the dying – nor could any burial be carried out in consecrated ground. It seems to have had not the slightest effect on the people generally nor on John, who retaliated by confiscating the church estates.

‡ Much trumpeted as the foundation stone of British democracy, it was in fact a critique of what the barons saw as the evils of John's rule. No sooner had he signed it than he was seeking ways to circumvent it, and it was never fully implemented. It was last cited as a legal authority in England in *Joyce* v *DPP* Court of Appeal [1946].

Sandwich in 1217, the French claimant withdrew, helped on his way by a hefty bribe.

Like his father, Henry tried to rule as an autocrat and, like his father, he fell out with his magnates as a result. He had, however, the sense to realize that he could not rule alone, and, by accepting his father's Magna Carta and, albeit under pressure, dismissing the large number of grasping relations of his French wife who had flocked to England to make their fortune now that the Holy Land, reconquered by the Muslims, was no longer an option, he was able to avoid being deposed. He too was no soldier, and in the Treaty of Paris in 1259 he gave up his claim to Normandy, Anjou and Maine and retained only Aquitaine, but as a vassal of the French king to whom he had to pay homage. Despite all this, he remained king for fifty-six years. Although the latter stages of his reign were again marred by rebellion and civil war, he did greatly improve the administrative machinery of government as well as promote Gothic architecture – his greatest artistic endeavour being the building of Westminster Abbey as a shrine to Edward the Confessor – and he did leave behind him a reasonably contented and more or less united kingdom, and an adult son who would begin to establish the military basis for a recovery of England's lost territories.

Historical revisionism is not confined to the wars of the twentieth century, and Edward I has come in for a good deal of it from some modern writers. On the positive side, all agree that he was tall, athletic and handsome, a good soldier and genuinely in love with his wife, Eleanor of Castile, which was unusual when royal marriages were contracted for political and dynastic reasons regardless of the personal preferences of the individuals involved. To his detriment, he took up arms against his father during the civil wars with the barons, changed sides at least twice, and was accused of breaking solemn promises and – even after having returned to his allegiance and when in command of the royalist forces at the Battle of Evesham in 1265 – of duplicity in the cornering of the rebel army and the death of their leader, Simon de Montfort, eighth earl of Leicester. This latter charge refers to Edward's flying the banners of captured nobles either to give the impression that they had changed sides or to convince de Montfort that his rebel troops had the royalists surrounded. That would seem a perfectly legitimate *ruse de guerre*, although the behaviour of another turncoat, Roger Mortimer, who is alleged to have killed de Montfort, cut off his head and genitals, and then sent the package to his own wife as a souvenir, would have been regarded as bad form even then.* Mortimer also killed a senior rebel commander, Sir Hugh Despenser, at the same battle, a matter that would resurface half a century later. Additionally, Edward had a vile temper, expelled the Jews from England in 1290 and profited thereby, and dealt with any opposition from the pope by fining his representatives in England.

Most of the criticism of Edward relates to his time as the heir, and contemporary chroniclers are less strident when writing about his reign as king – but then denigrating a prince is one thing, opposing an anointed king quite another. The probable truth is that Edward was no more self-seeking and avaricious than any other great lord of the time, and less than many. In the West of the early twenty-first century, we like to think that personal integrity and unselfishness are vital in the conduct of our daily lives, and most of us would put, or at least try to put, country and the common good before self. But this is not the norm in today's Third World, and it was not the norm in the medieval world. Then it would have seemed very odd indeed not to put the interests of one's own family before all else. We should beware of judging the past by the standards of the present.

One of Edward's first acts as king was to set up a commission to enquire into the very abuses that had precipitated civil war in his father's time, and he was assiduous in exposing and punishing corruption and misuse of office, provided that it was not his own. As many of the magnates claimed rights and privileges on the grounds that they had held them 'since time immemorial', Edward defined this as prior to the accession of Richard I in 1189. Thus, any claim less than eighty-five years old had to be proved by hard evidence, including the relevant documents, and even then was unlikely to be accepted. The administration of the realm was overhauled and an unprecedented flurry of legislation dealt with such matters as land tenure, debt collection, feudal overlordship, ecclesiastical jurisdiction, landlord and tenant relations, grants to the church and family settlements. The criminal law too was brought up to date and the statute

---

* Perhaps inevitably, considering de Montfort's claim to be fighting to obtain 'justice for all', by which he meant 'advantage to me and my friends', a cult around him rapidly grew up with miracles and apparitions aplenty. There is even a De Montfort University, whose antiquity dates back to 1993.

of Winchester of 1285 insisted upon the community's responsibility to lodge accusations of criminal conduct, ordered the roads to be improved and the undergrowth cut back to prevent ambushes by robbers, laid down what weapons were to be held by which classes to ensure the security of the kingdom, and made rape an offence for the king's justice rather than a local matter.

It is as a soldier and a castle builder that Edward is best remembered, and the early years of his reign saw the subjection of Wales and the virtual destruction of the Welsh nobility. While contemporary English propaganda may have exaggerated, accusing the Welsh of sexual licence, robbery, brigandage, murder, every crime on the statute book and many not yet thought of, the Welsh princes had neither the administrative machinery nor the legal system to govern the country, and Edward's campaigns of 1276 to 1284 brought the rule of (English) law and good (or at least better) government to a backward people. Edward's announcement that the Welsh wanted a prince and that he would give them one in his eldest son displayed to the people on a shield is, of course, pure myth, although he did bestow the title of Prince of Wales on his heir. However brutal and legally dubious Edward's subjugation of Wales may have been, modern Welsh nationalism has fed on a spurious legend of great warriors and an incorruptible native aristocracy that never existed. Then, in 1294, Edward's fifty-fourth year and the twenty-second of his reign, came war with France resulting from Philip IV's attempt to confiscate Aquitaine, simultaneous with a rising in Wales, and then a revolt in Scotland in 1297.

The preparations for the French war exposed the cracks in the feudal system of military service, which would linger on until the time of Edward III and briefly resurface under Richard II. Under it, the king had the right to summon those who held lands from him to give him military service for a specific period, usually forty days, although it could be extended, and these nobles with their retainers were supported by a militia of the common people, who again could only be compelled to serve for a specific period. Wars were expensive: the troops had to be fed, housed, transported and in some cases paid and armed. There was no permanent commissariat, and carts and horses and the supplies that they carried had to be bought or hired. It was generally accepted that the king could not finance a campaign of any length from his own income, and taxes and customs dues were usually agreed by an assembly of the great men of the realm, now increasingly being referred to as the parliament. Initially, such taxes were freely voted, but then, as Edward needed more and more money and more and more men to reinforce his garrison in Aquitaine, he began to take short cuts. Taxes were announced without consulting the parliament; the dean of St Paul's is said to have died of apoplexy on hearing that the levy on the clergy was to be half of their assessed incomes; merchants took grave exception to the compulsory purchase of wool at less than market price, which the king then intended to sell abroad at a large profit. Royal agents who collected taxes and scoured the country for supplies and grain were said to be accepting bribes for exempting some men and to be keeping a portion of what they collected for themselves. Many magnates summoned for military service refused to go: when Edward told the earl of Norfolk that he had better go to Aquitaine or hang, he replied, correctly as it happened, that he would neither go nor hang. By the time that Edward decided to take the field himself and sailed for Flanders in August 1297, the country was on the brink of civil war and there were those who feared a repetition of the barons' wars of Edward's father and grandfather. What saved him was a rising in Scotland.

The Scottish problem was not new, but, up to the death of the Scots' king Alexander III in a riding accident in 1286, relations had been reasonably cordial. William the Lion of Scotland had done homage to Henry II, and it was generally accepted that the English king was the overlord of Scotland, albeit that he was not expected to interfere in its administration. Alexander left no male heirs and his nearest relative was his six-year-old granddaughter, whose father was King Eric of Norway. Edward of England's plan, which might have saved much subsequent Anglo-Scottish enmity, was to marry the 'Maid of Norway' to his eldest son, Edward of Caernarvon, later Edward II, but, when the maid died in the Orkneys on her way to Scotland in 1290, the inevitable rival claimants appeared from all corners of the country. Civil war was avoided by the bishop of St Andrews asking Edward I to mediate between the starters, soon reduced to two: Robert Bruce (originally de Brus) and John Balliol, both descendants of Normans and owning lands on both sides of the border – Balliol rather more than Bruce. By a process that came to be known as the 'Great Cause', which appears at this distance to have been reasonably fair and legally correct, Edward found in favour of Balliol, who was duly crowned in 1292.

At this point, Edward attempted to extend his influence into Scotland as he had in Wales, and his overturning of decisions of the Scottish courts and attempts to enforce feudal military service from Scottish nobles, which Balliol did little to resist, led to a council of Scottish lords taking over the government from Balliol in 1295 and making a treaty of friendship with Philip IV of France. This could never be acceptable to England, with the threat of war on two fronts, and in a lightning and exceedingly brutal campaign in 1296 Edward destroyed the Scottish armies and accepted the unconditional surrender of the Scottish leaders including Balliol. Had Edward reinstalled Balliol and backed off from insisting on what he saw as his feudal rights, all might have been well, but, by imposing English rule under a viceroy, Earl Warenne, with English governors in each district and English prelates being appointed to vacant Scottish livings, and by adding insult to defeat by removing the Stone of Scone, on which Scottish kings were crowned, to England,* he ensured revolt was inevitable. It duly broke out in 1297 as Edward arrived in Flanders to intervene personally in the war against the French.

Almost immediately, all the resentment that had been building up against Edward for his unjust methods of financing the French campaign dissipated. War abroad against the French was one thing but revolt by what most English lords saw as English subjects was quite another. Robert Bruce, previously a loyal subject of Edward but dismayed by the failure to grant the throne to him, was easily dealt with by Warenne, but then a massacre of an overconfident English army at Stirling Bridge in an ambush skilfully conducted by William Wallace in September 1297 outraged and frightened the English government.†

---

* Placed under the coronation chair in Westminster Abbey, it has been part of the coronation of every English and British monarch since, including that of our present queen. It was returned to Scotland in 1996 but will be brought back to London for future coronations.
† According to the Chronicle of Lanercost, William Wallace had a sword belt made from the flayed skin of Hugh de Cressingham, the treasurer of England, killed at the battle. As leather made from human skin is far too frail to hold the weight of a sword, this seems unlikely.

Edward came to terms with Philip IV, returned from Flanders, and at the Battle of Falkirk in July 1298 slaughtered Wallace's Scottish army. It was the bloodiest battle on British soil until Towton in 1461 but it was not decisive. Although the Scots would not for a long time risk meeting an English army in open field, their hit-and-run tactics would drag the conflict on until 1304, when the majority of the Scottish leaders came to terms with Edward. Wallace himself was tried as a traitor and suffered the prescribed punishment: hanged until nearly dead, then disembowelled and castrated, and his intestines and genitalia burned in front of him before he was decapitated and his body divided into four parts, a quarter to be exhibited in different cities while the head was placed on a pike above Tower Bridge.

The respite only proved temporary, however. Robert Bruce, who had initially revolted in 1297 but then changed sides and supported Edward's subsequent campaigning, led another rising in 1306 and, having eliminated another claimant to the throne by murdering him, had himself crowned as king. More battles followed, and when Edward I died on his way to Scotland in 1307, exhorting his son on his deathbed to continue his conquest of the northern kingdom, the horrendous costs of warfare were revealed in the crown's debts of £200,000, or £124 million at today's prices.*

If Edward I has been subject to historical revisionism, then none is necessary for his son. Edward II was every bit as unpleasant and incompetent as the chroniclers claim. Although he inherited his father's commanding height and good looks and was a competent horseman, he had little interest in the other knightly virtues and corrupted the system of royal patronage. This latter depended for its success on the wide and reasonably fair distribution of land, offices and titles, thus retaining the loyalty of those who mattered, but Edward neglected the magnates who expected to be preferred and instead lavished favours and lands on his successive catamites.

Homosexuality was then a sin in the eyes of the church – it was equated with heresy – and generally regarded with horror by the laity. Still, Edward's proclivities might have been tolerated if he had kept them as

---

* The £ sterling was then worth twenty-four grams of gold, which at 2010 values is £619.20, or by the silver standard £82.50.

private as it was possible to be in a medieval court, but this he was unable to do. Some modern scholarship has suggested that Edward's relationships were not sexual but actually a form of blood brotherhood, and it points to the fact that accusations of homosexuality against Edward were only hinted at during his lifetime and not made openly until after his death. Edward and both his favourites were married and produced children, but all three had to produce heirs and anyway it is not uncommon for homosexuals to engage in occasional heterosexual relationships. While at the time it was not unusual for men to share a bed without any impropriety (indeed, soldiers in British army barrack rooms were required to sleep two or three to a bed until well into the nineteenth century), it was certainly unusual that Edward chose to sleep with a man rather than his wife on the night of his coronation. That the magnates had their doubts about Edward from a very early stage is evidenced by their insertion of a new clause in the coronation oath, whereby he swore to uphold 'the laws and customs of the realm'.

Edward's first favourite, who had been part of his household since he was Prince of Wales, was Piers Gaveston, a Gascon knight and son of a loyal servant and soldier of Edward I. Knighted by Edward I and then advanced by Edward II to the earldom of Cornwall (a title normally reserved for princes of the blood royal), Gaveston was intelligent, good-looking, a competent administrator and excelled at the knightly pastimes of hunting and jousting. All might have been well if he could only have restrained his wit and avoided poking fun at the great men of the kingdom. Had he deferred to the nobility and worked at showing them that he was no threat (and he appears to have had no political ambitions), he might well occupy no more than a brief footnote in history, but, as it was, he could not resist teasing the magnates, to whom he gave offensive and often apt nicknames of which he made no secret. Thus, the amply proportioned earl of Lincoln was 'burst belly'; the earl of Pembroke 'Joseph the Jew'; the earl of Lancaster, the king's cousin, the richest man in the kingdom and the proprietor of a large private army, 'the fiddler'; and the earl of Warwick, who would ultimately be responsible for Gaveston's premature demise, 'the black dog of Arden'.

Not only did Gaveston make no secret of his deriding the great men, but he also publicly humiliated them by beating them in jousts and took a prominent role in the coronation that should have been filled by men of far higher status. Gaveston married the king's niece, a union to which his birth did not entitle him, and, when Edward went to France to collect his own bride, he left Gaveston as regent. By his behaviour and by his position as the king's principal adviser, Gaveston was bound to make dangerous enemies: he was exiled once by Edward I and twice by Edward II under pressure from the magnates, who threatened civil war if the favourite did not go. Then, in 1312, Gaveston's return from exile for the third time did spark baronial revolt. He eventually fell into the hands of his enemies, principally the earl of Warwick, and, after a trial which was probably illegal, he was condemned to death and beheaded near Kennilworth on land belonging to the earl of Lancaster. As was the norm at the time, no one actually blamed the king for all the injustices and inefficiencies of his reign, but rather his evil counsellor – Gaveston – and Edward was then in no position to do anything about what he saw as the murder of his beloved Pierrot. Revenge was to come later.

Despite the removal of Gaveston, by 1314, baronial opposition to Edward's rule, or misrule, was growing. Having ignored his father's dying wish that he should complete the conquest of Scotland, Edward II had abandoned that nation to civil war and returned south. Now, hoping to restore the political situation at home by a successful war in Scotland, Edward summoned the earls to report for military service. The earl of Lancaster and a number of his supporters refused, on the grounds that Parliament had not approved the finance for the expedition, which was therefore illegal. Edward went ahead anyway and the result was a disaster when, at Bannockburn in June 1314, his army of around 10,000 was decisively defeated by a much smaller Scottish army commanded by Robert Bruce. Edward fled the field (to be fair, he wanted to stand and fight but his minders would not have it) and his army collapsed with perhaps a third becoming casualties. Disaster though it undoubtedly was for Edward, the battle was the trigger for a root-and-branch reform of the English military system which, as we shall see, would contribute much to the superiority of English arms in the Hundred Years War.

As the Scottish war dragged on without any prospect of a successful end, Edward's position weakened further. Scottish raids into northern England were increasingly ambitious, Berwick-upon-Tweed was under siege yet again,* and there was revolt in Wales. To make matters worse, new favourites began increasingly to engage Edward's attention and to receive favours from him. The Despensers, father and son, both named Hugh, were rather better bred than Gaveston had been, but were actually more of a threat, being even more avaricious than the previous royal pet and, in the case of Hugh the Younger, possessing both political ambitions and the ability to pursue them. There is less evidence for a homosexual relationship between Edward and Hugh the Younger than for one with Gaveston, but there can be little doubt that the friendship was rather more than just the comradeship of men both in their thirties.

As it was, the Despensers' methods of increasing their holdings of land varied from blackmail and intimidation of the courts to the threat and sometimes use of force and outright theft. In this, they particularly upset the Marcher Lords, who found estates in Wales and on the border that should have gone to them being acquired by the Despensers, while early on Hugh the Younger upset the earl of Lancaster when he was granted a potentially lucrative wardship which Lancaster had attempted to obtain for himself. Antagonism towards the Despensers exploded in 1321 when the Marcher Lords, aided by Lancaster and including one Roger Mortimer, attacked Despenser lands and properties. In Parliament in London, the lords laid the usual charges: removal of competent officials by the Despensers and their replacement by corrupt ones; refusing access to the king unless one of them was present; misappropriating properties; and generally giving the king bad advice. Edward, backed into a corner and faced with the united opposition of so many, had little choice but to agree to Parliament's demands and the Despensers were duly exiled.

Now began Edward's only successful military campaign of his entire reign. Lancaster, for all his titles and riches, was not a natural leader, a competent general or politically astute; he was indecisive and he too had his enemies. Once away from the London parliament, Edward recalled the Despensers, besieged and took Leeds Castle in Kent, executed the commander and his garrison, and marched north. Lancaster too moved

---

* Described by Robbie Burns as 'A bridge without a middle arch, a church without a steeple, a midden heap in every street, and damned conceited people', Berwick changed hands between England and Scotland thirteen times between the eleventh and fifteenth centuries.

north, possibly to seek sanctuary with the Scots, and on 16 March 1322 found his way barred by a royalist army at Boroughbridge, which held the only bridge over the River Ure. Unable to force the bridge, the earl of Hereford being killed in the attempt, and prevented by royalist archers from crossing at a nearby ford – lessons that would also be relevant to the great war that was to come – Lancaster's army melted away and the earl himself surrendered the next day. Tried as a traitor at Pontefract, Lancaster could have expected to have been pardoned with a fine or exiled at worst in deference to his royal blood (he was a grandson of Henry III), but now it was payback time for Gaveston, and the only concession to Lancaster was that he was beheaded rather than hanged, drawn and quartered.* Despite Lancaster's unpleasant traits, such was the unpopularity of the king and the Despensers that a cult rapidly grew up and royal guards had to be posted over Lancaster's tomb to prevent miracle-seekers approaching it. Now that he had dealt with Lancaster, Edward's revenge on the other rebels was bloody: eleven barons and fifteen knights were indeed drawn, hanged and quartered, four Kentish knights were drawn and hanged but not quartered, in Canterbury, and another in London, while seventy-two knights were imprisoned. From now until 1326, the Despensers' power, wealth and influence increased: their mistake, and the cause of their ultimate downfall, was in attracting the opposition of the queen.

Philip IV of France, known as 'the Fair' for his good looks, had three sons out of his wife Joan of Champagne before she gave birth to a daughter, Isabella, in 1295. As part of Edward I's search for a solution to the vexed question of Aquitaine, he married the French king's sister, Margaret, in 1299, his first wife having died in 1290, and had his eldest surviving son, the future Edward II, betrothed to Isabella. Their wedding took place in Boulogne in 1308, the year after Edward II became king, when he was twenty-four and his bride not yet thirteen. The earliest age permitted by the church for a girl to have sex in marriage was twelve, but practicalities ruled that she must have passed puberty. We do not know whether Isabella had passed that point at the time of their marriage – and if she had not, then there might be a charitable explanation for the non-consummation

---

* The term really should be 'drawn [tied to a hurdle dragged by a horse to the place of execution], hanged and quartered'.

of the marriage – but contemporary chronicles all describe her as being beautiful, so, if she was not yet physically capable of sexual intercourse, we may assume that she was within the next year or so. In any event, she did not conceive until 1312, when she was rising seventeen, which would indicate that Edward visited her bed but rarely. He did fulfil his dynastic duty, however, perhaps without much enthusiasm, and Isabella gave birth to the future Edward III in 1312, a second son, John, in 1316, and daughters Eleanor in 1318 and Joan in 1321.

Isabella must have felt humiliated and embarrassed by her husband's obvious preference for Gaveston over herself, particularly when she found Gaveston wearing the jewels given to Edward by her father, the French king, as wedding presents, and, worse, some of her own jewellery that had come over to England as part of her train. In spite of this, she seems to have done her best to support and help the king, albeit complaining to her father that she was kept short of money and that Gaveston was preferred over her.

Since the eighteenth century, Queen Isabella has been described as the 'she-wolf of France'. Reviled as a notorious adulteress, a rebel against her husband and an accomplice in his murder, only recently has she been reassessed, at least by some, as a tragic queen. Isabella certainly had much to contend with, and for most of her marriage to Edward II she was a loyal and supportive wife. She accompanied her husband on military campaigns (campaigns which almost always had disastrous results), and on several occasions she was entrusted with the Great Seal of England; she was literate and, with maturity, certainly capable of understanding the political nuances, both domestic and international, of her time. As the daughter of the king of France, and after the death of Philip in 1314, the sister of his successor Louis X, she was well aware of her status and determined to maintain it in the face of her husband's frequent neglect and casual cruelty.

Isabella's discovery of adulterous relationships involving the wives of two of her brothers with the connivance of the wife of a third and her eventual reporting of it to her father, Philip, in full knowledge of what the result might be, have been cited as evidence of a hard-heartedness in her character, but it is far more likely that she knew what the punishment for her might be if she concealed such knowledge. Margarite of Burgundy was the wife of Louis, later Louis X, and Blanche of Hungary was married to

Charles, later Charles IV. Both young ladies, aided and abetted by Jeanne of Burgundy, wife of Philip, later Philip V, were carrying on with two knights of the French court, the brothers Philip and Gautier d'Aulnay. All five were arrested and the brothers tortured until they admitted adultery – a particularly serious offence as it could call the whole royal succession into question. The wretched knights were publicly castrated with their organs thrown to the hounds, then flayed until almost dead, and finally decapitated. Margarite and Blanche were sentenced to life imprisonment in Château Gaillard, while Jeanne was put under house arrest.

Isabella's importance in British history lies not in whether or not her eventual conduct was justified, but in who she was and her place as a catalyst of the Hundred Years War. Gaveston's relations with the king, while shaming to the queen, did not seriously affect her property or her safety, while those of the Despensers certainly did. Until the rise of the Despensers, Isabella had supported her husband against his barons and in disagreements with her own father and brothers, kings of France. When the Despensers began to move against her, however, suspecting that she was in contact with their enemies, as she probably was, and when they persuaded the king to take back her property on the grounds that they should not, as an independent source of funds, be left in her hands as Anglo-French relations worsened, Isabella's attitudes began to change. She did retain the confidence of the king in political matters, for when war over Aquitaine broke out again in 1324, it was Isabella, with the approval of the overconfident Despensers, who was sent to France to mediate with her brother, Charles IV. Charles had succeeded his brother Philip V in 1322, when the latter had died of dysentery without a legitimate male offspring, and, while he was undoubtedly supportive of Isabella as his sister, he also saw her as a possible pawn that could be manipulated to discommode the English king.

The queen was well aware of the enmity of the Despensers but was clever enough to bid an ostensibly amiable farewell to Hugh the Younger on leaving Dover for France and to send him friendly letters from Paris. In her discussions with her brother Charles, Isabella seems genuinely to have wanted a solution to the issues between England and France that would benefit her adopted country and her husband, its king, while still being acceptable to the French. Inevitably, much centred around the homage that would have to be paid for any continental lands where the French would agree to English rule, and whether that would be simple homage, which acknowledged that the lands were held from the king of France; or liege homage, which carried with it a feudal obligation of service to that king – something that could never be acceptable to any English monarch. At one stage, Edward was prepared to come and pay simple homage in person, but then the Despensers, fearful for their own position if the king was out of the country, persuaded him not to go, and it was agreed, probably at Isabella's instigation, that Edward would grant his eldest son all his titles and lands in France and that the son, rather than the father, would go to France to pay homage. Whether this was a genuine attempt by Isabella to resolve the conflict, or whether it was a ploy to obtain control of the heir to the throne, is still the subject of debate – it was probably a bit of both. But in any event Edward, Prince of Wales, who was not quite thirteen, set sail from Dover with his entourage, including two bishops and a number of knights, on 12 September 1325 and paid homage to his uncle Charles at Vincennes on 24 September.

With a truce brokered and the English lands safe in the hands of the heir, there was now no need for Isabella and her son to remain in France and the king expected their return. At first, this took the form of enquiries as to their travel arrangements, with the queen giving various reasons why she should stay a little longer, but, as the king's enquiries became demands that she and his son should return, she made it clear that she would not set foot in England until the Despensers were exiled, as she feared for her safety if she returned. In the meantime, she began to become a focus for various disenchanted Englishmen and exiled nobles in France – something that was duly reported back to the king by emissaries sent to escort her back and by members of her own household whom she returned to England when the king stopped her allowance. The king of France, her brother, was initially happy to pay Isabella's bills, but then she became embroiled in scandal.

Roger Mortimer was born in 1287, into a family that was already enormously rich with lands in the Welsh Marches and mid Wales, southern England, the Midlands and Ireland, but, when his father died in 1304, his wardship was given by Edward II to Piers Gaveston. A wardship was immensely lucrative as all the income from the ward's estates was controlled by the guardian (and could be diverted to the latter's own purposes) until the ward reached his majority. The guardian also controlled his ward's marriage, and in 1306 Roger paid Gaveston 2,500 marks to claim his estates and income for the rest of his minority. As his minority had only two years to run, the payment of £140,000 in today's money (by the silver standard) indicates how valuable the estates were.

At first, Roger's life was like that of any other sprig of the nobility: knighted by Edward I in the same year as he reclaimed his estates and in the same batch as the Prince of Wales, later Edward II, he played an official role in the latter's coronation, served in Aquitaine, took part in the suppression of revolt in Wales, and served two terms as Justiciar of Ireland, where he was as successful as any English peacemaker could be in that lawless land. From 1320, towards the end of his second tour in Ireland, he became increasingly part of the opposition to the Despensers as they extended their holdings in Wales to what he and his fellow Marcher Lords saw as their detriment. In any case, it was said that Hugh Despenser the Younger was determined, in the manner of a Pathan blood feud, to wreak vengeance on Mortimer for the death of his, Hugh's, grandfather at the hands of Roger's at the Battle of Evesham in 1265. As we have seen, the success of the baronial opposition to the Despensers in 1321 was short-lived. The Battle of Boroughbridge on 16 March 1322 ended the civil war, but before that, on 23 January, Roger Mortimer and his uncle, Roger Mortimer of Chirk, had already surrendered to the king at Shrewsbury. They were sentenced to death but spared the terrible fate of so many of their fellow rebels when the sentence was commuted to life imprisonment in the Tower of London.

On 1 August 1323, in a Buchanesque adventure involving conniving jailers and drugged sentries, Roger Mortimer escaped from the Tower, obtained a boat in which he rowed across the Thames, stole or was given a horse, rode to Dover, found a ship to cross the Channel to France, and was welcomed at the court of Charles IV, then at loggerheads with Edward II over the usual vexed question of Aquitaine. Mortimer now joined the band of expatriates who were also in opposition to Edward II's England and clustered around the French court or that of the count of Hainault, whose territory bordered on Flanders and is now part of modern Belgium. His uncle, however, remained in the Tower, his lands forfeited, and died there aged seventy in 1326.

Roger Mortimer did not stay long in Paris and spent the next year or so in Hainault trying to raise troops and money to mount an invasion of England; in this, he was encouraged by the count and by disaffected elements in England who vowed they would rise if an invasion to remove the Despensers were to happen. Isabella probably first met Mortimer at the funeral of the old count of Valois, when he came to Paris in the entourage of the countess of Hainault. As both he and Isabella were united in hatred and fear of the Despensers, it was natural that they should meet and that Roger should confer with the English opposition now coalescing around the queen.

Remarkably quickly, their relationship became more than a political alliance, and by at least early 1326 it was generally assumed that they were sleeping together. While it was considered normal for married men to have mistresses (and Mortimer had been separated from his own wife for three years), for a lady to have extra-marital affairs was regarded as a heinous crime and for a queen to do so was treason of the worst sort. One can only assume that Isabella knew this perfectly well but that she was motivated by years of sexual frustration and resentment of her husband's actions towards her and his predilection for unsavoury favourites. She was a mature beauty of thirty-one and the thirty-nine-year-old Mortimer was, after all, everything King Edward was not: he was heterosexual, decisive, outgoing and audacious, and he shared her interest in culture and the arts. We might not blame either of them today, but at the time both were playing a dangerous game. Once news of their relationship reached England – and it did so remarkably quickly – Edward redoubled his efforts to force his son to return to his allegiance, even if the boy's mother would not. Letters were sent to the king of France, to the pope, to his son and to anyone who might listen, but to no avail.

Rumours of invasion were rife, and throughout the summer Edward issued commissions of array calling up troops, sequestered ships to watch the maritime approaches, ordered coastal defences to be put in order, seized Isabella's remaining lands and confiscated her funds lodged in the Tower, attempted to arrest Mortimer's mother (she was tipped off and went into hiding), and locked up anyone else he could lay hands on who might be sympathetic to the queen or who might oppose the Despensers. Eventually, having failed to persuade Charles IV to cooperate, Edward declared war on France in July 1326. At last, Edward's appeals to the pope in Avignon bore fruit: John XXII had hoped to keep the peace between England and France and had sent nuncios to try to mediate between Isabella and her husband, but he could not condone adultery and wrote to Charles IV to tell him so. Charles, no doubt mindful of what had happened to his ex-wife Blanche and her illicit lover, agreed to expel Isabella and her lover, but it would seem to have been done in a gentlemanly way, with the couple given plenty of notice and Isabella allowed to take with her all her possessions and the funds provided by Charles. It seems that she now accepted, if she had not done so before, that it was not just the Despensers that were her enemies, but her husband, the king of England, as well. Since his escape from the Tower, Mortimer had always hoped to overthrow Edward II, and Isabella became part of the plan too, for it was she who possessed the strongest card – the king's son, Edward, Prince of Wales. After a diversion to Isabella's county of Ponthieu to raise further funds, she and Mortimer were welcomed in Hainault in August.

Young Edward was now betrothed to Philippa, daughter of the count of Hainault, with a dowry of men, money and ships to be placed at Isabella's disposal immediately, and troops raised by Mortimer and those provided by Hainault began to gather at the assembly port of Dordrecht, south-east of Rotterdam. There were no French troops involved: Charles IV was fully engaged campaigning in Aquitaine, and Isabella and Mortimer both knew that the way to make their support in England evaporate overnight would be for a single French soldier to land on English shores. Edward II was well aware of what was being planned, and on 2 September he ordered the earl of Norfolk to raise 2,000 troops from East Anglia to defend the port of Orwell in Suffolk. We do not know whether Edward's intelligence service, such as it was, had discovered that port to be the intended landing area or he concluded that an invasion mounted from the port of Dordrecht would probably make for Orwell, but in any event the troops were never raised and the earl, the king's half-brother, went over to Isabella. Edward himself does not seem to have checked that his orders were being obeyed.

At Dordrecht, Isabella, Mortimer and her army embarked on ninety-five ships and put to sea on 22 September 1326. The army was a mix of Flemish, German and Bohemian soldiers, mainly mercenaries but with some unpaid volunteers hopeful of making their fortunes, and a gaggle of English exiles and emissaries sent by Edward II who had then sided with Isabella and stayed. Estimates of their numbers vary from a high of 2,757 (Walsingham) to a low of 500 (Chronicle of Meaux), but, given the capacity of the ships of the time and the need to transport horses and equipment, the force was probably around 1,500 strong. It was a tiny army with which to mount an invasion, even by medieval standards, but Isabella had good reason to expect indigenous support once she landed, and she and Mortimer had probably concluded a secret treaty with the Scots – one that was to come back and haunt them – to ensure that Robert Bruce, styled King Robert I, did not invade northern England while Isabella was dealing with Edward II. In the event, the campaign was even easier than Isabella and Mortimer could have hoped. After two days being tossed about in a storm, the invasion force landed somewhere near the mouth of the River Orwell on 24 September unopposed by the king's ships, which were either not in the vicinity or had mutinied against the Despensers.

Most of the nobility had now accepted that the influence of the Despensers was intolerable and that the king would not reform. The time had finally come to remove this ineffective and capricious monarch and replace him with his son. Many, perhaps most, of the queen's contemporaries had some sympathy for her position and thought her more sinned against than sinning, and public opinion soon swung in her favour as more and more of the barons and their troops rallied to her. Edward's support melted away, and he, the Despensers and what adherents they still had fled to Wales, where they no doubt hoped for support from the Despensers' tenants there. It was not to be, and, when the garrison of Bristol surrendered on 26 October, Hugh the Elder was taken, tried for numerous offences, and executed the following day, with his head sent for public exhibition to Winchester.* Then, on 16 November, the king and Hugh the Younger were captured at Llantrisant, near Caerphilly. Appropriately enough, their captor was Henry of Lancaster, brother of Thomas, who had been executed after Boroughbridge in 1322. Hugh Despenser was taken to Hereford, condemned to death as a traitor, a heretic and a sodomite, hanged from fifty-foot-high gallows, cut down while still alive, castrated,

---

* He was earl of Winchester. The Lanercost Chronicle says he was ninety years old when executed, which seems unlikely.

disembowelled and finally beheaded. The king was sent to Kenilworth and on 20 January 1327 was persuaded to abdicate in favour of his eldest son, who was duly crowned Edward III on 1 February.

The deposed Edward was now transferred to Berkeley Castle, and there were a number of plots to rescue him, some real, many more imagined. Then, during a parliamentary session at Lincoln, it was announced that Edward had died on 21 September 1327. Whether or not he did die then and, if he did, the cause and manner of his death have intrigued historians ever since. All the reliable evidence would seem to point to the fact of his death at Berkeley Castle in the autumn of 1327. At the time, it was stated to be from 'natural causes', but, as Edward was only forty-three, this seems unlikely. A lurid account – written thirty years later but probably circulating orally shortly after the king's death, and sniggered over by schoolboys ever since – says that he was killed by having a red-hot poker or spit shoved up his bottom. This too seems unlikely and was more probably intended as a cautionary tale against homosexuality (Edward was reckoned by contemporaries to be the buggeree in his relationships). But in any case, why bother? The body of a dead king would have to be put on public display to avoid claims that he had been spirited away and was in hiding (and such tales of Edward II did arise), and charred flesh in the nether regions would surely be noticed during the removal of organs as part of the embalming process. It seems much more likely that the wretched Edward was smothered, a means of dispatch which would have left no marks on the body. In any case, the body was displayed in Gloucester from 22 October and buried there in the presence of Isabella and the new king shortly afterwards.*

On 30 January 1328, Edward III married Philippa of Hainault, daughter of the count of Hainault. She was now sixteen years old and described by the chronicler Froissart as being 'full feminine' – past puberty. It was to be a genuinely happy marriage, despite Edward's later womanizing, but at this early stage there was to be little time for domestic bliss, for the new regime faced difficulties enough.

---

* While this author is not convinced, a strong case is made by Ian Mortimer for Edward II's not being done to death but surviving for many years incognito in Italy (see Mortimer, *The Perfect King: The life of Edward III*, Jonathan Cape, London, 2006).

The Battle of Sluys, 1340. In many ways the most important battle of the whole war, as it finally destroyed any French ability to invade England. The illustration, from the Chronicles of Jean Froissart, shows how the English (on the left) were able to fight a land battle on ships, rather than a sea battle which they might well have lost.

2

STATING THE CLAIM

The first problem facing the new regime in England and the one most in need of a conclusion was the ever-present running sore of the Scots. Robert Bruce had adhered to his promise not to raid England during Isabella's invasion and subsequent campaign, but now, with the deposition of Edward II, his assurances no longer held, and bands of ferocious Scots were raiding the northern English counties. It seemed that a short and successful war would cement the popularity of the new dynasty, so Edward, his mother and Mortimer began to gather an army in York. The assembly was marred by an argument between English archers and the servants of Flemish men-at-arms sent from Hainault. Fuelled by the endemic English dislike of foreigners, the argument turned to a fight and then to a slaughter, with the archers shooting indiscriminately at anyone who appeared alien. When order was restored, there were three hundred dead in the streets of York, mainly Hainaulters. It was perhaps an omen for the campaign, which began with the English army floundering about over an inhospitable terrain where it mostly poured with rain, trying to find the Scots, who had no intention of fighting an open battle; and ended with an exhausted English army withdrawing. Edward was furious and was said to have wept in frustration.

Now it was increasingly clear to Isabella and to Mortimer that this was an unwinnable war. Even in the glory days of Edward I's Scottish wars, the Scots had always eventually returned to the fray, and the incessant border raids and the consequent punitive expeditions were a drain on resources and funds that England could ill afford. English emissaries began to negotiate with the Scots, and the result was the Treaty of Northampton, ratified by Edward III in May 1328. The treaty acknowledged Scottish independence and the position of Robert Bruce as king; gave up English overlordship of Scotland (claimed by English kings ever since the Conquest); agreed to the return of various relics, including the Black Rood (a sliver of wood that the Scots believed was from the cross on which Christ was crucified), the Ragman (a parchment admitting submission to Edward I, with the seals of most of the great men of Scotland affixed to it), and the Stone of Scone; and agreed the marriage of Robert Bruce's four-year-old son, David, to Isabella's seven-year-old daughter, Joan. In return, Robert Bruce agreed to pay an indemnity of £20,000, or £1.65 million in today's money (silver standard), for Scottish raids into England and to support England against any enemy except the French. As there was no other likely enemy, this was a rather hollow promise.

In hindsight, the treaty was a piece of pragmatic common sense. If the Scots could not be brought to heel, then give them what they wanted in exchange for perpetual peace and join the two crowns by a marriage deal. Additionally, security in the north would mean that Edward could pursue a French war without constantly having to look over his shoulder. Unfortunately, that was not how it was seen in England. The 'Shameful Peace' had given away a princess, acknowledged the success of treason, given up the English crown's hereditary privileges over Scotland and, crucially, failed to address the rights of English lords who held lands in Scotland. As by the treaty they now had no rights there, these lords styled themselves the 'Disinherited'. The young Edward made no secret of the fact that he disapproved of the treaty, saying that it was all his mother's and Mortimer's doing, and that he frowned on the wedding of his sister and would not attend the ceremony. No doubt some of this was a swift adoption of sloping shoulders once he realized the extent of public opinion, and in any case the London mob prevented the abbot of Westminster from releasing the Stone of Scone. Almost overnight, Isabella's popularity began to wane, and by extension that of Mortimer.

Hot on the heels of the conclusion of the Scottish war came the news of the death of Charles IV, the last of the Capetian kings who had ruled France for over three hundred years. All three sons of Philip IV, the Fair, had ruled in succession after him and none had produced sons that survived infancy. The next-born child of Philip was Isabella, and she was swift to send emissaries to Paris to register her claim. The stage was set for the Hundred Years War.

When Charles was on his death bed, his wife was pregnant. The king was said to have decreed that, if the child was a boy, then he would succeed, and, if not, the crown of France should pass to the thirty-five-year-old Philip of Valois, count of Anjou and Maine, the son of Charles of Valois, who was a brother of Philip IV. When, two months later, in May 1328, the child was still-born, Philip summoned a carefully chosen assembly of the nobility of France to decide the succession. His own claim was based on his being the grandson of one king and the cousin of three others, whereas Edward III's mother Isabella was the daughter of a king and the sister of three others; thus, if the succession was to be decided by consanguinity, her claim was the stronger. The so-called Salic Law, which was supposedly part of the legal code of the ancient Merovingian Franks and which forbade descent through the female line, was not trotted out and relied upon until very much later, but it is true that there had never been a queen regnant of France, and when the question had last arisen, in 1316, the girl's guardian had conveniently withdrawn her claim. Isabella's emissaries, Bishops Orleton and Northburgh, argued that there was no legal justification for excluding her. They pointed out that the greatest duchies, such as Aquitaine, could be and had been inherited by females, and that other kingdoms – Hungary, Bohemia – had been ruled by females of cadet branches of the Capets. Furthermore, they argued, even if there was justification for excluding a woman, this argument could not be extended to Isabella's son, who was the closest male descendant of Philip the Fair. This was a sensible shift – claiming the throne for Edward rather than for his mother – for, if the latter's claim was pressed, then in logic her dead brother's daughters would also have a claim.

Whatever the legal arguments might have been, the French were determined not to have Isabella on their throne, nor to accept her fifteen-year-old son. Not only was Edward of England a foreigner (although he would not have considered himself such) but he was a mere boy and would simply be the figurehead for his mother and her very dubious (in French eyes) lover, Mortimer. Philip of Valois, on the other hand, was a vigorous adult and a member of one of the greatest families of France. Accordingly,

Isabella's representatives found little support for her claim. Philip of Valois was proclaimed king of France as Philip VI, and the burgomaster of Bruges, who was unwise enough to voice his countrymen's support for Edward, was mutilated and hanged as a warning to others.

Isabella would never relinquish her and her son's claim to the throne of France, but for the moment there was very little she could do about it. The unpopularity of the Scottish treaty, the arrival of a queen consort, and Mortimer's acting in the very way that had persuaded him to oppose and eventually to rebel against Edward II were all conspiring to reduce her influence. The regency council of state ruled in Edward's name, with neither Isabella nor Mortimer having any official role. As the queen mother, Isabella was of course entitled to make her views known and to be consulted, but, while Mortimer could no doubt have had himself appointed to the council, he seems to have preferred to remain in the background and to exercise power over the king through the boy's mother, which did at least allow him to avoid blame for unpopular decisions. When the new king of France demanded homage for Aquitaine and Ponthieu on pain of invading Aquitaine, Isabella's first reaction was to refuse, but, when Philip began to seize the incomes of the wine trade, Edward had no option but to cross to France in 1329 and pay homage in Amiens cathedral. Technically, the act of homage would negate any claim to the French throne, but later it was argued that Edward had not removed his spurs or his crown, nor had he knelt, so the act was meaningless. In any case, he had not done it freely but in the face of *force majeure*. For the moment, however, neither Edward nor his mother was in any position to press his claim.

The rule of Isabella and Mortimer, at first greeted with acclaim as a relief from the unstable and increasingly oppressive reign of Edward II, was now beginning to be viewed with as much dread as Edward's and the Despensers' had been. It was obvious to all that Isabella controlled the young king, and Mortimer controlled Isabella. Isabella's lands and incomes increased, largely at the expense of the new queen Philippa, who was yet to receive the queen's dower still held by her mother-in-law, while Mortimer too acquired more land and riches and, by having himself created earl of March, set himself above all other Marcher Lords in precedence. As Isabella was intelligent enough to realize the opposition that such tyrannical behaviour had aroused during her late husband's reign, one can only suppose that she was in such thrall to Mortimer that she could not or would not curb his ambitions. Even when Mortimer enticed Edmund, earl of Kent, into a bogus plot to rescue his half-brother Edward II – supposedly imprisoned rather than dead – and then had him executed as a traitor, Isabella failed to rein him in. But when rumours began to circulate about her being pregnant by Mortimer – which, if true, was a scandal of enormous proportions – the young king had had enough of being controlled by Mortimer through his mother.

On 15 June 1330, with the court at Woodstock, Queen Philippa gave birth to a son, Edward of Woodstock, the future Black Prince. That same summer, the court moved to Nottingham, and Mortimer issued writs for a meeting of the great council of the realm, with nobles being warned that staying away would attract heavy penalties. Quite what Mortimer hoped to achieve at the council can only be a matter of speculation, but he was aware that he was unpopular, that the young friends of the king were urging him to assert his authority, and that, with the king approaching his majority and with a healthy heir apparent, the rule of Isabella and Mortimer was under threat unless they managed somehow to persuade or intimidate the council into extending it.

The castle at Nottingham, built by William I and improved and extended by his successors, was a formidable structure, and when Mortimer offended the barons still further by informing them that only the king, Isabella, Mortimer and their personal guard were to be accommodated in the castle, with all others lodged in the town, he must have felt that he was quite secure – particularly when Isabella brought new locks for the gates and doors leading to the keep, where the royal family was quartered, and had the keys delivered to her personally each night when the doors had been locked and sentries placed on them. Such tight security did not save them. On the evening of 19 October 1330, the magnates left the castle at the conclusion of the day's business and the gates were duly locked. Later, a group of the king's supporters, led by the governor of the castle, whose soldiers had been replaced by Mortimer's men, entered the castle by way of a tunnel that ran from the town into the castle keep, where they were met by the king and taken to Isabella and Mortimer's apartments. The king remained outside while his party burst in to find Mortimer in discussion with the chancellor, the bishop of Lincoln. In the ensuing scuffle two of

Mortimer's bodyguard were killed, and Mortimer and the bishop were seized and dragged out through the tunnel. Isabella, meanwhile, is said to have cried in French for her good son to have pity on dear Mortimer – although, as she is said to have called from an adjoining apartment, it is difficult to see how she could have known that the affair had been orchestrated by the king. Next morning, Mortimer's associates were arrested and the party was taken to the Tower, while the king called a parliament to meet at Westminster and announced that henceforth he would rule fairly and with the advice of the great men of the kingdom. He was just eighteen years of age.

In November 1330, Parliament duly met in London. Mortimer was condemned unheard and sentenced to death, along with two of his most notorious adherents. On 29 November, he was drawn to Tyburn on a hurdle and hanged, as were his two collaborators on Christmas Eve. All three were spared the more exotic refinements of a traitor's execution and were permitted burial. Edward had taken pains to ensure that no mention of his mother was made in the trials, and she was merely pensioned off to live in some style at Castle Rising. A cursory and unsuccessful attempt was made to find those suspected of murdering Edward II and those complicit in the judicial murder of the earl of Kent, but all had fled abroad except for Sir Thomas Berkeley, the owner of Berkeley Castle where Edward II had met his end, who was put on trial but cleared. There were no more executions. In disposing of the old regime, Edward III was a lot more lenient than his father or Mortimer had been, and in due course many of Mortimer's adherents were pardoned and their lands and titles restored.

Edward now had to rectify the oppression of his father's reign and that of Mortimer and Isabella. Many of the officials of the two previous regimes were given a short period in the wilderness but then re-employed if they were able administrators, as many of them were. All land grants made since his accession – made by Edward in name but by Isabella and Mortimer in reality – were cancelled, and laws forbidding duels, unofficial tournaments and the bearing of arms in Parliament were strengthened. Outside the immediate control of the king and his government, England was a lawless land: brigandage was rife, and justices, whether those of Edward II or Mortimer, were corrupt. The exhibition of various body parts of notable persons acted as a salient reminder of the dangers of choosing the wrong side in what had been a violently fluctuating political landscape. Great lords maintained private armies and often behaved very much as they liked, even if they were constantly obliged to jockey for position depending on whose star was in the ascendant at any particular time. Whether Edward III saw war abroad as a way to channel English aggression to the common good, or he was mainly concerned with what he saw as his rightful inheritance through his mother, is irrelevant. In any event, it is clear that from very early on he was intending to take on the French king. Before he could do that, however, he had to ensure that his back door was secure and that, if he took an army to France, he was not going to be invaded by the Scots.

It took Edward four campaigns to be sure that Scotland was safe, but he had to maintain the fiction that the Scots were the aggressors, otherwise by the Treaty of Northampton he would have to return the £20,000 reparations paid by the Scots but actually a loan to them from the pope – a sum long since spent by Isabella. Initially, he hid behind the Disinherited, those holders of lands north of the border who had lost out in the Northampton settlement. They, led by Edward Balliol, son of the deposed king John Balliol, raised an army and landed in Scotland. Openly Edward III condemned the move, refused the Disinherited passage over English territory, and confiscated the estates of their supporters in England (quietly returning them a few months later). At the same time, Edward agreed to liege homage for his French lands, promised various marriage settlements between the French and English royal families, and agreed in principle to going on crusade with Philip. Initially, with Scotland divided and ruled by a regency for the six-year-old king David Bruce, the Disinherited made startling progress, and, although he had by no means conquered all of Scotland, Edward Balliol was nevertheless crowned at Scone in September 1332 and promised homage to Edward III for the whole country. English pretence of non-intervention began to unravel with the arrival of King David and his court as refugees in France. Nevertheless, as the pope was anxious to prevent the two major Christian powers from going to war and had granted the French king a tax on the clergy to fund the projected crusade, a peace of sorts was maintained save for a few insignificant French raids on the Channel Islands and the landing in Scotland of a handful of French horsemen.

Then, in 1333, there was a resurgence of the Bruce faction, which captured Berwick and embarked on the age-old Scottish sport of launching raids into England. Edward was able to claim that it was the Scots, not he, who had broken the treaty, and in went an English army that soundly trounced the Scots at Halidon Hill. Further expeditions followed in 1334, 1335 and 1336 until Edward was able to penetrate to the farthest reaches of the Highlands – much deeper than his illustrious grandfather had ever been able to do, and this time the English did not fall into the trap of trying to fight a guerrilla war with a conventional army. It was increasingly clear to Philip of France that Edward of England not only had no intention of abiding by the Treaty of Northampton, but that he had no intention of joining a crusade either. This entirely correct assessment was reinforced by the presence at the English court of Robert of Artois, who was on the run from Philip of France.

Robert of Artois had once been one of Philip's closest friends and advisers; now he was his implacable enemy. When Robert's father, the duke of Artois, died in 1299, the dukedom had passed not to the then fourteen-year-old Robert but to his aunt, the old duke's sister. Once he was old enough to argue the point, Robert had devoted all his energies to getting the dukedom passed to him. He had tried litigation, persuasion, bribery, blackmail and outright violence, but nothing had worked. He had married Philip's sister, and, when Philip became king of France, Robert saw his opportunity and wormed his way into the new king's counsels to the extent that for a period the king would make no decision without consulting him. Robert then made his move and persuaded the king to confiscate the duchy of Artois while his claim was examined anew. Unfortunately for Robert, his aunt died in 1329 and the inheritance passed to the duchess of Burgundy, who, by virtue of her husband being one of the great lords of France, was a much tougher proposition than an aged aunt. Matters were not helped when Robert's documents purporting to prove his right to the duchy turned out not only to have been forged but also to have been forged under his instructions. Philip had been made a fool of and was furious. A criminal prosecution failed when Robert fled the jurisdiction, hiding out in the Low Countries or anywhere else that would give him shelter and railing against the French king, threatening revolution and the death of the royal family by witchcraft. The understandably vindictive Philip, meanwhile, banned him from all French territories, confiscated his lands, and tried in vain to have him kidnapped or assassinated. Eventually, in 1334, Robert turned up in England, where he was received with interest – but little else – in the court. Edward III was still, at this stage, anxious to placate France, so Robert was ordered to keep his head down and cease his propaganda against Philip, which for two years he did.

By 1336, things had changed. Edward had secured his northern borders against the Scots and had quietly built up a series of alliances with states bordering France, some owing allegiance not to Philip VI but to the Holy Roman Emperor Louis IV,* who was rather less holy now that he had been excommunicated but powerful nonetheless. The enthusiasm of these allies was directly proportional to their distance from France: the German states, with the River Meuse between them and France, were all for it; the count of Flanders, next door to France, was less so. The threat of stopping exports of English wool was deployed to bring the Flemings into line. In France, litigation in the courts was chipping away at the rights of English cities and bishoprics in the disputed lands, and, thanks to the pope, Philip was the owner of a large fleet of ships.

Since 1309, the papacy had been based in Avignon in southern France, whither it had moved to escape the infighting and machinations of the great Roman families who had hitherto dominated the office. From then until the return to Rome in 1378, all the popes would be French, and so would an increasing number of cardinals, often relatives of the reigning pope. Although the south of France was very different in both language and culture from the north, where king and government lay, the English tended to assume that popes were in the French king's pocket and, while paying lip service to the papacy, regarded any secular actions by it with suspicion. Pope John XXII was querulous and superstitious but a shrewd amasser of riches, and, when he died in December 1334, his treasury was found to be full to overflowing. John's successor, Benedict XII, concealed behind an obese and drunken exterior sharp political antennae, and in order to keep the peace in Europe and to direct the warlike tendencies of the French and English externally towards the recovery of the Holy Land, rather than internally towards each other, he had happily financed the

* Or perhaps more properly Ludwig IV, of the Wittelsbach dynasty.

building of a fleet to transport the crusading army. Then, in March 1336, the pope cancelled the crusade and rescinded his authorization for the clergy to be taxed to finance it. Benedict had concluded that he could not keep the peace between England and France, and that, if Edward of England was not going to join an expedition, then the French king could not take his army abroad. So Philip now had a fleet to use for other purposes, and the ships began to move from Marseilles to the Channel ports. The English knew very well that the move could only presage a sea-borne invasion of England, and Edward began to take measures to deal with it.

Although English kings had long styled themselves 'Lords of the English Sea', by the time of Edward III it was an empty title, and at this period of English history there was no great maritime tradition to fall back on. From 1066 until King John lost his lands in France, England controlled directly or through alliances the whole of the Atlantic coast, and, while navies were occasionally raised after that when invasion threatened, they were swiftly disbanded when the threat had passed. It was not that the English were unaware of the security of their sea routes – ships plying between Bordeaux and England hugged the coast rather than cross the Bay of Biscay, hence the importance of a friendly Brittany – it was just that they could not afford to spend much on it. Edward III owned but a handful of ships, with masters (often unpaid for long periods) but no crews, and in the event of a naval threat the defence of the nation at sea depended, in theory at least, upon the Cinque Ports. By ancient decree these ports were required, in exchange for various customs and taxation privileges, to provide fifty-seven vessels between them for fifteen days. In fact, most of the ports had silted up, many of the ships they could provide ostensibly for war were in fact fishing vessels, and evasion of their obligations was widespread. In practice, the king would have to requisition ships from elsewhere – Great Yarmouth was now far more important as a port than any of the Cinque Ports and most of the ships would come from there.

Command of English navies was vested in two admirals, that of the North and that of the South. The posts were usually held either by soldiers, who knew a lot about fighting on land but little about war on the sea, or by influential magnates, who might know very little about any sort of war. Most of the ships impressed for the English navy were cogs, thought to have originally developed from Viking longships. Cogs were wide-beamed, shallow-draught merchant vessels with one mast and a square-rigged sail, built of oak and with a stern rudder. Divided into various sizes ranging from 'up to 10 tons' to 'over 120 tons', most were relatively small, although there were cogs of 300 tons.* Being square-rigged, the cog could not sail into the wind, nor was it very manoeuvrable, but it could carry a considerable quantity of cargo, was reasonably resistant to bad weather and heavy seas, and could put in to estuaries and bays that a ship with a deeper draught could not. Most of those assembled to counter the threat of the French fleet were of 100 tons displacement, sixty feet long and twenty wide, with a crew of twenty-five sailors and a fighting element of archers or men-at-arms. Once the cogs were taken into the king's service, fore and stern castles – wooden towers front and rear – and crows' nests were added. These were manned by archers and stone-throwers, for English naval tactics were simple: ram any enemy ship, sink it or board it, attack the crew and chuck their bodies overboard, dead or alive.

On 24 May 1337, King Philip announced the confiscation of Aquitaine, stating this to be as punishment for Edward's failure to fulfil his obligations as a vassal of the French king and for his sheltering of Robert of Artois. It is this act that can be taken as marking the beginning of the Hundred Years War. The English response was to despatch an advance party to the Low Countries to prepare for the reception of an English army which Edward intended to land there later in the year. Eighty-five ships crewed by 2,000 seamen and carrying 1,500 soldiers and a large cargo of wool, which would be sold to pay for the escapade, set sail from Sandwich in November under Sir Walter Manny.

Admiral of the North and responsible for all ports from the Thames to Berwick, Manny was an early example of the sort of men who would make their reputations and fortunes in the coming war. A younger son of minor Hainault aristocracy, he originally came to England as a page to Queen Philippa. Having progressed from being her carver, responsible for her food, to looking after her greyhounds, he was knighted in 1331 and came to prominence as an up-and-coming soldier in Edward Balliol's army of the Disinherited that invaded Scotland in 1332. He then served in all of Edward

---

* By comparison, HMS *Victory*, Nelson's flagship at Trafalgar in 1805, displaced 3,500 tons, and HMS *Warrior*, the Royal Navy's first ironclad launched in 1860, displaced 9,000 tons.

III's Scottish campaigns, did well, and received honours and lucrative appointments as a result. In his mid- to late twenties in 1337, he appears to have been personally brave, unheeding of danger, reckless, flamboyant, as greedy as everyone else at the time, but a competent commander and a good leader of men withal.

Instead, however, of going straight to Dordrecht, on the Rhine south-east of Rotterdam, as he should have done, Manny decided to embark upon a private frolic of his own. First, he attacked the port of Sluys and was repulsed, whereupon he raided the island of Cadzand, east of Zeebrugge, where he captured enough notables to earn himself a tidy sum in ransom later. He then looted the town and burned most of the inhabitants to death, having first locked them up in the church. Lucrative though the venture was to Manny, it achieved little of military value. Having at last landed his party at Dordrecht, the admiral returned to England to prepare to transport the main army.

On 16 July 1338, Edward of England sailed from Walton-on-the-Naze, south of Harwich on the Essex coast. After landing at Antwerp and much to-ing and fro-ing to secure local alliances, the king eventually processed to Coblenz, where in a lavish ceremony in September the Holy Roman Emperor Louis of Bavaria – whose anti-French and anti-papal stance was reinforced by a hefty English bribe – appointed Edward as overlord of all the emperor's fiefs west of the Rhine. Even Edward's flat refusal to kiss the emperor's foot could not mar the occasion. It was now too late for campaigning that year and so, having promised the rulers of the minor states supposedly now allied to him large subsidies for the provision of troops, Edward ordered them to concentrate their contingents north of Brussels in July the following year. The English court settled down in Antwerp for the winter, leaving the king's clerical staff to reply to the remonstrance of the pope, who objected to Edward's dealings with the excommunicated emperor and his giving of succour to Robert of Artois. The pope pointed out that previous English kings had come to grief by trusting too much to foreign advice, a clear reference to Edward's father's fixation with Piers Gaveston.

Far from the allied armies being on parade in July, it was not until September 1339 that Edward's army was ready to move, and even then not all the promised participants had turned up. The campaign was

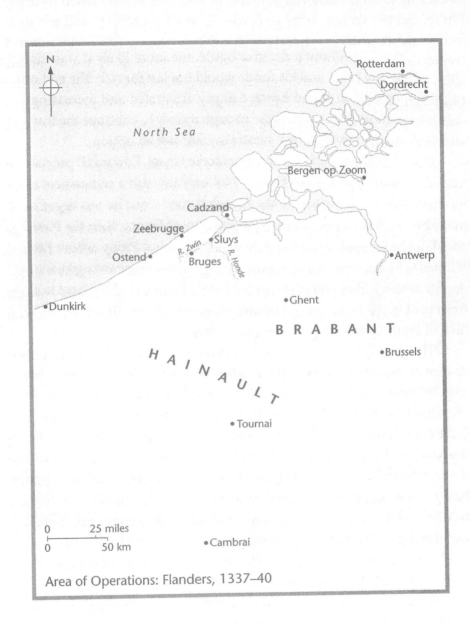

N

North Sea

Rotterdam
Dordrecht

Bergen op Zoom

Cadzand

Zeebrugge
Ostend
R. Zwin
Sluys
Bruges
R. Honde
Antwerp

Dunkirk

Ghent

B R A B A N T

Brussels

H A I N A U L T

Tournai

0   25 miles
0   50 km

Cambrai

Area of Operations: Flanders, 1337–40

exhausting and expensive, and it achieved nothing. Much manoeuvring in Picardy around Cambrai, St Quentin and Buironfosse failed to bring Philip and the French army to battle. A win for Philip would not gain him England, whereas a defeat could lose him France. The longer Edward stayed in France without a decisive battle, the more likely it was that his allies would slip away, and his funds would not last forever. The end of the campaigning season found Edward angry, frustrated and increasingly in debt. His priority now was to raise enough money to continue the war, and also to persuade Flanders that neutrality was not an option.

On 23 January 1340, in the marketplace in Ghent, Edward III proclaimed himself king of England and France. Not only was this a restatement of his mother's and his own claim to the French throne – one he was egged on to make by Robert of Artois – but, if he was king of France, then the Flemings could not be accused of treason if they fought against Philip, whom Edward claimed to be a usurper. More importantly, given that there were genuine legal doubts as to whether English kings held their French lands in liege homage from the king of France or in full sovereignty, if Edward III was the rightful king of France, then the question was irrelevant.

The French fleur-de-lys was now incorporated into the English royal coat of arms, quartered with the English lions (or leopards), and Edward took as his motto *Dieu et Mon Droit* – 'God and my right' – which has remained the motto of English and then British sovereigns to this day. Oddly, perhaps, Philip did not object to the incorporation of the fleur-de-lys – as the grandson of a French king, Edward was entitled to use it – but he did object to the lions, the symbol of a poor offshore island, being placed in precedence over the arms of the great kingdom of France. In England itself, Edward's claim was not universally approved; there was widespread distrust and indeed hatred of France, and Parliament had to enact a statute saying that in no circumstances, now or ever in the future, could any Englishman be subject to the laws of France.

Although Philip had no intention of meeting the English army in open battle in northern France, fighting was going on in Gascony, French forces were besieging English castles in the Agenais, and they were active at sea too. Between 1337 and 1339, Rye, Folkestone, Dover, Harwich, Plymouth and the Isle of Wight were all subject to sudden French landings, followed by a brief period of pillage, rape and murder before the raiders set fire to what would burn and took to sea again. In 1338, they took most of the Channel Islands and held them until 1340, and also in 1338 they captured England's largest ship, the king's own cog *Christopher*, along with the *Edward*. While the English responded by equally bloody raids on Le Tréport and Boulogne, no town on England's east and south coasts was safe from French raids, usually by galleys which, being powered by rowers, were less subject to wind or tide than were English cogs.

In addition, Edward's financial situation was precarious. So far, the cost of procuring allies and sending an English expeditionary force to Europe and keeping it there had been met by loans, mainly from Italian bankers and English and Flemish merchants, but these sources were drying up. Some loans were coming due for repayment, more recent loans went only to repay old ones, new ones could only be obtained at exorbitant rates of interest, and the wool brought over by Manny had not fetched as much as had been hoped. Things were so serious that Edward had actually pawned the crown of England in Bruges. He had to tilt the balance of the war in his favour quickly, and the only solution was to raise more money from England and to bring over an army large enough to force a battle. In February 1340, a month after proclaiming himself king of France, Edward returned to England to raise funds. It was a humiliating departure: he had to agree to his queen and a number of his nobles remaining behind as surety for the loans, and he had to promise that he would return with the money or, if without it, that he would subject himself to detention until it was found.

In the almost two years that Edward had been out of England, Parliament had increasingly begun to question the cost of the war, laying down all sorts of conditions before granting yet another tax. Edward met Parliament in March 1340 and deployed his extraordinary ability in managing public opinion to charm the legislators. Explaining that, if the money was not raised, then his honour would be destroyed, his lands in France lost, and he himself imprisoned for debt, and assuring all that he had no intention of combining the two kingdoms nor of taking any action in England in his capacity as king of France, Edward asked for, and received, a tax of a ninth.* This, in addition to more loans squeezed from

---

* This meant one in every nine sacks of wool, sheaves of grain and lambs, and one ninth of the value of every town dweller's moveable goods.

the London merchants and a levy on the clergy, would be sufficient for him to carry on the war. He did not even discuss Parliament's conditions, agreeing to them all without argument.

The troops being assembled to reinforce those already in Europe were a mix of men raised by feudal array, volunteers and paid professionals, both men-at-arms and archers. The reported numbers of men in medieval armies are notoriously unreliable, and the number of English ships said by contemporary chronicles to have been mustered for the crossing vary from 147 (Lanercost)[3] to 260 (Le Baker).[4] But as the number of French ships is generally agreed to be around 200 and all chroniclers of both sides agree that the French fleet outnumbered that of the English, then 150 is probably the most the English could have had. If we allow that around 50 ships would have been carrying horses, stores and the ladies going out to join the queen and that a 100-ton cog could carry at most 100 men of whom 25 would be crew, then the maximum number of soldiers might have been around 5,000, in the proportion of three archers to two men-at-arms.

By the time Edward and his fleet were ready to leave England, in June 1340, the English knew that the French fleet had been moved to Sluys, now silted up but then the main port for Bruges, north-east of it at the mouth of the Zwin on the south side of the Honde estuary. As the only purpose of stationing the fleet there would be for an invasion of England, or at the very least to prevent an English army from crossing the Channel, Edward decided that he would meet the threat head-on and, rather than avoiding the French ships and landing at Dunkirk or Ostend, would do battle with them.

This was an audacious plan indeed, and, when Edward suggested it, his chancellor, Archbishop Stratford, argued strongly against it; and when he could not change the king's mind, he resigned his office and returned the Great Seal of England to the king.* Edward summoned his most experienced admiral, Robert Morley, and asked his opinion. Having previously served Edward II and been party to the coup that deposed him, Morley initially served on land in Edward III's Scottish wars before taking to the sea. He had shown himself a most accomplished organizer and leader of raids on the French coast and had been appointed Admiral of the North in February 1339.

---

* He was replaced by his brother, so the family was hardly disadvantaged.

Morley pointed out the dangers of the king's plan and advised against it, and this opinion was backed up by the very experienced Flemish seaman John Crabbe, originally a mercenary pirate in the Scottish service who had been captured by the English and changed sides and was now the king's captain. Edward lost his temper and accused all three of plotting against him, telling them that they could stay at home but he was going anyway. He was mollified only when Morley and Crabbe announced that much as they opposed the caper, if the king went, then so would they.

The story of the Battle of Sluys – the first major engagement of the Hundred Years War – is not one that springs to the lips of every English schoolboy, but in its way it is as significant as the defeat of the Spanish Armada in 1558 and the Battle of Trafalgar in 1805. For if it had been lost, the 20,000 troops that Philip of France was amassing to invade England would have found nothing at sea to oppose them and precious little on land once they got there. Like Admiral Jellicoe at Jutland over half a millennium later, Edward III was the one man who could have lost the war in an afternoon.

Up to this point, despite the improving English ability to mount coastal raids, the French had been superior at sea, and had the Great Army of the Sea, as Philip termed it, been in the Channel a year earlier, things would have been very different. Then, not only would the French have mustered many more ships overall than they did now, but also they would have had many more galleys, swift and manoeuvrable and far more suited to war at sea than the sluggish English cogs. Fortunately for the English, the combination of a revolution in Genoa that had resulted in a regime no longer inclined to hire galleys and crews to the French, and English raids that had burned beached galleys at Boulogne, had left the French with only six galleys, four of their own and two Genoese. In addition, the fleet had twenty-two oared barges, not as manoeuvrable as the galleys but more easily handled than the cogs nonetheless, seven sailing ships specifically built as naval vessels, and 167 requisitioned merchantmen.[5] Manning the ships were around 19,000 soldiers and sailors, although only about 500 crossbowmen and 150 men-at-arms were professional soldiers, the rest being mariners, militia and recently impressed recruits.

Knowing that Edward was intending to sail for the Low Countries, the best alternatives open to the French admirals were to blockade English ports or to catch the English fleet at sea and annihilate it. In the event, they did neither. The two French admirals, Quiéret and Béhuchet, elected to take up a defensive posture across the mouth of the three-mile-wide estuary running south-west from the island of Cadzand, deploying their ships in three lines, chained together. Béhuchet, a short, fat Norman, had been a civil servant before showing considerable ability as a leader of raids on the English coast, and Quiéret too was an experienced sailor; but the two men did not get on personally. Both should have known better, for they were relinquishing the opportunity of fighting a sea battle, something at which the French were better than the English despite their shortage of galleys. Instead, they were affording the English the chance to fight a land battle on ships – and the English were very much better at fighting on land than the French. The third commander of the Great Army of the Sea – a Genoese mercenary named Pietro Barbanero, Barbenoire, Barbevaire or Barbavera, depending on the source – was the most experienced practitioner of naval warfare of them all. He urged that such a defensive deployment gave no room for the ships to manoeuvre and that the fleet should put to sea and make use of its numerical advantage to fight the English well away from the shore. He was ignored.

The English fleet sailed from the mouth of the River Orwell at first light on 22 June 1340, with the king aboard the cog *Thomas*, and hove to off the Flemish coast the following morning at (according to Edward's despatches) the hour of Tierce, or 0900 hours.* The two fleets could see each other. Edward first ordered the church militant, in the shape of the bishop of Lincoln, to go ashore, ride the ten miles or so to Bruges, and encourage the Flemings to attack the French from the shore once the English fleet attacked from the sea. Three knights were also landed to observe and report on the French fleet. By early next morning, 24 June, Edward knew the strength and disposition of the French fleet, and he had also received the bishop of Lincoln's unwelcome news that the citizens of Bruges were adamant that on no account should the English attack such a huge French fleet, for to do so would court disaster. Rather, they said, Edward should wait a few days until he could be reinforced by Flemish

---

* Tierce was a monastic office said at the third hour of the day, the day beginning at what we term 0600 hours.

ships. The king ignored this advice, but, since to attack at once would mean sailing into the sun, Edward decided to tack out to sea and position himself where the wind and the tide would be at his back. This and the redisposition of the fleet into attack formation took most of the day. Some sources say that the manoeuvring was interpreted by the French as an English retreat and that they began to unchain their own ships in order to pursue; and Barbanero certainly advised a move out to sea. In any event many French ships were still chained together and their fleet was still in a defensive posture when the English, with the wind, the tide and the sun behind them, struck.

Edward had arranged his fleet in line abreast, with one ship full of men-at-arms – infantry – flanked by two of archers. The archers were on the fore and stern castles and in the crow's nests, and, as the fleets closed, a storm of arrows began to cause casualties among the French. Their crossbowmen replied, but there were insufficient of them and with their much slower rate of fire they were ineffective. When the lines of ships crashed into each other, the English sailors swung their grappling irons and the infantry began to board. This was difficult, as many of the French ships were higher than those of the English, particularly the Spanish vessels of Philip's Castilian ally, but once on board the raw sailors were no match for the English men-at-arms, most of whose fighting skills had been honed by their participation in the Scottish wars. With sword, mace, short spear and bill, the English infantry captured ship after ship in the first line and recaptured the cog *Christopher*. Once the colours of Philip of Valois were struck and replaced by the lions and fleur-de-lys of England, panic set in amongst the second line of smaller ships and less experienced crews. By nightfall, most of the ships of the second French line had been captured and those of the third were trying to make their escape. Many soldiers and sailors jumped overboard to avoid the ferocity of the English attack, but a good number of those who managed to swim ashore were bludgeoned to death by the waiting Flemings. Those who could not swim (most, in fact) were drowned, as were many who could swim but were weighed down by their armour. In the darkness some French ships got away, including Barbanero's galleys, but next morning any remaining in the estuary were swiftly accounted for, and altogether 190 French ships were captured or sunk.

It was a great and overwhelming victory. Edward, and most contemporary chronicles, attributed it to the grace of God, but in truth the French were beaten by their decision to throw away their advantages in numbers and seamanship by confining themselves to the estuary, by the superiority of the English archers' firepower, and by the experience and fighting abilities of the English infantry once they had boarded the French ships. Sources vary as to the extent of the butcher's bill. Most of the chronicles give figures between 20,000 and 30,000 French dead, which are far too high. But while a beaten army on land can run away, the only escape at sea is into it, so there may have been as many as 10,000 French dead, wounded and prisoners, or about half the total number engaged, and for days afterwards bodies were being washed ashore. Quiéret was killed in the fighting, but Béhuchet was recognized and held by his captor in the hope of ransom. It was not to be: the scourge of the English coastal towns was not going to get away so lightly and Edward had him hanged on the mast of his own ship. English casualties – remarkably light considering the intensity of the ship-to-ship fighting – were between 400 and 600 killed and wounded, including the king himself, who sustained minor wounds to his thigh and hand.* While the French could and would still raid English coastal towns, the threat of a full-scale invasion had gone.

To the English, all the auguries for a successful campaign in northern France now seemed favourable. So Edward decided to capture the frontier city of Tournai himself, while Robert of Artois, with Flemish troops bolstered by a small contingent of English archers, would take the city of St Omer. All came to naught. Robert was unable to take St Omer and had to retire back to join Edward, and Edward was unable to take Tournai as he had no siege train. He also had his usual problems over money and had once more to appeal to Parliament in England for another subsidy. There, public opinion, while supportive of the war, was fiercely opposed to yet more taxation; as one chronicle put it, 'Wherefore you shall know the very truth: the inner love of the people was turned into hate and the common prayers into cursing, for cause that the common people were strongly aggrieved.'[6] A grant was forthcoming, however, but not enough

---

* Among those killed were four knights: Thomas de Mouhermere, Thomas de Latimer, John Butler and Thomas de Poynings (Lanercost).

to keep the armies in the field, nor to conduct a lengthy siege, and in mid-September, with the weather deteriorating, supplies running low and the less committed allies beginning to hedge their bets, the pope proposed a truce to last until the summer of 1341. Edward was glad to accept and slink back to England. It was an inglorious end to what had been such a promising start; it would not be for another six years that Edward III would achieve such a devastating victory as that of Sluys, and then it would be on land.

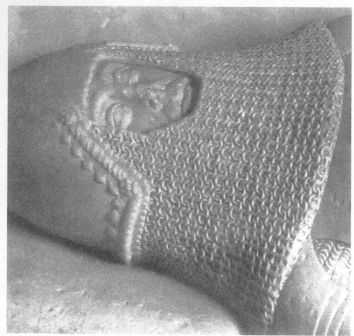

The tomb of Sir Thomas Cawne in the church of St Peter at Ightham, Kent. Descended from a Chaune who came over with the Conqueror, Cawne originated in Staffordshire and built a manor house in Ightham in 1340. He died around 1374 and while he is not shown on Wrottesley's roll local legend has it that he fought at Crecy. Note the camail, the chain mail protection for the neck and shoulders, fastened to studs in the helmet. Cawne's sword and dagger have long gone, possibly a legacy of Reformation vandalism.

3

FROM OBLIGATION
TO PROFESSION

The story of the Hundred Years War is in many ways that of the professional versus the amateur, with the increasing professionalization of English armies followed, usually all too late, by those of France. By the time of Edward I, the English military system, a fusion of the pre-Conquest Anglo-Saxon military organization with Norman feudalism, was beginning to creak. The Anglo-Saxons had depended on semi-professional household troops employed directly by the king and supported by the *fyrd* or militia, a part-time force which was embodied when danger threatened and could be required either to operate solely within its own shire or, like those elements which accompanied King Harold to Stamford Bridge and down again to Hastings in 1066, nationwide. The Norman feudal system depended on the notion that all land belonged to the king and was granted to his supporters, who in turn owed him military service. This service was expressed in terms of the number of knights the landholder, or tenant-in-chief, was required to provide for a fixed time, usually forty days. Often the tenant-in-chief would sub-allocate land to his tenants, who then took on the military service obligation. Each knight was required to provide his own equipment – armour (initially mail, giving way progressively to plate), helmet, sword, shield and lance – and at least one horse. Each knight brought his own retinue with him: a page to look after and clean his armour, a groom to care for his horses, and probably a manservant to look after him. Often there would be numerous armed followers, frequently described as esquires, or well-bred young men aspiring to knighthood. Bishops and monasteries also had a military obligation, usually, but not always, commuted for a cash payment in lieu. The number of knights required for each land holding fell steadily during the post-Conquest period, presumably because knights and their equipment became more expensive, and by 1217 a total of 115 tenants-in-chief are recorded as producing between them 470 knights.[7]

When Edward III came to the throne, the English peerage had not developed into the modern system of baron, viscount, earl, marquis and duke. It was Edward himself who created the first English duke – his eldest son, the Prince of Wales. After the Conquest, the Normans took over the existing Anglo-Saxon title of earl (from the Scandinavian *jarl*), although it was given to Normans and not to those who held the rank before the Conquest; and William I introduced the rank of baron, which came below an earl. The term 'knight' did not have the exactitude that it does today, when we have two types of knight: the knight bachelor, who is dubbed by the monarch and entitled to be described as Sir Thomas Molesworth and his wife as Lady Molesworth, and who holds the title for his lifetime only; and the hereditary knight baronet, also entitled to be described as Sir Thomas but with the abbreviation 'Bart.' or 'Bt.' after the name. The latter honour is relatively recent, having been introduced by King James I as a money-raising scheme in 1611.

During the medieval period, the honours system was much more elastic. A military knight had not necessarily been dubbed but was able to afford the cost of knight's equipment and was probably a landholder. Assuming that he did reasonably well, he would almost certainly be dubbed eventually, often on the eve of battle. A knighthood banneret, a title that lapsed in the seventeenth century, could only be awarded on the field of battle and only if the king was present;* it entitled the holder to display a rectangular banneret, as opposed to the triangular pennon of lower-ranking knights, and his own coat of arms or heraldic device. The men who filled the knightly class were brought up and trained for battle, but it was battle as individuals – tourneys and jousts for real, if you will – and under the feudal system there was real difficulty in getting them to act as a team or to persuade them to adopt a common tactical doctrine. The knights – whether dubbed or not – were what we would call the officers of

---

* Although sometimes men qualified if the king's standard was on the field even if the monarch himself was not.

the army, while the Other Ranks were provided by commissions of array, or conscription from able-bodied men of the hundreds or shires. Again, these were only required to serve for a limited period, and there were frequent arguments over whether or not they could be compelled to serve outside their own locality, and whether it was a local or national (that is, royal) responsibility to feed and pay them.

When the king knew personally all or most of the landholders in the kingdom, the feudal military system worked reasonably well. It sufficed for dynastic squabbles and raids from Scotland, but, as time went on, it could not cope with expeditions abroad or with sieges that lasted more than forty days, nor could it provide permanent garrisons. Men could not reasonably be expected to be absent from their homes during the planting season, nor for the harvest, and this greatly restricted the scope and duration of any military campaign. Even as early as the reign of Henry II, in 1171, the king faced his rebellious sons with forces that, while largely composed of men carrying out their feudal dues, included 'knights serving for wages'. Given that English kings would increasingly fight their wars abroad, mainly in France or in Scotland, and that soldiers would be required to be away from home for far longer than the feudal system allowed, the transition from a feudal host, where the officers served as part of their obligation to their overlord, to an army where all served for pay was an inevitable progression. Once soldiers (of any rank) serve for pay, rather than almost as a favour, they can be ordered to arm themselves and fight in a certain way; they can be sent to where the king wants them rather than where they want to go or not go; and, as long as the money holds out, loyalty is assured. It was Edward I who began this professionalization of the army, and eventually he paid everybody except those whom we would term generals. It was his efforts that laid the groundwork for the great victories of his grandson Edward III, against French armies which were usually far larger but still raised under a semi-feudal system.

One way of raising soldiers, once the feudal system had irreparably broken down, was to hire foreign mercenaries, and there were lots of these ready to sell their services to the highest bidder. Most of the mercenary bands were from areas where nothing much grew, like Brittany; or where there was overcrowding, such as Flanders or Brabant; or where other career paths were limited, as they were in Genoa. The difficulty was an inherent

English dislike of foreigners (some things don't change), so, while there were contingents from Brittany and Flanders in English armies abroad, there were very few actually employed in England. Even the Welsh, who provided large numbers of soldiers for Edward's wars, tended to be mustered and then marched off to the embarkation ports as speedily as possible.

It was not only the move from feudal to paid service that marked a revolution in military affairs, at least in England, but the composition of armies too. During the feudal period, the major arm was the heavy cavalry, composed of armoured knights on armoured horses who provided shock action and could generally ride through and scatter any footmen in their way. As socially the cavalry were regarded as several cuts above the infantry, who were often a poorly equipped and scantily trained militia, this held true for a very long time. The cavalryman wore mail or latterly plate armour, carried a sword, lance and shield, and was mounted on either a destrier or a courser. The destrier, or great horse, was not, as is sometimes alleged, the Shire horse or the Percheron of today. Rather, it was similar to today's Irish Draught: short-coupled, rather cobby, with strong quarters and well up to weight, the destrier was probably between fourteen and fifteen hands,* although some of the horse armour at the Royal Armouries at Leeds is made for a horse of fifteen to sixteen hands.† The courser was similar, but lighter and cheaper. Destriers are sometimes said to have been entires, and the Bayeux Tapestry certainly shows them as uncastrated, but this seems unlikely. An uncastrated horse is far less tractable than a gelding or a mare, and the depiction of the complete animal in paintings and tapestries of the period may simply be symbolic – our horses are male and rampant, and so are we.

There has been much discussion of the role of the stirrup in equestrian warfare. Some authorities state that it was only with the invention of the stirrup that the cavalryman could be anything other than an appendage to an army: useful for reconnaissance and communications but incapable of serious fighting, because only when able to brace against the stirrups could

---

* Horses are measured without shoes from the top of the withers vertically to the ground, the unit of measurement being the hand of four inches. Thus, a horse described as being 14h 2 means one of fourteen hands and two inches.
† But this may be intended for a parade horse, rather than one to be ridden in battle.

a man deliver a weighty blow without falling off. It is probable that those who make this assertion have little experience of riding. While the stirrup is a useful aid to balance when the horse does something unintended and unexpected, it is by no means essential and it would have been very difficult to fall out of a stirrupless Roman saddle, with its high pommel and cantle. Similarly, the armchair nature of the medieval saddle, with or without stirrups, made for a very safe seat except if the horse fell, when the rider, rather than being thrown clear as he would hope to be in a modern saddle, would be trapped under the horse, risking a broken pelvis or his throat being cut by an opportunistic infantryman. All the depictions of the armoured medieval cavalryman show him riding with a straight leg and very long leathers, so he could not brace against the stirrups in any case. It seems that the usefulness of the stirrup was in mounting the horse when there was no mounting block available or when the weight of armour made it impossible to vault astride the withers.

In addition to his warhorse, the armoured warrior would also have a palfrey, a hack to be ridden when not in battle and not encumbered by armour, and a packhorse to carry his kit. Fodder for a minimum of three horses per man and rations for him and the host of camp-followers, to say nothing of the cost of horses and armour, made the armoured knight a very expensive fellow, but it was not cost that forced his decline and eventual banishment from the battlefield altogether, but advances in technology and the quality of the infantry.

During the Welsh wars, the English began to have doubts about the merits of an army composed mainly of heavy cavalry: the hills and valleys of Wales did not lend themselves to flat-out charges or to wide envelopment, and the Welsh infantry spearman was generally able to put up a stout defence unless surprised and scattered. There were other pointers: at Courtrai in 1302, a Flemish infantry army had roundly defeated the flower of the French heavy cavalry by digging ditches across the approaches to their position and then standing on the defensive. The French duly charged, the impetus was destroyed by horses falling into or breaking legs in the ditches, and the Flemish won the day. As far as the English were concerned, it was Bannockburn that began to bring it home to thinking soldiers that well-organized and equipped infantry, however ill-bred, could see off the mounted host if they could bring their enemy to battle on ground of their choosing. There, on 23 June 1314, Robert Bruce's Scottish army took up a dismounted position at one end of a flat field, with both his flanks protected by woods and marshes. His men dug holes and ditches, three feet deep by three feet wide, across the inviting approaches, camouflaged them with wooden trellises covered with grass and leaves, and waited. Having had his vanguard repulsed on that day while trying to move round the Scottish flank to reach Stirling and relieve its siege, Edward II ordered, as expected, a cavalry charge on 24 June. It was a disaster. The Scots infantry did not flee, and by presenting a wall of pikes they prevented even those horsemen who did negotiate the obstacles from getting anywhere near them. Eight years later, Sir Andrew Harcla's wedge of pikemen supported by archers stopped Thomas of Lancaster's infantry and cavalry getting across the only bridge over the River Ure at Boroughbridge, while an attempt to put cavalry across by a nearby ford was stopped by archers alone.

Very few radical advances in tactics come all at once or are the product of one commander's thinking. The shift towards reliance on infantry in England and Scotland was not a sudden one but a product of experimentation and discussion at home and abroad. Many Scots took service as mercenaries in Europe and would have brought home ideas from Flanders, and the costs of the mounted arm would have forced rulers to consider cheaper alternatives. But there can be little doubt that the rout of Bannockburn accelerated English thinking, while skirmishes at home gave scope for trying out various combinations of archer, horse and foot.

That the English had absorbed the lessons of Bannockburn and Boroughbridge was duly confirmed at Dupplin Moor and Halidon Hill. At Dupplin Moor, six miles south-west of Perth, on 11 August 1332, the 1,500-strong army of the Disinherited – nominally commanded by Edward Balliol but with English advisers there with the unofficial blessing of Edward III – defeated the Bruce army of 3,000 commanded by Donald, earl of Mar. The Disinherited lost two English knights and thirty-three men-at-arms. The Scots losses are unknown but included three earls and must have been many hundreds. On 19 July the following year at Halidon Hill, two miles north-west of Berwick-upon-Tweed, an English army of around 4,000 led by Edward III in person roundly defeated Sir Archibald Douglas's 5,000-strong Scots army. Again, English losses were negligible

– one knight, one esquire and ten infantrymen of various sorts – while Douglas and five Scots earls were killed and an unknown number of lesser nobles and soldiers, perhaps as many as 1,000 all told. After Halidon Hill, there was no one left in Scotland capable of raising an army and Robert Bruce's kingdom was effectively at an end.

Both Dupplin Moor and Halidon Hill had a number of factors in common which enabled English armies to inflict crushing defeats on greater numbers, and those factors were to be incorporated in English military doctrine for the Hundred Years War. In each case, archers formed the largest portion of the armies and the victorious commanders chose to stand on a piece of ground where their own flanks were secure and which restricted the frontage of the enemy. At Dupplin Moor, the Disinherited took up a defensive position at the head of a steep-sided valley, while at Halidon Hill Edward's right flank was covered by the sea and on his left was marshy ground with a river flowing through it. In both cases, English forces fought on foot, including Edward himself at Halidon Hill, in two ranks with archers on the flanks, and in both cases the archers concentrated their arrow storms on the advancing Scots flanks, forcing them to close in towards their centre and reducing their frontage and hence their shock effect still more. By the time the Scots finally reached the English infantry line (or failed to do so at Halidon Hill), they had suffered so many casualties from the archers that their cohesion was broken and they were repulsed and fled. The pursuit was taken up by the English remounting their horses and following the defeated Scots. The policy of dismounting and standing on the defensive on carefully chosen ground, using archers to prevent outflanking moves and to break up enemy attacking formations, and presenting a solid mass of infantry in a two- or four-deep line to meet the attacking remnants was the recipe for the great English victories of the war. It was only when the English overreached themselves, and the French finally began to learn from their own defeats, that English military supremacy began to wane.

Technology came in the shape of the longbow. Bows and arrows are as old as prehistoric man: simple missile weapons, they are depicted in Palaeolithic and Neolithic cave paintings, and archaeological excavations have uncovered bows and arrows dating back to the third millennium BC.[8] Bows were in use by Roman auxiliaries and light hunting bows were used by both sides at Hastings in 1066. Quite how and where the short bow, drawn back to the chest and with its limited range and penetrating power, mutated into the English longbow is uncertain: it would not have been a sudden change, and the longbow may have first been used by the southern Welsh in the second half of the twelfth century, although the evidence is scanty. It was anyway gradually, and eventually enthusiastically, adopted by the English, and, as a reluctance to spend money on defence is not confined to twenty-first-century British governments, its cheapness would have appealed. The longbow would become the English weapon of mass destruction; it was consistently ignored by England's enemies, who would consistently be slaughtered by it. From the time of Edward I's Assize of Arms in 1285, all free men were required to keep weapons at home and to practise archery regularly at the village butts, for the longbow was not something that could be picked up and used by anybody. Rather like Scottish pipers, archers began to develop their skills as children, gradually increasing the size and 'pull' of their bows as they grew up. Exhumed bodies of medieval archers show greatly developed, or over-developed, shoulder and back muscles.

The standard longbow was made of yew wood, either native English yew or imported from Ireland, Spain or Italy, and approximated in length to the height of the archer. Thus, there would not have been very many that were six feet in length, as modern reproductions are. Rather, the average would have been around five feet two or three. While originally the same craftsman would manufacture bows and arrows, this soon diverged into two trades, the bowyers who made bows and the fletchers who made arrows, each with their own guild. The bow had a pull of around 100 pounds and shot a 'cloth yard' arrow out to an effective range of about 300 yards. There is dispute over exactly how long a cloth yard was, the measurement being one used by Flemish weavers, many of whom were encouraged to come to England by Edward III. Definitions vary from 27¼ to 37 inches, the latter supposedly codified by Edward VI, the short-lived son of Henry VIII, while some sources describe an arrow as being an ell in length. As an English ell was 45 inches, this seems unlikely. Whatever the length of the arrow – and the shorter seems more realistic – its construction was a skilled affair, requiring the fletcher to obtain good straight wood for the shaft, usually ash, to cut it to the correct length, and to affix the arrowhead and the feathers to stabilize the arrow in flight. Three pinion feathers per arrow were required and generally came from a goose. As a goose only had six feathers that were suitable, three on each wing, which regrew annually, and as many hundreds of thousands of arrows were ordered during the wars, the goose population in the kingdom must have been considerable.

Arrowheads came in two basic types: one to pierce flesh with broad barbs; the other, much narrower with a sharp point and no barbs, to penetrate armour. While the arrow was said to be capable of going through an inch of oak at a hundred yards, it would not have gone through plate armour except at relatively close range and at a flat trajectory. The usual way of employing archers was to mass them and have them shoot volleys at a 45-degree angle, thus obtaining maximum range and ensuring that they struck from above. While this might not immediately kill armoured cavalrymen, it would wound them, panic their horses and generally discourage an enemy from pressing home his charge. As a competent archer was expected to be able to discharge ten arrows a minute, the 5,000 or so archers that Henry V had at Agincourt in 1415 could produce a horrifying arrow storm of 25,000 arrows every thirty seconds.

The other missile weapon in general use was the crossbow. This was made of a composite of wood and horn, and even steel, and shot a bolt, or quarrel, of iron, steel or ash with more force to a greater range and with more accuracy than the longbow; but the effort and the length of time needed to pull the bowstring back to engage with the trigger meant that its rate of discharge was only around two quarrels a minute. The English generally only employed the crossbow as a defensive weapon in castles and fortified places. It could, however, be shot from behind cover, unlike the longbow, and unlike the longbow required little training to use. In the field, crossbowmen carried a large shield, a pavise. As tall as a man and with an easel-type leg at the back allowing it to stand up unsupported, this afforded the crossbowman cover while he reloaded. The French did have some longbowmen but presumably considered the training and development not to be worth the effort. Still fighting their wars with a feudal host, they employed large numbers of mercenary crossbowmen, to their detriment as we shall see.

In England, contracts for very large numbers of bows and arrows were placed. In 1341, when the king had returned from France and was gearing up for another foray there, 7,700 bows and 12,800 sheaves of arrows were purchased and stored in the Tower of London.[9] A sheaf was twenty-four arrows, so the astonishing total of 307,200 arrows, with the feathers of 153,600 geese, was still only three minutes' shooting for the 10,000 archers that Edward was intending to take to France. The rate of purchase continued throughout the war, and, in 1421, the crown bought and stored in the Tower 425,000 arrows, to which 212,500 geese had contributed. A sheriff would receive written instructions from London to obtain a certain number of bows, arrows and bowstrings from his bailiwick, and he would place the order with local craftsmen, receive the finished product, box them up and despatch them to the Tower. Bows might be 'white' – that is, in natural wood – or painted, although this latter could refer to some form of preservative oil, as paint would soon flake off when the bow was flexed. The accounts of the chamberlain of Chester Castle show that he paid one shilling and sixpence (£0.075) for a bow, and one shilling and fourpence (£0.064) for a sheaf of arrows.[10] Today a replica longbow costs around £300 and arrows are £130 a sheaf. While in 1346 Edward would take foot and mounted archers to France, thus reducing his speed of movement, the foot archers would be phased out over time, and by the following decade most archers would be mounted – that is, they would move on horseback while dismounting to fight. Archers were protected by an iron or steel helmet and wore a 'jack', a short, quilted jacket sewn with iron studs. An archer-heavy army was ideal for the English: bows and arrows were cheap, laws were enacted to ensure that the male population remained proficient in their use, and they were an early example of English armies using technology as a force multiplier when opposed by far more numerous enemies.

The other major element of the English military machine was the man-at-arms, the successor of the heavily armoured mounted knight. Men-at-arms were mainly of gentle birth, ranging from actual knights or those hoping to become knights to esquires or minor gentry, usually in the proportion of one knight to four others.[11] Like the mounted archers, they moved on horseback but fought on foot. As the transition from mounted to dismounted battle took place, the shield they carried grew smaller and eventually was dispensed with altogether. Men-at-arms were still well protected, although, unlike their French equivalents, mainly in mail, rather than plate, armour. While they were equipped with swords – and a variety of axes, maces and daggers were also carried – their main weapon was the halberd, or half-pike. The chronicles are lacking in details about exactly how the men-at-arms fought, but it is likely that they were drawn up in two or four ranks, depending on the frontage to be covered, close together but not so close that they could not swing their weapons, with each man taking up two-and-a-half feet or so of frontage. Another infantry element was the spearman, or light infantryman, many of whom were Welsh. They formed up in schiltrons or phalanxes to present a hedge of spears to an attacker who, once impaled on a spear, would be finished off with what were described as knives but were in fact short swords. Finally, the infantry included skirmishers and scouts, lightly armed with javelins and daggers, whose main occupation when not scouting seems to have been cutting the throats of enemy wounded. They were recruited from Wales, Cornwall and Ireland, with a few renegade Scots.

While the heavy cavalry component had almost disappeared in English armies, there was still a requirement for light cavalry, and these were the hobelars, shown in the muster rolls as *armatti*, who were lightly armed and mounted on ponies or on what today would be considered light hunter types. Their role was not to charge the enemy but to reconnoitre, patrol, find routes, forage for rations, collect intelligence and provide communications. With so much of the army now mounted, there was of course a requirement for grooms and farriers to accompany it, to say nothing of the huge amount of forage that would have to be either shipped with the army or bought or sequestered on the ground. Other specialists would be miners for siegework, armourers to repair weapons and suits of armour, masons and carpenters to construct defences and build bridges, bowyers and fletchers to repair and replace the archers' necessities, and even a military band. Edward III may also have had some early cannon, or gunpowder artillery, although the details are vague.

The army that Edward was gathering was made up of three types of soldier: those belonging to retinues, either the king's or those of magnates; paid contingents raised by individual contractors; and men summoned by commissions of array. There were two sorts of retinues: those composed of household troops and those of men who were indentured. Household retinues consisted of those men who were tenants of the lord and whose families owed a feudal obligation to him. These personal retinues would become less important as the war went on, but in the 1340s they were still significant. Indentured retinues – sometimes unkindly referred to as 'bastard feudalism' – were those raised by an individual, who had to be of the rank of banneret or above, and its members were employed on contract, occasionally for a specific period but more often to serve the lord in peace and war for life. The contract was written, laid down the wages and expenses to be paid, stipulated exactly what type of service was to be provided, including whether it was to be within England only or abroad, and usually included the proviso that a certain proportion of any ransom or plunder acquired was to go to the lord. Service was owed to that particular lord and could not be transferred to anyone else without the agreement of both parties. The contract was sealed and both parties kept a copy. Members of indentured retinues were required to be of the rank of knight or esquire and to wear the lord's badge or uniform.[12] The retinues varied in size from that of the earl of Northampton, who in 1341 undertook to provide seven bannerets, seventy-four knights, 199 men-at-arms, 200 armed men (spearmen and hobelars) and 100 archers, or the earl of Derby, who in 1342 agreed to muster five bannerets, fifty knights, 144 esquires and 200 mounted archers, both forces a mix of household and indentured retinues; to less well-off members of the gentry like John Beauchamp, who produced one knight (himself), five esquires, six men-at-arms and four mounted archers.[13]

As knights still had a feudal obligation, it was in the government's interest to have lots of them, and there were various regulations to persuade those of means (lands worth £40 a year) to accept knighthood. To those who were going to war, whether as part of an overlord's retinue or of their own volition, knighthood was an advantage, for not only did it double the man's pay but a captured knight was also more likely to be held for ransom rather than slaughtered out of hand. That said, the expense of armour, horses, servants and the other trappings of gentility did deter some, and fines were levied against those who turned knighthood down. When the king was strong and admired – Edward I, Edward III, Henry V – there were few who resisted becoming knights and contributing to the war effort, while when kings were weak or unpopular – Edward II, Richard II, Henry VI – the contrary applied.

Contract forces raised by the king and the government were similar to indentured retinues but without personal loyalty to an individual lord.

They were the first true professional or career soldiers and might be considered the national army, as opposed to local or private armed bodies. An individual, usually referred to as a captain, contracted to produce a certain number of soldiers of a stipulated type for a prescribed period of time to serve in a particular area; terms and conditions of service were laid down and agreed. Like indentured retinues, numbers varied widely, from Edward Montagu, captain, who in 1341 agreed to provide six knights, twenty men-at-arms, twelve spearmen and twelve archers for forty days in Brittany for a total of £76,* to men like Sir Hugh Calveley, who could recruit a thousand soldiers to serve in the same area.

In the early stages of the war, soldiers raised by commissions of array – a system of conscription that had changed little since Saxon times – outnumbered those in retinues or under contract, although as time went on the army would become more and more composed of professionals. With the exception of those living in coastal areas, all males aged between sixteen and sixty were liable to conscription organized by arrayers, who might be sergeants-at-arms (royal servants and more like mobile inspectors and trouble-shooters rather than the senior non-commissioned officers they are today), knights of the king's household or local officials. Using the local authorities to select men was administratively simple but invited corruption, as local arrayers sought or were offered bribes to exempt those who did not wish to go, and often the men selected were quite unfit for military service. Sergeants-at-arms or the king's own officials were less susceptible to corruption, and, because they had military experience themselves and knew the sort of man they wanted, they tended to get a better quality of recruit.

Even then, there were problems. Often the best men had already been recruited either into a local lord's retinue or into an indentured company. And despite various statutes, not everybody possessed weapons, which had to be provided or paid for locally, and it was a stipulation that those who did not serve were required to contribute towards the cost of those who did. Because of the difficulty of finding sufficient men by array, there had to be

---

* The going rate was £80 (see pay rates below), so either Montagu was finding the rest from his own pocket, or he had persuaded his men to take a cut in pay and was hoping to make up the shortfall from plunder.

incentives. These included assurances to pressed men that they could keep a certain proportion of the value of goods captured, usually up to £100, which was twenty years' salary for a foot archer, and pardons for outlaws. If a man who was ordered to appear before the courts on a criminal charge consistently failed to appear, then he was declared outlaw, or 'without the law', which meant that, technically at least, he could be killed with impunity depending on the seriousness of his alleged offence. Outlawry only applied to the man's county, so someone on the run had only to escape to the next county to be safe from retribution, but, as an outlaw's goods and chattels were forfeit to the crown, it was not a comfortable state. The king, and only the king, could grant pardons in exchange for military service, although sensibly the pardon was usually withheld until the service was complete and the man's good behaviour attested to by his commander. In the year 1339/40, a total of 850 charters of pardon were granted for military services rendered, of which around three-quarters are estimated to have been to murderers. Altogether, perhaps up to one-tenth of an English army was made up of criminals working their passage to forgiveness.[14]

Men raised by commissions of array were organized into vintenaries, or twenties, under a vintenar or junior officer, usually a knight but, if not, someone of military experience. Five vintenaries made a centenary commanded by a centenar, who was mounted even if his troops were not. The nearest modern equivalent is the platoon and the company. We have little knowledge of how these men were trained, but clearly there must have been a training syllabus over and above weekly archery practice. While soldiers of the time did not march in step, they would have been required to move with a measured pace at a set rate of paces per minute, in order that they could change formation without losing cohesion. The men would have been made to become accustomed to moving and fighting as part of a team, to obey orders without question, to understand military terminology, and to handle their weapons as the army demanded. Development of physical fitness and training in living in the field would not have been as important as it is for young British recruits today, but some understanding of field hygiene and first aid would presumably have been instilled.

Soldiers wearing a uniform are recognizable and hence easier to control and discipline – they also find it more difficult to desert. While there was not as yet a national uniform in the modern sense, many contingents were equipped to a common standard of dress, and many of the richer magnates, and even localities, vied with each other in the provision of uniform clothing. Mostly, the men seem to have been clothed in various shades of white, but the Welsh contingents were clothed in hats and quilted tunics that were white on one side and green on the other, while the men of London wore red and white stripes. But even if units were all uniformed to a greater or lesser extent, recognition in the heat of battle cannot have been easy, given the number of contingents in the army and the plethora of individual coats of arms on bannerets' surcoats – to say nothing of the standards and banners displayed by barons, earls and formation commanders. Edward III eventually reverted to his grandfather's practice of ordering all to wear an armband of the red cross of St George.

By now, it was recognized that, lingering feudal obligations notwithstanding, officers and men of an army had to be paid. Rates of pay, varying somewhat depending upon the success or otherwise of recruitment, were expressed as daily rates (as British army rates of pay still are). A duke (and at first there was only one – the Prince of Wales) got thirteen shillings and fourpence (£0.67); an earl eight shillings (£0.40); a knight banneret four shillings (£0.20); a knight bachelor two shillings (£0.10); a man-at-arms who was not a knight one shilling (£0.05); an English vintenar, a hobelar and a mounted archer sixpence (£0.025); a Welsh vintenar, a dismounted archer and an English light infantryman threepence (£0.0125); and a Welsh spearman twopence (£0.0083). Taking the numbers that they might command, then the duke might be a brigade commander, the earl a battalion commander, the banneret a company commander and the knight a platoon commander. Thus, the ratio of pay was 7:4:2:1, which in terms of responsibility is probably about right.*

While of less importance after the Battle of Sluys, it was still necessary to guard against sea-borne raids, and this was the responsibility of the Keepers of the Maritime Lands, officials in the counties bordering the sea. Appointed by the king, they organized and commanded the Garde

---

* The modern-day comparison is 3¼:2¼:1¾:1, which bears little relation to what the job actually entails but does illustrate the reluctance in a democracy with universal suffrage to pay senior commanders what they are worth.

de la Mer, which combined dedicated coastal observers with a warning system and a call-out in the event of a French landing. The warning system consisted of a line of beacons along the shore and stretching inland, which were to be ignited if a landing was about to take place; pitch was preferred to twigs in the beacons as being less likely to be affected by rain. Each beacon was attended by between four and six men, who manned an observation post consisting of two or three wine barrels filled with sand and stacked on top of each other, with a watcher perched on top looking out to sea. Churches were ordered that under normal circumstances only one bell was to be rung, as the ringing of all the bells was the signal that a landing was happening. Men living in the Maritime Lands – defined as the coastal strip extending three leagues (nine miles) inland – were exempt from military service outside that area, while owners of estates within the area were reminded that they must live on them, as they provided the officers in the event of a call-out of the militia to counter an invasion. There were also arrangements whereby the militia of inland counties could be deployed to coastal counties if invasion threatened. One of the difficulties was the need to prevent residents of the Maritime Lands from leaving them, as many who lived on the Isle of Wight and in Portsmouth and Southampton – areas regularly raided by the French – not unnaturally tried to do. The arrangements had changed little from pre-Norman times, and, while such a system could cope with minor raids, it is doubtful whether it could have done very much to counter a full-scale invasion. Fortunately, after Sluys, it did not have to.

While Edward was raising money and an army to return to France, which he would do in 1346, the English military machine was not idle, for there were momentous happenings in Brittany that England could not ignore. Brittany had always been important to England: strategically placed between Normandy and Aquitaine, it controlled the coastal sea route between England and Bordeaux, one along which the lucrative trade in grain one way and wine the other could flow and thereby avoid the treacherous storms of the Bay of Biscay. It was very much in England's interests that Brittany should be at best an ally, and at worst neutral, in any struggle with France. Although technically vassals of the king of France, dukes of Brittany issued their own coinage and underwent a ceremony suspiciously similar to coronation; they had always managed to retain independence to a greater or lesser degree, depending on how much control French kings could exercise over a relatively remote province. When Bretons aggrieved by a decision of the duke or his courts appealed to the *parlement* in Paris,* as they were legally entitled to do, dukes generally ignored the findings, and there was very little that the king could do.

Duke Arthur II, who ruled from 1305 to 1312, married twice. By his first wife, Marie, viscountess of Limoges, he had two sons: Jean III, who succeeded him in 1312, and Guy, who died in 1331. By his second wife, Yolande, countess of Monfort, he had one son, John de Montfort. Duke Jean III died in 1341 without legitimate issue. Guy, who predeceased him, had a daughter, Jeanne de Penthieve. The candidates for the succession, therefore, were Jeanne and her half-uncle John de Montfort. Both John de Montfort and his mother Yolande had always felt that they had not been granted the landholdings to which their position and birth entitled them. John had spent most of his time out of the duchy as a vexatious litigant pursuing lawsuits in the Paris courts and in Flanders, where he believed that he was entitled to certain landholdings by virtue of having married a daughter of the count of Flanders. On hearing of the death of Duke Jean III, John de Montfort accepted the support of Edward III – whether at his initiative or at Edward's is disputed – but if Edward was king of France, as he said he was, then he was entitled to decide the succession. Philip VI, however, called an assembly in Paris which decided in favour of Jeanne. As she had been married since 1337 to Charles of Blois, a stout supporter of the Valois, this came as no great surprise, even if only a few years previously Philip had argued strenuously against inheritance through the female line. John intended to press his claim by force of arms, but at first few Bretons rallied to his cause – after all, he had hitherto shown little interest in his claimed birthright. It was the advance of a large French army towards Brittany to assist Charles of Blois to take possession that forced the population to take sides. In general, the leading nobles supported the French candidate, while the lesser, Breton-speaking gentry supported Montfort, probably because they resented French encroachments on their independence. In addition, many of the merchants and those who lived

---

* Not, as might be expected, a parliament in the English sense but the supreme royal court and supposedly superior to all duchy and provincial courts.

near the ports and profited from trade with England also threw in their lot with him.

At first what was now a civil war did not go well for the Montforts. The French army, commanded by John, duke of Normandy, Philip VI's son, concentrated at Angers and moved to the Brittany frontier, capturing Champtoceaux on the Loire and laying siege to Nantes, which capitulated on 18 November when John de Montfort was captured. Negotiations now began – what might Montfort accept as compensation for giving up his claim? – but, as the anti-French party had other issues besides the question of succession, the war went on and Rennes and Vannes fell to the French in the spring of 1342. Just when it looked as if the Montfort cause was doomed, Montfort's wife, Jeanne of Flanders, a formidable woman described by the chronicler Froissart as having 'the heart of a lion and the courage of a man', took herself to England and prevailed upon Edward III (who would have needed little persuasion) to intervene with troops. The redoubtable Sir Walter Manny, with forty knights and 200 archers, was first to land in Brittany in March 1342, followed in July by William Bohun, earl of Northampton, with fifty knights and 1,000 archers.

Northampton now took over command of the entire force and, somewhat ambitiously given the size of his contingent, laid siege to the town of Morlaix. When in September a French army under Charles of Blois approached to raise the siege, Northampton abandoned his lines, marched his troops by night four miles north-west of Morlaix, and positioned them in a well-chosen defensive position across the French line of advance, with his back to thick woods and his flanks protected by further woods and by ditches he had his men dig. Adopting the tactics of Bannockburn, he also had his men dig ditches and pits, concealed by grass, across the front of his position and on all likely avenues of approach, and then formed his men into one dismounted line. Contrary to what had become and would continue to be the standard English defence tactic, he did not employ his archers on the flanks but included them in the infantry line, presumably because, had he not thus augmented it, the line would have been too thin to withstand attack. As it was, assuming that all ninety knights and 1,200 archers were still on parade, then he could have presented a two-rank frontage of 600 yards, but, given the lack of heavy weapons (halberds, two-handed swords, maces) among the archers, it is perhaps more likely that he formed them in three or even four ranks, offering a frontage of 400 or 300 yards. In any event, when a portion of the French army, which may have been as much as 5,000-strong, appeared on 30 September and launched their usual successive charges of heavy cavalry, the horsemen could not negotiate the ditches and pits and the result was chaos and slaughter. At least fifty French knights were killed and perhaps 150 captured, and the rest fled the field. Wisely, given the small force under his command, Northampton did not pursue.[15]

Northampton was soon reinforced by the king himself, who landed at Brest in October with 5,000 men. Soon the castles and fortified places along the coast were in Anglo-Breton hands, but both John, duke of Normandy, and his father Philip VI, who had now arrived in the area with more troops, adopted delaying tactics and refused to give battle, playing for time until Edward ran out of money or patience or made a major mistake. Vannes was eventually betrayed to Edward, but not before a number of attempts to take it by assault had failed, including one led by Robert of Artois in which he was wounded and, while supposedly recovering, caught dysentery, which killed him. His body was brought back to England and buried in London. Vannes now became the Anglo-Breton administrative headquarters, but otherwise the stalemate lasted until January 1343, when a truce was brokered which allowed the status quo to remain and both kings to withdraw so that negotiations could begin in earnest under papal supervision. Now John de Montfort, no doubt exasperated by the lack of progress, broke his parole, escaped from imprisonment and fled to England, where he did homage to Edward – who had narrowly escaped shipwreck on the way home – as king of France. John then returned to Brittany in 1345, determined to galvanize the struggle, and promptly died in September of that year, the cause of death probably gangrene from what had been thought to be a minor wound. In any case, the Montfort hopes now rested in John's five-year-old son. From now on it would be the English who kept the war of succession going, partly to ensure a friendly or client Brittany, but also to give Edward another point from which he could attack France when hostilities were resumed.

Meanwhile, in England, preparations for the next expeditionary force to France continued. While the army would attempt to live off the land in enemy territory and by local purchase in the country of an ally, the men would have to be fed while they waited to embark, while they were at sea, and on landing until other arrangements could be made. Royal commissaries would purchase the necessary rations in bulk and have them delivered to the muster stations or ports of embarkation, or this might be delegated to the admiral in command of a fleet. Meat would usually be salted beef, pork, bacon and mutton, although beef on the hoof could also be bought and transported, while vegetables would be peas, beans and oats. Wheat would be bought but ground into flour before delivery; cheese was bought by the 'wey', a wey being twenty-six stones; and large quantities of dried fish, mainly herring, were also supplied. The potato was, of course, unknown and its equivalent was bread, which was the staple for medieval man, who did not (unless he was very rich) eat from a plate but from a 'trencher', a flat, boat-shaped piece of bread. As wheat, which produced white flour, would only grow in ground that was well manured, white bread was restricted to the rich (the officers), while the lower ranks made do with black bread made from rye, or loaves made from barley or even from ground peas. Water was generally contaminated, unclean and the bearer of all sorts of diseases, and so was only drunk *in extremis*. Instead, people drank ale, which was brewed from barley.* The barley was soaked until it germinated and produced malt, which was dried and ground and then mixed with hot water and allowed to ferment. The result was only very mildly alcoholic – certainly not of strength to have any effect – and the ration for a soldier or a sailor was one gallon per man per day. Many households brewed their own ale, and, although brewing was one of the few commercial activities open to women, there were very few brewers who could supply the quantities needed by an army or a fleet. In 1340, when Yarmouth contracted to supply thirty ships for forty days to ply between England and Flanders, the 60,400 gallons of ale for the 1,510 men of the ships' crews came from just three suppliers at a cost to the treasury of one penny a gallon.†

From late 1345 and into the spring of 1346, soldiers were ordered

---

* Beer, which is made from hops, was drunk in Europe at this time but not in England. In modern usage, the terms 'beer' and 'ale' are interchangeable, except to the purist.
† Today, a gallon of real ale (admittedly much stronger than its medieval ancestor) costs £22, an inflation factor of 5,280. On the other hand, a gallon then cost a third of a day's pay for a foot archer and today costs about a third of a day's pay for a mid-band private soldier, so perhaps the ale standard is the most accurate comparator of monetary values yet.

to muster points and then to the ports of embarkation, while the king's sergeants-at-arms were ordered to 'arrest' shipping and have it prepared to transport the army to France. The requisition of ships in this way was not popular with owners or merchants, as it interfered with trade. Nor could it be done quickly: the ship would have to unload its cargo, often in an unintended port, and then be moved to Portsmouth, Winchelsea or Sandwich, prepared for the transport of troops and horses, and then loaded with rations and equipment to await the arrival of the troops. Ships that were to become horse transports had to have extra-wide gangways installed and stalls built on board for the horses. In Hampshire alone, orders were placed for twenty gangways and 1,000 hurdles to make the partitions for the stalls, plus nails, rings to tie the horses to and rope for halters.

Soldiers conscripted by commissions of array were to be from the counties 'citra Trent' – south of the River Trent – only, as the Scottish threat could not be discounted. The men were ordered to muster points in their own localities and then, when enough had reported to justify detaching an officer or vintenar to command them, sent off to one of the embarkation ports. On 2 January 1346, thirty men from Salisbury were despatched to Sandwich and took six days to cover the 130 miles; men from Stafford took seven days to cover the 140 miles to the same port; and men from Shaftsbury took twelve days to get to Winchelsea via Southampton, a distance of 155 miles. Men were therefore expected to march up to twenty miles a day along rough roads and tracks while carrying their weapons and personal kit. In an age when the only means of locomotion was by horse or on foot, physical fitness was not a problem. When the arrayed soldiers arrived at a muster point and waited there, and again while they were on the march to a port, their wages were the responsibility of their counties, but, once they arrived at that port, they went onto 'king's wages'. As in some cases they had to wait for long periods until other contingents arrived or until the weather was suitable, their presence was no doubt welcomed by prostitutes and tavern-keepers, although perhaps not so enthusiastically by others. Modern-day Aldershot is not so very different.

The total numbers assembled by Edward for his 1346 invasion of France are not easy to come by: many original records, pay rolls and the like have been lost and chroniclers seem to have plucked a number out of the air, nearly always wildly exaggerated. The best guess is that Edward's army totalled around 16,500 combatants,[16] perhaps slightly more, plus specialists (standard-bearers, trumpeters, chaplains, physicians, farriers, miners, gunners, artisans various and the bishop of Durham, whose pay rate was six shillings and eight pence, or £0.33 a day). Of this figure, some 7,700 were men of retinues, either feudal or indentured or contracted companies, while around 8,600 were men raised by commissions of array. With eight earls, fifty-five bannerets, 599 knights and 1,821 esquires, it was somewhat over-officered by modern standards, but, as only the earls, bannerets and some of the senior knights would actually command sub-units of any size, the ratio of officers to soldiers is not too different from present-day arrangements. The army contained around 2,500 men-at-arms and 2,200 mounted archers, all in retinues or contracted, 5,000 foot archers, 3,000 Welsh spearmen and 1,200 hobelars, all arrayed. Each Welsh vintenary had an interpreter, as many of the men spoke no English. Given that in battle only the earls and the bannerets would be mounted (so that they could see what was happening) and that all others would fight on foot, then the army would field nearly 8,000 infantry and, with the royal bodyguard (of Cheshire bowmen), about the same number of archers.

Edward had originally ordered that ships and men be assembled at Portsmouth and the subsidiary embarkation points by 14 February 1346. However, when it became apparent that the ships would not be ready in time, this was extended to the middle of Lent (23 March in 1346), then to two weeks after Easter (30 April), when another, supposedly final delay of two weeks was ordered. Even then, high winds and foul weather meant that embarkation could not begin until July, and the process of loading something in the order of 20,000 horses and the last of the fresh rations took several days. As the king was responsible for replacing or paying for horses lost in battle, each horse as it was loaded had its description (height and markings such as star on forehead, white off-pastern, and so on), owner and value noted. This latter could vary from a hobelar's hack at £1 to a knight's warhorse at £10. Before the king embarked, the ceremony of handing over the Great Seal took place on the altar of the church in Fareham, Hampshire, and at last, on 5 July, the ships with their cargo of men, horses, equipment and stores set sail from their respective ports to rendezvous off the Isle of Wight. Once the entire fleet was assembled, messengers were sent to London, Dover, Winchelsea and Sandwich with the royal command that no one was to be permitted to leave the country for eight days – a measure intended to prevent French spies from reporting the movement of ships, something that could hardly be concealed from watchers on land. The fleet now headed for France. Edward III was about to earn his place as one of England's greatest soldier kings.

The Battle of Crécy, 1346. A highly stylised version from the Chronicles of Froissart, where neither the ground nor the dress of the combatants has any similarity to reality. It does, however, show how the crossbowman winding his windlass could not approach the rate of discharge of the archer. The Oriflamme of St Denis, indicating no quarter, was present as shown.

4

CRÉCY

When Edward with his army and fleet left the Isle of Wight, he had a number of possible courses open to him. He could have landed in Flanders, where since the Battle of Sluys the inhabitants were firmly allied to the English; or in Aquitaine, where Henry, earl of Derby and Lancaster, was holding out against French depredations; or in Brittany to join Sir Walter Manny and the Montfort party. In all of those locations friendly troops could have ensured an unopposed landing and a secure base whence to advance inland, but in the event Edward chose none of these obvious courses but instead elected to land where there were no friendly troops in a province that was steadfastly French and whose ruler was Philip VI's son. Edward would, of course, have been well aware that Philip would be expecting an invasion, but, like General Sir Frederick Morgan planning for his D-Day nearly 600 years later, it was imperative that he concealed the actual landing zone and so he headed for Normandy. To land in Normandy was certainly taking a chance, but not so much of a chance as might initially appear. For, while there would be no friendly troops to meet him, there would be no enemy ones either, as most had been sent off to Aquitaine, and, by opening up yet another front, he would force the French to disperse their forces even more and prevent them from concentrating. Added to that, there was the richness of the Norman countryside and of its cities. The former, with the harvest just in, would provide provisions in plenty, while the latter would yield rich pickings in plate, jewels, coin and ransom.

The sea-borne journey from England to Normandy in 1944 was highly unpleasant for the men involved, but it was far worse in 1346.

In 1944, the journey took much less time, and, although the men had to try to avoid being sprayed by each other's vomit – for just about everyone was sea-sick to a greater or lesser degree – at least they were not surrounded by ever larger piles of horse droppings, nor did they have to try to feed and groom the increasingly fractious animals. One consolation in 1346, however, was that horses have no facility to regurgitate. Bad weather blew Edward's fleet back almost all the way to the coast of Cornwall before the winds changed, and, although the ships had left the English ports on 5 July, it was not until 12 July that they sighted the Norman coast and began to disembark in the bay of La Hougue (now Saint-Vaast la Hougue) on the eastern side of the Cotentin peninsula. It took three days to land the men, horses and stores, and, while unloading was going on, ships that had discharged their cargo moved to Barfleur, three miles up the coast. Here the sailors found and destroyed seven French warships, before setting fire to the town itself, having first removed all portable valuables.* A few disaffected Norman knights appeared and threw in their lot with the English, and their local knowledge would be useful, for time was now of the essence.

Edward was intending to embark upon a *chevauchée*, literally a 'mounted raid', which involved moving rapidly through enemy territory doing as much damage as possible but avoiding pitched battle. The purpose was partly economic and partly to terrorize. The destruction of property, the levelling of buildings, the reduction of fortifications, the burning of crops, the removal of gold and silver, and the killing of people all damaged the economy by reducing the amount of tax that could be levied, while at the same time enriching the invading army. Terror could persuade the population to change its allegiance and spelled out a message to the enemy ruler: come to terms or this goes on and will be repeated. Particularly relevant too, at this period in history, was the damage to Philip's honour and reputation if he could be shown to be incapable of defending his subjects. Leaders of such raids usually aimed to start from a secure base and slash and burn their way to another secure area, or to a port where they could

---

* Froissart says the English did not burn the town, but he was not there, whereas Michael de Northburg, one of the royal clerks (quoted in George Wrottesley, *Crecy and Calais*, Harrison and Sons, London, 1898), was there and says it was burned.

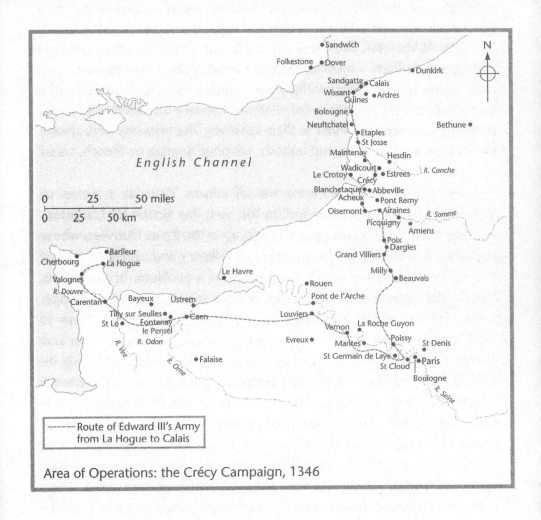

Area of Operations: the Crécy Campaign, 1346

re-embark, before an avenging army caught up with them. Edward would have been intending to sweep up from Normandy to the English county of Ponthieu, at the mouth of the River Somme, and then, depending upon the French reaction, either to return to England or to move into friendly Flanders. At the time, there was little distinction between enemy soldiers and enemy civilians – indeed, the line between them was blurred when most males had a military obligation – and, although there was still a vestige of chivalry present in the relations between the nobility of either side, this was rarely extended to their inferiors. The peasants were always the victims in these raids, and nobody, whether English or French, cared very much about them.

By 18 July, the English army was all ashore. That day it moved to Valognes, eleven miles away, and on the next day struck for Carentan, another twenty miles away, but was held up at the River Douvres, where the locals had destroyed the only bridge. Infantry and cavalry could, of course, cross the river without too much of a problem, bridge or no, but, for the baggage train of wheeled vehicles which carried the tentage, stores, rations and accumulated loot, a bridge was needed. Many of the Norman bridges were of stone, which would have taken time and energy to destroy, so many had one span in wood that could easily be demolished when necessary – and as easily repaired. Edward's engineers rebuilt the bridge during the night, and on 20 July the English were in Carentan, where a large quantity of provisions and wine fell into their hands. They then burned the town, although Edward is said to have attempted to prevent it, and next day reached the River Vire, where again the bridges giving access to Saint-Lô had been torn down. Once more, the engineers repaired one of the bridges, and on 22 July Saint-Lô was in English hands and again was put to the torch, but not before 1,000 butts of wine had been confiscated. Edward made no attempt to save Saint-Lô, for he was particularly infuriated to find the heads of three Norman knights on pikes above the main gate – they had been captured fighting for Edward in Brittany and executed as traitors. Edward's view was, of course, that they had been fighting for their rightful king – him – and in any event one just did not execute captured knights.

Bayeux escaped the fate of the other towns on the army's route: its citizens had taken the precaution of sending emissaries pledging allegiance to Edward well before the army got anywhere near the town. By 25 July, the army was approaching Caen, a city bigger than any in England except London, having covered ninety miles in seven days – very fast going when the delays in bridging the rivers and plundering the towns and villages for miles either side of the route are considered. The advance would have been led entirely by mounted knights, men-at-arms and archers, while the foot-borne elements would have followed on, and if the engineers (carpenters and masons) were on foot, as they probably were, then they had made excellent progress indeed. A portion of the dismounted troops had been left behind to support the fleet, which now sailed along the coast with the soldiers moving parallel to it, looting and burning every coastal village and farmstead until from Cherbourg to Ustrem (Ouistreham) there was not a house standing nor a farm animal alive, while any stores of grain or other provisions not loaded onto the ships were burned. The purported reason for this devastation was to destroy French naval power in the Channel, to which it undoubtedly contributed, but there was a personal profit motive too. Discipline in the navy was clearly not what it should have been, for, despite orders that all ships were to remain in Norman waters, some of the crews – some sources say as many as a hundred – loaded their ships to the gunwales with loot, then took off for England to realize their newfound wealth.

Caen was a much more formidable obstacle than the towns captured so far, which had been defended only lightly or not at all. The city itself was centred on William the Conqueror's castle. This was an immensely strong fortification, but the town below it was not well suited to defence, as its eleventh-century walls were by now in disrepair and in some places falling down. To the north-east and south-west of the castle and about 800 yards from it were respectively the Abbaye aux Dames and the Abbaye aux Hommes, the latter the burial place of William the Conqueror. The commercial heart of the city and its most prosperous suburb lay 600 yards south-west of the castle on the Île Saint-Jean, centred round the church of Saint Jean, which is still there, and was unwalled but entirely surrounded by the waters of the Rivers Odon and Orne and their branches. Those rivers are still there too, but their courses have changed, particularly that of the Odon, which is now underground for much of its traverse of Caen, while the minor branches of both rivers have long dried out. Then the Odon ran from south-west to north-east along what is now the Rue des Alliés, with the church of Saint Pierre, which still survives, on the north side and a bridge, the Porte Saint-Pierre, crossing the river beside the church. The axis of the Île was the road now named the Rue Saint-Jean, which runs, as it did then, south-east to north-west. On the southern side, the Orne ran pretty much as it does now, although the Bassin Saint-Pierre was not built until 1845.

For days, refugees had been pouring into Caen, and by the time the English army had reached Fontenay-le-Pesnel, just east of Tilly-sur-Seulles – about twelve miles from Caen and on a ridge that would become frustratingly familiar to another British army during the Normandy campaign of 1944 – the constable of Caen, the garrison commander, knew that death and destruction was coming his way, and coming soon. He had perhaps 1,200 soldiers, men-at-arms and mercenary crossbowmen recruited from Genoa, and decided to hold only the castle and the Île Saint-Jean. To abandon the old city was sensible enough – its walls would not have withstood an assault even if he had had sufficient men to cover all the approaches, which he did not – and, while both abbeys were stoutly walled, he considered that he could not afford to attempt to hold them. The bishop of Bayeux, with around 200 men-at-arms and 100 crossbowmen, was placed in the castle, while the remainder of the garrison withdrew to the Île and prepared to defend it with the help of those citizens who could bear arms. As the bridge at the Porte Saint-Pierre had been designed to defend against an assault coming towards the castle from the south-east, not away from the castle from the north-west, a barricade of upturned farm carts, church benches and blocks of stone from building sites was constructed on the north bank to prevent the English from crossing the bridge, and barges were moored along the bank of the Odon with crossbowmen on the decks and in the fore and stern castles. That night, an English friar and professor of theology, the Augustinian Geoffrey of Maldon, arrived at the old walls with a letter from Edward. In it the king promised to spare the lives and goods of the citizens if the city would surrender to him. The council of Caen rejected the demand, the bishop of Bayeux tore up the letter, and the wretched Geoffrey was flung into the castle jail.

The English army, divided as was customary into three divisions or *batailles* (literally, 'battles'), marched at first light and drew near to Caen at mid-morning. The vanguard, commanded in theory by the Prince of Wales, took possession of the Abbaye aux Dames to the north-east, while the main body, commanded by the king, formed up around the Abbaye aux Hommes, with the third division somewhere north of the castle. Edward was preparing to reconnoitre the city prior to formulating a plan for its capture, when events overtook him. Some soldiers of the Prince of Wales's division saw an undefended gate in the eastern walls of the old city, made a rush for it and, having got there, realized that beyond it the city itself was deserted, all the garrison and most of the occupants having decamped to the Île Saint-Jean. The earl of Warwick, supposedly the Prince of Wales's adviser but in reality the commander of the division, led more troops into the old city and was unable to prevent the men from beginning to loot the empty houses and setting on fire those that did not look as if they offered rich pickings. As they advanced further within the old walls, the leading soldiers spotted the French men-at-arms manning the barricade on the north side of the Porte Saint-Pierre and a scuffle developed. At this point, the king, watching from the Abbaye aux Hommes, realized what was happening and sent an aide to tell the earl of Warwick to pull back until a coordinated attack could be mounted. The earl duly had his trumpeter sound the retreat, and, when that was ignored, the earl, on the principle that, if you can't stop them, you might as well join them, threw himself wholeheartedly into the battle for the bridge.

What had begun as an accidental encounter now developed into a full-scale assault. As the Odon was low at that time of year, archers and Welsh spearmen began to wade across the river and attack the crossbowmen on the barges moored on the opposite bank. That line of defence gave way, the English infantry were in, and the French defenders of the bridge, realizing that they were about to be cut off and attacked from the rear, abandoned the bridge and withdrew back into the Île. Now the slaughter began. Once the bridge was open, the English men-at-arms and spearmen swarmed across and began killing anyone they met, soldier or civilian. The fighting was particularly brutal in the narrow streets and inside houses, and, while the men-at-arms would accept the surrender of a nobleman or an obviously prosperous civilian, the archers and spearmen were in a bloodlust and killed indiscriminately. French knights, conspicuous by their armour and rich trappings, would seek out an English knight to surrender to, knowing that only then would their lives be assured.

The castle was never captured and simply ignored, and by late afternoon it was all over and the looting began. The chronicles differ widely over the casualty list. It was said that 5,000 French were killed; that 2,500 French bodies lay on the streets and in the houses, stripped and disfigured so that they were unrecognizable; that 500 bodies were buried in a mass grave in the grounds of the church of Saint Jean; that 250 knights and esquires and a large number of rich merchants were taken prisoner; and that only one English esquire died of wounds some days later.[17] The figure of the French dead is almost certainly too high, although the sources do agree on the number of prisoners taken. The number of English dead is similarly almost certainly too low; there must have been losses among the archers and spearmen who waded across the Odon to get at the crossbowmen on the boats, and the Lanercost Chronicle tells of civilians hurling stones and beams on the advancing English from the upper storeys of their houses.

The English stayed at Caen for five days. Once the army was back under control, after an initial orgy of plunder and rape, it could replenish its baggage train, collect the valuables of Caen, tend to its wounded, bury the dead, and – an opportunity of interest to those of a less rapacious nature – go and gaze at the tomb of the Conqueror. English and later British armies would gain a reputation for misbehaviour on capturing a town – a reputation that would last well into the nineteenth century – but, as English soldiers tended to look for alcohol first and women second, the incidence of rape was generally less than that practised by other nationalities; it was hangovers, rather than the threat of the hangman, that usually brought soldiers back to their allegiance relatively quickly. While pausing at Caen, Edward sent orders back to England for the arraying of 1,200 archers, mainly from East Anglia, and directed that contracts should be placed for 2,450 bows and 6,300 sheaves of arrows. Not all the men and equipment would have been replacements for losses in battle, but some of them surely were.

At the same time, 100 ships were to be impressed to replace those that had deserted, and the prisoners were sent off to England from Ustrem under the guard of the earl of Huntingdon and a detachment of archers.

Prisoners of rank were an important asset in medieval warfare and, like the prizes taken by the Royal Navy in the eighteenth and nineteenth centuries, gave the captor the chance of making a great deal of money. A man who could afford it was held for ransom and not released until his family or his subjects had paid up. While the practice of holding men for ransom was a very old one, neither the Welsh nor the Scottish wars had produced very much profit for those taking a prisoner – blood and stones, feathers and frogs spring to mind – but the Hundred Years War was a very different matter. Rich burgesses who had little money could buy their freedom with furs, jewels or plate, rich knights could do so with money, poorer ones with horses or armour or land, and knights with nothing at all might actually agree to serve their captor for an agreed period of time. Arrangements for the allocation of ransom money were usually specified in the indentures, and could range from one-third to one-half payable to the man's lord. In the contract companies, the rule was that the man handed over one-third to his captain, who in turn handed over one-third of his accrued takings to whomsoever he was contracted to (usually the king). Prisoners could also be sold on by a captor who wanted instant cash or who did not want to be responsible for looking after the prisoner through the often years-long process of extracting the ransom. Some of the ransoms demanded, and paid, were very high indeed. At Caen, the constable, the count of Eu, surrendered to Sir Thomas Holland, who then sold his prisoner to the king for £12,000, who ultimately extracted a lot more than that for the release of the count. Sir Thomas Daniel, who took the surrender of the count of Tancarville, the chamberlain of Caen, was less fortunate: as he was a member of the Prince of Wales's retinue, he had to hand his prisoner over and be content with £666 down and a pension of £26.13.4 (twenty-six pounds, thirteen shillings and fourpence) per annum for life – not bad, but hardly beyond the dreams of avarice. The prince eventually received £6,000 to release Tancarville.[18]

The army was now ready to move on. Edward ordered that the recently impressed 100 ships and archer reinforcements were to rendezvous with him at the port of Le Crotoy, in Ponthieu, which gave him the option of taking the army off should the situation warrant, but Le Crotoy was a good 140 miles away, and first he would have to cross the River Seine, a far greater obstacle than any encountered so far. He might, of course, have moved parallel to the coast, keeping in touch with the fleet, which could have transported the army across the mouth of the Seine to Le Havre (this town posed no threat, its resident warships and the town itself having already been burned by the fleet). But Edward wished to strike inland, to show the French that the Valois usurper could not protect them, so the army marched east, burning and looting as it went. The next obvious target would have been Évreux, but that town had a strongly fortified castle with a garrison and the king did not want to get tied down in siege operations at this stage – he had to keep moving, and so he next took the unfortified but prosperous cloth-making town of Louviers. From here both Froissart and Northburg list the towns on the English army's route,[19] but in an order which makes little sense, involving as it would have done a great deal of doubling back to no discernible purpose.

After Louviers, the intention seems to have been to cross the Seine at Pont-de-l'Arche and to advance on Rouen, then, as now, a major Norman city. Intelligence soon informed Edward that Rouen was well garrisoned by a substantial body of men-at-arms under the count of Harcourt (whose brother, Sir Godfrey Harcourt, was serving in Edward's army) and the count of Dreux, with a sizeable outpost in Pont-de-l'Arche, and in any case the bridge over the river at Pont-de-l'Arche had been pulled down. The army now moved along the left (south) bank of the Seine, heading for Vernon, looking for a crossing point and moving ever closer to Paris, while a scratch French force (which for a time at least included Philip VI) moved along the north bank destroying the bridges. Vernon was well fortified and, although the English took the fortress of Longueville on the approaches to it, they could not take the town itself and without the town the bridge could not be reached.

The only success to be plucked from the search for a bridge so far was a totally pointless but rather gallant little venture by the thirty-six-year-old Sir Robert de Ferrers, a Staffordshire landowner whose command consisted of one banneret, three knights, twenty-five esquires, thirty-two mounted archers and three foot archers. Ferrers, or some of his men, found a boat on the south side of the Seine. Ferrers packed as many men as he could into it, crossed the river and approached the castle of La Roche-Guyon on the north side of the river. The defence works of the castle were (and are) formidable and Ferrers could not possibly have taken it with the few men he had with him. The commander of the garrison, however, panicked, thought that Ferrers's little band was the vanguard of the whole English army, and instead of withdrawing into the keep, where he could have held out for months against any attacking force, surrendered the castle and its inhabitants. The only English casualty was Sir Edward Atte Wode, who was killed by a stone thrown from the castle walls. Ferrers agreed not to take the captured nobles prisoner in exchange for a promise that they would pay their ransoms later, recrossed the river and rejoined the army. His escapade was of no military significance whatsoever, but it demonstrated yet again the inability of Philip VI to defend his subjects on his own territory, something that had already been made clear south of the Seine.

Philip had already made a half-hearted attempt to negotiate when a French bishop was sent to offer Edward the county of Ponthieu and the confiscated parts of Aquitaine, provided that he would hold them as a vassal of the (Valois) king of France. This was, of course, quite unacceptable. From Vernon, the English army moved off to the next possible crossing, at Mantes, but having got there they very sensibly ignored the sizeable body of French men-at-arms drawn up outside its walls and continued along the river, bypassing any town or castle that was defended, while razing to the ground anything that was not. The next bridge was at Poissy, only twenty miles from Paris, and Edward got there on the evening of 12 August. That same day, Philip VI ordered the bridge to be broken and left a few soldiers to watch the site, while the main French army marched round the bend of the Seine to the last bridge before the city, at Saint-Cloud. Although the bridge at Poissy had been torn down, the piles were still in place, and Edward ordered the engineers to bridge the river using the piles. While timber was cut and hauled to the river, strong patrols were sent off to lay waste the various palaces and hunting lodges that were scattered among the Parisian suburbs to the south of the river. Within two days there was a whole line of destruction running all the way from Saint-Germain-en-Laye south-east to Boulogne on the outskirts of the city. Inside the capital there was panic, with citizens being formed into hastily organized parties to build barricades across the streets and troops deployed to restore order.

Philip, meanwhile, was at Saint-Denis, the burial place of French kings to the north of the city, where he was assailed by differing advice on what to do next. The tactic of avoiding battle until the English ran out of money or men was not working; the opportunity to cross the Seine and defeat the English south of the river had been missed, another front had just been opened from Flanders, Aquitaine was not subdued, and Philip could never afford to neglect what might be happening in Brittany. Orders were sent out to the cities and towns to send all available troops to Paris, as Edward's army crossed the Seine by the reconstructed bridge at Poissy and marched north. Its advance guard, commanded by Sir Godfrey Harcourt with 500 men-at-arms and 1,200 archers, all of them mounted, ran into a French army marching south. These were the troops provided by the city of Amiens marching to Paris as ordered, and, although they put up a stout defence, they were no match for the now battle-hardened, or at least massacre-hardened, Englishmen. Many of the Amiens burgesses were killed or taken for eventual ransom, but of more importance was the capture of their baggage train, which was well stocked with rations, wine and clothing.

The next stop for Edward's army was Beauvais, where the usual looting and burning was entered into with gusto. The Abbey of Saint-Lucien was set on fire – whether deliberately or accidentally is not known, although the former seems more likely – and, as Edward had issued orders that no church buildings were to be damaged, he was not pleased. He ordered the hanging of those responsible, said to number twenty but in all probability a lot less than that – soldiers were expensive assets and could not easily be replaced. It is likely that the punishment was dealt out to one or two known trouble-makers as a warning that, while plundering and burning was officially encouraged, discipline was still required and men were not to overstep the mark.

The army moved on, through Milly (probably Marseilles-en-Beauvais) and Grandvilliers to Poix, taking the lightly held castle at Dargies on the way. At Poix they found not one castle but two, neither garrisoned, and when a deputation of the town's inhabitants appeared and offered to pay a large sum of money, to be collected and delivered in the morning, if the town was spared being put to the torch, Edward agreed. Alas, when the army moved off the next day leaving a small party behind to collect the ransom, the locals decided not to pay after all and a fight developed. The English were getting the worst of it when a messenger on a fast horse caught up with Edward and recalled the army. Now the town was looted and burned, and those who had taken up arms were hanged.

Edward's next halt was at Airaines, about three miles from the River Somme, which he would have to cross before he could make contact with the fleet. Here, not only did it seem that all the bridges had again been destroyed, but it was reported that Philip had now assembled an army considerably bigger than Edward's, had left Paris and by a series of forced marches of up to twenty-five miles a day was close behind. By now, most of Edward's foot-soldiers were mounted on captured horses, but even so the constant halts to plunder, and the need to forage far and wide for food for the men and fodder for the horses, slowed the English down. It was now imperative to get across the Somme and either join with the fleet or head for Flanders, where an allied army had just taken the town of Béthune. The major bridges were in Amiens and Abbeville, however, both of which were strongly held by French troops, and the main French army commanded by Philip was moving into Amiens.

In just over six weeks, the English army had covered 400 miles – considerably more for the foragers and looters – and was now tired, short of provisions, and for the first time in the campaign beginning to encounter partisans. Civilians, emboldened by the knowledge that the Valois army was closing up, began to ambush small foraging parties and kill any soldier foolish enough to leave the line of march on his own. Like their successors almost six centuries later, during the German occupation, these members of the resistance made little difference to the course of the war, but they were a nuisance and meant that sentries had to be doubled and the size of patrols increased.

Edward halted around Oisemont and scouting parties searched along the banks for a crossing, but from Pont-Rémy, just east of Abbeville, to Picquigny, just west of Amiens, the bridges were down and the fords guarded. All along the north bank French troops swarmed and all attempts by English detachments to get across were repulsed. Then Edward was informed of a ford at Blanchetaque, between Abbeville and the mouth of the Somme, which could apparently be crossed at low tide. It is unclear – the sources vary – whether this information came from a prisoner offered his freedom and that of twenty of his chosen companions, or from an English soldier who had served in the area before. On 23 August, the

English army began to move to a concentration area at Acheux, eight miles from the river, and that same day the French army began to move west from Amiens along the south bank of the river. Their hopes were high: the English could not cross the river, and the French would trap them with far superior forces and destroy them.

Sometime during the night of 23/24 August, the English army marched, intending to get to Blanchetaque at low tide. Loading the baggage wagons and the sumpter horses in the dark took longer than it should have, and the army was late. When the troops arrived at the river on the morning of 24 August 1346, the sun was up and the tide in: neither man nor horse could wade across, and they had to wait until the tide turned once again. The deep and fast-flowing water was not the only problem, however, for Philip also knew about Blanchetaque and had sent one of his more competent commanders, Godemar du Fay, with a mixed force of men-at-arms, Genoese crossbowmen and light infantry to hold the north side of the river and prevent a crossing. Froissart, with the chronicler's usual exaggeration, puts Godemar's detachment at around 12,000, but it was probably nearer 500 men-at-arms and around 1,000 infantry including the Genoese.[20] The French were drawn up in three ranks and it was clear that they were there to stay.

For several hours, the English and the French could do little but stare at each other, but then, some time after Prime (0600 hours), the tide had gone out sufficiently for the earl of Northampton to lead 100 men-at-arms and about the same number of flanking archers into the river. The Genoese crossbowmen began to loose their bolts, which caused some casualties until the archers got within range. Once the archers began to shoot from about 150 yards, gaps began to appear in the French ranks and covering volleys allowed the English men-at-arms to reach the northern bank. Once they were on the bank, they held a narrow bridgehead while more and more of Edward's soldiers swarmed across, covered by the archers. Then the balance shifted, and the English had more men across than the French had to oppose them. Godemar du Fay, realizing that the day was lost, ordered a retreat which soon became a rout, as the English men-at-arms mounted their horses and pursued the fleeing French almost to the gates of Amiens. By the time that detachments of the main French army arrived at the southern end of Blanchetaque, Edward's army, with its men, horses, wagons and accumulated loot, was long gone,* the tide was in again, and pursuit was impossible. On the evening of 24 August, the French army returned to Abbeville to cross the Somme there, while the English camped in the forest of Crécy.

There can be little doubt that Edward III wanted a battle, and he wanted it to be decisive, but he wanted it on his own terms. Ponthieu had been English by inheritance since 1279, even if Philip had confiscated it; there was an escape route if needed, either to Flanders or to the coast, where Edward could have rendezvoused with as much of the navy as had not deserted to realize their plunder;† and most important of all, there was a possible battlefield that fitted all the requirements of English battle procedure shaped from the experiences of Bannockburn, Dupplin Moor and Halidon Hill.

There has, though, been some debate among historians over the exact location of the battlefield of Crécy. On the assumption that everyone knew where a battle took place, the chroniclers tended not to give more than a cursory description of the location – they were more concerned with embellishing tales of knightly chivalry – and archaeological evidence is either not there or impossible to find. Only when firearms appear on the battlefield can archaeology, by finding where a line of musket balls has landed and therefore from where they were fired, work out fairly accurately what happened. Metal-detector enthusiasts are often surprised that arrowheads, broken swords, spurs, discarded helmets and the like are rarely found on a medieval battlefield. But all these were valuable items, even if broken, and if the field was not thoroughly gleaned by the victors, it was by the local inhabitants, so that in a very short space of time no artefacts would be left.‡ The only evidence for the traditionally accepted site of the battle – apart from what the chroniclers report, and that can be

---

* Blanchetaque, or Blanche Tarche, was so called because the water ran over white marl, hard enough for wagons to cross even when the tide was out. Today the lower reaches of the Somme have been diverted into a canal, so the ford is long gone, but it was roughly opposite the present-day hamlet of Petit-Port.

† As no mention of them is made in any of the sources, we may assume that the 100 ships and archer reinforcements called for had not yet arrived at Le Crotoy.

‡ The obvious exception is Towton, 1461, but it was fought on muddy ground in a snowstorm, so much battlefield detritus was trampled into the ground and not found by contemporary scavengers.

read in several ways – is in local tradition and in place names. The best argument for accepting the area of the gently sloping valley to the north-east of Crécy-en-Ponthieu as the site of the battle is that, if Edward wanted a battle (and all the available evidence is that he did), then he could not have found a better place to have it – assuming that he wanted to force the French into attacking him, as English tactical doctrine said he should. There is simply nowhere else within a day's march – and the French were but a day's march behind – that offers anything like the advantages of the Crécy position.[21]

Between the villages of Crécy and Wadicourt there is a ridge along which runs the modern D111. The ridge forms the side of a valley that slopes north-east to south-west between the ridge and the village of Estrées-lès-Crécy, just off a Roman road that is now an extension of the Chausée Brunehaut. Behind the ridge was a wood, and running from Crécy south-east along the side of the valley is the River Maye, while on the northern side of the valley was a steep bank. Assuming that the French would approach from the south or the south-east, it was a perfect defensive position. Edward's army spent the night of 24 August in and around the woods south and west of the ridge of Crécy. On the morning of 25 August, the king and his senior commanders reconnoitred the ground on horseback, looking at every possible line of approach. The plan was simple: the army would take position on the ridge and dare the French to drive them off it.

The strength of Edward's army at Crécy, like that which landed at La Hougue, is and has been the subject of much debate. No two chroniclers agree and all tend to exaggerate. The historian Andrew Ayton has produced a convincing assessment of numbers and breakdown by arms of the army on landing in Normandy, and this seems the most accurate analysis that we are likely to get. According to him, Edward started off with around 16,500 all ranks, all arms. There had not been a pitched battle so far, and, while the chroniclers repeatedly state that no, or very few, English were killed, there must have been a steady attrition from the storming of small towns, the killing of foragers by grumpy farmers, the battle for Caen, and the crossing at Blanchetaque, to say nothing of men wounded and unable to rejoin the banners, accidents (there are reports of burning houses collapsing on top of the

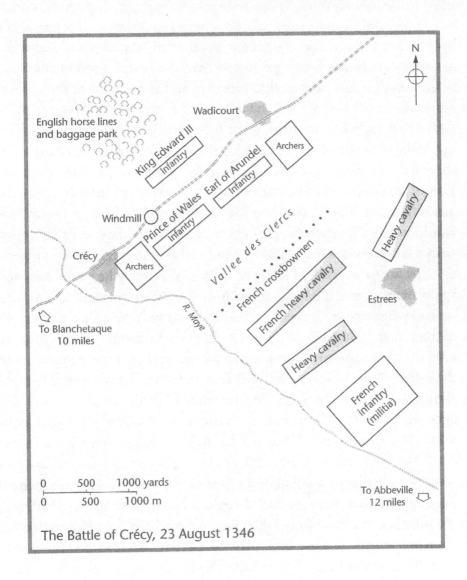

N

English horse lines
and baggage park

Wadicourt

King Edward III
Infantry

Earl of Arundel

Archers

Prince of Wales
Infantry

Infantry

Windmill

Heavy cavalry

Crécy

Archers

Vallee des Clercs

French crossbowmen

French heavy cavalry

Estrees

To Blanchetaque
10 miles

R. Maye

Heavy cavalry

French
infantry
(militia)

| 0 | 500 | 1000 yards |
| 0 | 500 | 1000 m |

To Abbeville
12 miles

The Battle of Crécy, 23 August 1346

arsonists), disease, sickness and desertion. On top of that, the escort to the prisoners sent back to England under the earl of Huntingdon must be deducted. While it can only be a very rough approximation, it does not seem unreasonable to allow for a reduction in the size of the army of between 10 and 15 per cent. As the knights, esquires and men-at-arms were rather better protected than the rest, we might suggest a reduction of 10 per cent in that category and 15 per cent of the archers and spearmen. Most of the hobelars, not overly involved in skirmishing so far, had probably survived. If the foregoing is anywhere near correct and if the majority of the knights fought as armoured infantrymen with the earls and bannerets commanding sub-units of varying size, then Edward at Crécy could field around 4,500 armoured infantry, perhaps 4,000 light infantry – assuming that the hobelars, whose mounted role would now be in abeyance, fought as spearmen (they were equipped with a lance, sword and helmet) – and rather more than 3,000 archers.

The army was still in its three battles, of roughly the same size, and again there is much debate about how they were formed up. We can probably dismiss the suggestion that the soldiers formed up and fought in their mixed-arm retinues. This would make no military sense, diluting as it would the battle-winning arrow storms and creating weaknesses in the infantry line. It is far more likely that, for all the advantages of fighting alongside men they knew and had marched with, the archers would have been separated from the men-at-arms and the light infantry. The chronicler Jean le Bel, from whom Froissart takes much of his account, has all three battles in line, and even eminent modern scholars, relying on original sources, have the battles deployed either as le Bel describes or one behind the other. It would have certainly been unusual to have all three battles in the front line, for there would then have been no depth to the position – if the enemy had pierced the line, there would have been nothing behind to stop them. Similarly, if all three battles had been engaged simultaneously, there would have been no reserve, and a commander without a reserve is unable to influence the battle once it begins. Conversely, the placing of the battles one behind the other would have reduced fighting power considerably and been unlikely to cover the frontage.

The length of the ridge along which Edward arrayed his army is about 1,500 yards, which, allowing room for the archers and gaps between sub-units, would have needed 2,400 infantrymen if they had formed up two ranks deep, and 4,800 in four ranks. The frontage could only have been covered by one battle if the men were formed in two ranks, and this seems most unlikely: it would not have been sufficient to withstand the shock of an assault by mounted or dismounted men. If the chronicles and the paintings can be relied upon at all (doubtful, I accept), then the description of hand-to-hand fighting would indicate that the men were formed in at least three and probably four ranks, which would predicate two battles forward. If we rely on the theory of inherent military probability, and what we can extract from the sources, then the most likely deployment would seem to have been two battles forward in four ranks – the vanguard of the Prince of Wales on the right as the senior commander after the king, the rearguard under the earl of Arundel on the left, and the centre, commanded by the king, in the rear. While the three battles were given the titles vanguard, centre and rearguard, this did not, rather confusingly, mean that they necessarily occupied those positions. As the king was in overall command, it made sense for him to be in the rear, from where he could control the battle. In the event, he made use of a windmill on the ridge as a command post: in this way he could look over the two forward battles and, if necessary, easily deploy the rear one as a reserve or reinforcement.

As for the archers, here too there is discussion over their deployment. It has been suggested that the archers were formed in line either in front of or behind the infantry. This again makes little sense: they would impede the infantry and cause chaos as they tried to avoid a closing enemy, and the formation would dilute the effect of their shooting. There can be little doubt that the archers were placed as they were at Dupplin Moor and Halidon Hill – that is, on the flanks, where their shooting could have prevented any outflanking move, forced an enemy to close into his centre, and so reduced his momentum that, if he did get as far as the infantry line, he could easily have been repulsed.

What is more problematical is whether or not there were archers in the centre as well as on the flanks. For if each battle was allocated its own archers, then it is perfectly likely that archers were positioned on the flanks of each battle, and in that case some would be in the centre of the English line. In most paintings and in many of the original sources, the archers are shown or described as being in a wedge shape, and, as the commander or commanders of the archers would have to balance concentration of arrows with the area over which they fell, then a square formation would seem best. If there were 1,500 or so archers on each flank, then they could have been formed into two squares each of thirty-eight men across and the same deep. If each man occupied a circle with a radius of two yards – enough room for him to place his arrows on the ground and draw his bow – then each square would need a frontage of around seventy-five yards, and in the heat of battle the square might well have become a lozenge or a wedge. If archers were deployed on the flanks of the battles, rather than on the flanks of the army, then each battle would have been flanked by squares each of around fifty yards across, and to an oncoming enemy it would have appeared that the mass of archers was in the centre of the front line. On balance, it would seem likely that the archers were on the flanks of the army only, but one cannot dismiss the possibility that there were some in the centre as well.

Having ridden around the area and decided upon his plan of action, Edward ordered pits and holes to be dug across the cavalry approaches and had the baggage wagons drawn into the woods of Crécy-Grange on the north side of the ridge, where they were used to form a laager inside which the army's horses were put. As there may still have been as many as 20,000 horses, any lost having been more than compensated for by those captured or plundered, the stabling area would have been enormous. There was neither time nor material to build stalls, so hitching rails would have been put up; and, in order to prevent horses fighting or kicking each other, they would have had to be tied up a good twelve feet apart, with each line of rails eight feet behind the one in front of it. This indicates an area of 500 yards by 400 yards for stabling alone, and the animals would have had to be fed and watered – a labour-intensive task which would have been partly undertaken by non-combatants, although it is probable that numbers of hobelars were detached to guard the laager and look after the horses at the same time. By morning on 26 August, all was ready. The soldiers heard mass and the priests heard confessions. The men were then told to sit or lie down in their positions while breakfast was cooked by fatigue parties and brought up to the lines.

Meanwhile, the French army under Philip spent the night of 25 August at Abbeville. As with the English army, we can only make an educated guess at its strength. All sources, English and French, agree that the French were far more numerous than the English. Their heavy cavalry (composed of the nobility) is variously reported as numbering from 12,000 to 30,000, the (mounted) men-at-arms from 60,000 to 100,000, and the crossbowmen from 2,000 to 15,000. The lowest multiple given by any of the chronicles is that of le Bel, who says that there were four times as many French as there were English. If we err on the conservative side and take a multiple of three, and if we accept that it is most unlikely that Genoa and northern Italy could have produced more than 2,000 crossbowmen at Crécy, given that they also provided garrisons in other parts of the French lands, then we might hazard a guess at the French army consisting of around 30,000 heavy cavalry and mounted men-at-arms in the probable proportion of one noble to four men-at-arms, plus those 2,000 crossbowmen. Not all those men would have been at Abbeville on the evening of 25 August: units and retinues kept arriving during the night and into the next day.

Philip knew that the English were somewhere in the vicinity of Crécy, and on the morning of 26 August the French army began to move north in that direction. Ahead of them went a small reconnaissance party of four knights to report the location, strength and intentions of the English. They reported back that the English army was deployed on the ridge between Crécy and Wadicourt, that they looked as if they were prepared for a battle, and that there were no indications that they might move off. Furthermore, the leader of the reconnaissance party suggested that it would be a sensible idea for the French army to concentrate and rest until the following day, when they would be in a much better position to destroy the English upstart. This very sound advice was echoed by Philip's senior commanders and accepted by him. Many French units were still on the march from Abbeville, others were still coming in from other parts of the country, and a large allied contingent from Savoy would not arrive until sometime the next day. Philip was always a cautious commander – in hindsight too cautious perhaps – but he was absolutely right to heed the advice given and to issue orders that the army was to advance no farther but to bivouac and be prepared for battle the next day. By now, the leading French units had reached the valley, about 1,000 yards from the English position. They could see the English and the English could see them. It was late in the day (probably not as late as Froissart thought – Vespers or dusk – but perhaps 1700 or 1800 hours), and the English would have been watching more and more French soldiers of various types crowd onto the field. Even the greenest Welsh spearman could do the maths, but, as Edward rode along the lines shouting words of encouragement, his men were quite confident in their ability to hold off the French host.

As Philip's orders to hold hard were delivered to the troops in the vanguard, they obediently halted, but, as the orders were relayed farther back, the recipients were unhappy: they wanted to get forward where they could see the enemy, and then they might halt. The result was a scrum of major proportions, as those behind pushed and shoved to get forward and those in front tried to hold their positions. In an aristocracy-heavy army, where every man felt himself the equal of every other and instant obedience to orders was an extraordinary concept, there was a general feeling of wanting to get on with the battle – at least among the mounted element who had let their horses do the work of the march from Abbeville. It was soon apparent to Philip and his marshals that the task of holding the army back was an impossibility, and so the battle might as well start now.

The crossbowmen were ordered forward to lead the French advance. Unlike archers, who except at very close range shot their arrows at a high angle and so could be arrayed in ranks all shooting at the same time, crossbowmen fired on a flat trajectory and, as they could only reload standing up, were obliged to shoot one rank at a time. Tactically, the intention was that volleys of bolts from the crossbowmen would so disorganize the enemy line, not least by killing large numbers of men in it, that those who remained would become easy prey for a charge by the mounted knights and men-at-arms. While we do not know exactly how the crossbowmen were deployed, it is logical to suppose that they would have acted in the same way as did men armed with matchlocks in a later age. If the rate of discharge was two quarrels a minute, the front rank could discharge its weapons and then move to the rear to reload while the next rank stepped forward and did the same. A formation three ranks deep could therefore loose a volley every ten seconds. If the French army's crossbowmen did advance in this way, then, allowing a yard of front per man, the 2,000 crossbowmen would have covered a frontage of around 700 yards. In view of what happened to them, it is likely that they did not bring their pavises with them. These may have still been in the baggage train; alternatively, given that the crossbowmen were ordered to move forward rather than shoot from a defensive line, they may have found their shields too cumbersome to bring with them.

The trumpets sounded and the drums pounded as the crossbowmen began to move towards the English line. Crossing the floor of the valley and beginning to climb the gentle slope, they would have halted as soon as they were within range, perhaps 200 or 250 yards away. The English probably allowed them to discharge their first one or two volleys, but, shooting uphill and with the setting sun in their eyes, they cannot have hit very much. Then the English archers replied. The captains and the vintenars would have bellowed 'Nock – draw – loose!' and the deadly arrow storm began. Within thirty seconds, the astonishing number of 15,000 arrows would have come raining down from the sky. The archers did not have to hit a specific target; they simply had to ensure that their arrows landed within what a later age would describe as a beaten zone – an area that encompassed the lines of crossbowmen. Relatively densely packed as the Genoese would have been, it is not unreasonable to posit that one in three arrows hit something; and that being so, it would not have taken very long before the crossbowmen were thrown into confusion – some dead, many wounded, and with no cover and no escape except backwards.

The crossbowmen would not have been helped by the arrival of one of those sudden and violent summer thunderstorms common in this part of France, which would have wet their bowstrings and caused them to stretch, thus reducing considerably the propulsive power of their weapons.* For them to stand where they were and shoot back would plainly have been suicide, but even those at the rear who were more able to move would have found their retreat blocked by the packed lines of mounted knights. As it

---

* The rain would surely have had the same effect on the longbowmen's bowstrings. But it takes only a few moments to change the string on a longbow (and archers carried spare bowstrings, often coiled inside their hat or helmet) and much longer to replace it on a crossbow.

was, the obvious chaos and, to French eyes, cowardice of these despised foreign and low-born mercenaries encouraged the commander of the leading French battle, the count of Alençon, to order a charge. Whether he actually ordered his men to ride over the crossbowmen, as some of the chronicles allege, or whether what happened was simply collateral, is irrelevant: the wretched crossbowmen could not get out of the way of big heavy men on heavy horses, and many were trampled underfoot or knocked flying.

A horse will go to almost any lengths to avoid stepping on anything alive,* but, packed closely as they were and with head and face armour restricting their vision, the animals had little option. Allowing three feet of frontage per horse, that first French charge may have begun with 300 or 400 riders. After they had negotiated their way past the fleeing crossbowmen or galloped through them, their cohesion was lost and, instead of coming on in a controlled line at the canter, they were now a mob of individuals, all anxious to strike the first blow. And then the arrow storm began again. Clouds of arrows coming down at an angle out of the sky might not have killed many riders, but it would have unnerved them and it would certainly have panicked their horses. Again, an arrow whacking into a horse's unprotected quarters would not kill it, but it would very likely make it rear and dump its rider, or whip round, bolt and take him into the next county, and that is exactly what happened. Those riders who managed to stay aboard and keep their horses pointing in the right direction then had to face archers shooting directly at them. At 100 yards or less, a bodkin point – the needle-like arrowhead designed for just this purpose – would go through armour or, with just a bit of luck, could penetrate through the slit in a visor and kill its wearer.

The French launched charge after charge, and the archers shot volley after volley, with runners replenishing their arrows from the baggage train. As more and more Frenchmen fell and more and more terrified loose horses galloped screaming hither and thither, what had originally been a smooth and open approach to the English line became an obstacle course

---

* Stand by a fence at a National Hunt race meeting and see how the horses twist and turn in mid-air to avoid fallen jockeys. This author, having been thrown from a green mount, has had the whole hunting field gallop over him with no injury except to his pride.

of dead and wounded men and horses. Welsh spearmen, meanwhile, laid down their lances to come out and kill the wounded. Some French men-at-arms did get as far as the English lines, and occasionally fighting was fierce, but the defensive line held, and the pole arms – halberds and short lances – wrought great slaughter among those unlucky enough to be hooked by them. Edward had specifically said that the dead were not to be looted and that no prisoners were to be taken: he did not want to risk men leaving the line tempted by fat ransoms.

We can probably dismiss the tale of a knight of the Prince of Wales's retinue coming to the king and asking for help, as his son was hard pressed, to be met by a refusal and the admonition: 'Let the boy win his spurs.' It is surely inconceivable that the king would refuse to support the sixteen-year-old heir to the throne when he had an uncommitted reserve to hand. On the French side, we can probably also dismiss the blindness of the king of Bohemia, whose badge of three feathers and motto *Ich dien* was adopted by the Prince of Wales and has been the crest of Princes of Wales ever since. John, count of Luxembourg, king of Bohemia, claimant to the thrones of Poland and Hungary and elector of the Holy Roman Empire, lost one eye from disease in 1336, but it is almost certain that he could see perfectly well with the other. He was killed at Crécy, aged fifty, supposedly having demanded that his household knights take him into the thick of the battle so that he could strike a blow with his sword. His son was also present but survived, having wisely scarpered when it was evident that all was lost, to become the Holy Roman Emperor Charles IV.

The furious battle went on through the evening, but, by the time darkness fell, there were precious few French knights or men-at-arms left. Those who had not been killed were slipping away, and even Philip had to accept the hopelessness of the cause when his advisers insisted that he too should quit the field. He went, leaving the oriflamme of Saint-Denis – the royal banner of the kings of France, only taken out of the Abbey of Saint-Denis in time of war – abandoned on the ground.* He paused first at the château of La Broye, where he is said to have hammered on the gate shouting (according to Froissart): '*Ouvrez, ouvrez, chastelain –*

---

* According to the chronicle of Geoffrey le Baker, writing in 1357/8, if the oriflamme was raised, it signified that no prisoners were to be taken.

ç'est l'infortuné roi de France' ('Open, open, it is the unfortunate king of France'). Now, in the gloaming of that August night, the heralds and the priests moved down into the valley to identify the dead – hence the name later bestowed on it: the Vallée des Clercs.

It was a great and glorious victory. The flower of French chivalry lay dead on the field, and, while numbers are imprecise, it is clear that at least 1,500 and perhaps as many as 2,000 of the nobility were killed, and many thousands of the infantry levies and crossbowmen. Among the dead were at least eight members of the extended royal family, including the count of Alençon, whose impetuosity was a major contribution to the disaster, the counts of Blois, Harcourt (whose brother was one of the senior commanders in the English army) and Flanders, and the duke of Lorraine. Only the figures for the dead English men-at-arms have survived – forty – and we might extrapolate that to perhaps 150 archers and spearmen as well. It was certainly a remarkably cost-effective battle.

It is easy to say that, rather than the English winning the battle, the French lost it. Certainly, their lack of cohesion, the confused command arrangements, the failure to allow the whole army to assemble out of sight of the English lines, the misuse of the crossbowmen, and the impetuosity of individual commanders and knights were major factors in the result of the battle. Having said that, the English had deliberately selected a position which allowed them to fight the battle in the way they did best: protected flanks, a narrow frontage, the use of missile weapons to break up the enemy assault, and a dismounted infantry defence (and commanders who could not depart the field because they had dismounted could only boost the morale of the soldiers under their command). These principles were vital, and significant, for they formed the basis of English tactical doctrine for the whole of the war. English armies moved on horseback but fought on foot; provided they could do so on ground of their choosing, they were unbeatable until, very late in the day, the French were able to develop field artillery that could counteract the hitherto overwhelming firepower of the longbow. Above all, perhaps, it was the discipline and teamwork of a professional or quasi-professional army under a respected and charismatic leader that won the day – and would have won the day even if the French had had a coherent plan and had been commanded as they should have been.

Crécy was a seminal battle. It proved that an English army properly deployed and well led could defeat a far larger host that clung to the now-outmoded feudal system. The lessons were there for the French to see; that they failed to do so would cost them dear in the years ahead.

The tomb of 'blind' King John of Bohemia in the Cathedral of Notre Dame, Luxembourg. Erected in the mid-seventeenth century over the original grave, the inscription points out that John was the son of the [Holy Roman] Emperor Henry VII, the father of Emperor Charles IV and the grandfather of Emperors Wenceslas and Sigismund. He was, of course, killed at Crécy in 1346, not in 1340 as shown.

5

TRIUMPH AND DISASTER – CALAIS AND THE BLACK DEATH

The English army did not attempt to pursue the remnants of Philip's host as it straggled away towards Amiens on the night of 26 August. They were exhausted and needed time to rest and recuperate, and it was not until the following day, a Sunday, when the heralds had completed their grisly task of identifying the dead nobles, that they realized the extent of their victory. At least two French contingents arriving to join their army and with no inkling that the battle was over were quickly seen off with more slaughter. However, true to the code of behaviour between gentlemen, the body of John of Bohemia was washed and wrapped and sent back to Germany, while those of the princes and the more important nobles were transported to the monastery of Maintenay, ten miles to the north. A truce of three days was announced to allow the locals to find the bodies of the common soldiery, which were stripped and buried in grave pits in the valley. Spin is not only a twenty-first-century political ploy and a report of the battle was sent back to England by fast cutter. Embellished somewhat, the account, combined with a report of the capture of Caen, was to be read out in every church, and in a very short space of time all over England there was genuine delight and pride in the great victory over a hated and feared enemy. Now Parliament and the people might grumble at the prospects of more taxes to keep the war going, but they would pay up for what they could see was a continuing success.

Meanwhile, in Amiens the hunt for the guilty was on. The fault lay with evil counsellors, corrupt officials, the weather or even the displeasure of the Almighty, and it was always easy to blame the foreigners. The Genoese crossbowmen were all traitors and were to be hunted down and killed, and many of them were massacred before it was pointed out that they were valuable assets who might be needed elsewhere, whereupon Philip rescinded his order. In any age, a military commander who cannot identify his mistakes is doomed to repeat them, and the French refusal to face facts and recognize that their way of waging war was obsolete in the face of rapidly discharged missile weapons and professional dismounted infantry was to cost them dear in the future. It was inconceivable that well-born French nobles could be defeated by low-born archers – 'gens de nulle valeur', people of no worth, as one French chronicler put it. And in any case, by refusing to take prisoners for ransom the English were not playing fair, while the behaviour of the Welsh in despatching the wounded was very bad form indeed.

On 29 or 30 August, the English army set off again, burning and pillaging as it went. The areas around Hesdin, Saint-Josse and Étaples were all reduced to smouldering heaps of rubble, while anything that looked like being properly defended was bypassed. The question was what to do next. Despite the capture of Caen and the great victory of Crécy, underneath the propaganda and the jubilation there was not a great deal to show so far, at least nothing of any permanence. Despite Edward's insistence that he had come to France to claim his own, French troops relatively quickly reoccupied the areas that the chevauchée passed through, and stern punishment was meted out to those Normans who had thrown in their lot with Edward, including the garrison of Caen, who were rounded up and executed. What was needed was a concrete and obvious advantage, something that could be held and shown to be a lasting gain from the war, and that meant a city that was not part of the English lands in France. Edward would capture Calais and annex it to the English crown in perpetuity.

Calais, with a population of about 8,000, was not then a town of any great commercial significance. Its harbour was small and liable to silt up, and most travel between England and Europe was through Wissant or Boulogne, both of which had much better and more easily navigable approaches. For all that, it was the nearest French port to England and might be developed, and it had for years been a scourge of English trade as a nest of piracy. From the French point of view, although it was only a minor trading post, the town was close to the border with Flanders and important as a military base to guard against Flemish incursions, and it had been well garrisoned and stocked with enough provisions to withstand a long siege. Moving through Neufchâtel and Wissant, the English army reached the heights of Sangatte on 3 September, from where they could see their objective.

It is unlikely that Edward ever thought that he could take Calais by a *coup de main*, for it was well sited for defence. To the north was the harbour and the open sea, to the west was a river with only one bridge, the Neuillet bridge, and to the east and south was marshland criss-crossed by streams and rivulets that constantly changed their course. Within those natural defences was a series of well-constructed walls, themselves protected by moats, and at the western end was the castle, with its own separate system of walls, towers and ditches. The English did not even attempt to assault the walls, but instead prepared for a long siege. This was standard practice since, before the development of effective cannon, it was very unusual for a medieval castle or fortified town to be taken by assault. Far more often it was starvation, disease or treachery that forced capitulation, and it was common for a besieged commander to agree with the besieger that, if not relieved by a certain date, he would surrender the fortress. If, however, a castle or fortress had to be assaulted, there were three ways in: over the walls, through the walls or under the walls.

Assault over the walls could be achieved by the use of belfries or scaling ladders, or both. The belfry was a three- or four-storey wooden tower on wheels or runners. Packed with archers and men-at-arms, it would be pushed up close to the wall until the attackers could leap from the top storey onto the wall. It was a very old stratagem – the Romans had made frequent use of belfries – and it took much time and labour to place them in position. Once packed with men, a belfry was very heavy and the ground had to be levelled and a road built to allow it to be pushed along. All this preparation would be obvious to the defenders, who would try to set the belfry on fire with fire arrows or by throwing burning balls of straw soaked in pitch at it, and mass their own men on the walls as it approached. While the belfry was still theoretically on the equipment tables of a medieval siege train, it was hardly ever actually built or used.* Scaling ladders were easier to make and to conceal until the last minute, but, unless there were sufficient archers or crossbowmen to keep the defenders away from the walls, this too was a dubious way of earning a living, particularly for the first man up the ladder.

Attacking through the walls meant creating a breach, and this could only be done with a battering ram or a bore, both of which were very slow and vulnerable to boulders and, once again, fireballs hurled onto them from above. Going under the walls involved the use of miners. Rather than attempt to tunnel beneath the walls and then emerge inside the castle, like the demon king popping up through a trapdoor in a pantomime, miners would try to collapse the walls. The mining team would tunnel under the wall, supporting the roof of the tunnel by wooden pit props.† The tunnel would then be packed with combustible materials (dead pigs, having lots of body fat, were a favourite) and ignited. Once the pit props had burned through, the tunnel would collapse and the walls above with it.

There was a variety of machinery which could be used to hurl projectiles at the walls or into the besieged town. The mangonel relied on the energy of twisted ropes – human hair was regarded as the best material for mangonel ropes – to hurl a stone or fireball from the end of a beam. The springal, little different from the Roman *ballista*, was a giant crossbow, but, like its hand-held baby brother, it was slow to load and only effective if used in massed batteries. The trebuchet relied on a counterweight on a beam with a huge sling on its end and could deliver seriously large stones against or over a wall, while the petrary was an enormous catapult. It was claimed that the mangonel could be used to

---

* The French did make one for the siege of Breteuil in 1356. It took a month to fill in the moat, and when the belfry was finally pushed up to the walls, the defenders set it on fire.
† Edward's miners were from the Forest of Dean. Thanks to their skill in tunnelling under walls, by royal decree of Edward I any male born within the Forest of Dean who had worked in a mine for a year and a day was granted the right to mine anywhere in the forest without a licence – a right still enjoyed today, although as most boys are now born in the local hospital, which is not in the forest, there are fewer and fewer who are eligible.

propel dead horses into towns in an early version of biological warfare, and the chronicler Froissart avers that, when the French were besieging Auberoche in Aquitaine in 1345, they captured an English messenger sent out to contact relieving forces, killed him and returned his body over the walls with a petrary – a somewhat unlikely tale. Edward may have had some early cannon in his siege train, and there is some evidence that three may have been on the field at Crécy. Descriptions are vague: they may have fired stone balls or large darts, but, as the secret of casting gun barrels was as yet unknown and the manufacture of gunpowder imprecise, they will have done little but frighten the horses and were probably more dangerous to the gunners who served them than to the enemy. If they did exist, they seem to have played little part in the siege of Calais.

At Calais, going over or through the walls was not an option as the moats and ditches protected the approaches; mining was ruled out because the soil was waterlogged and siege engines were too heavy to be moved over the marshy ground. Starvation was the only answer and the English were quite prepared to wait. At long last the requested reinforcements arrived from England and the fleet under Sir John de Montgomery, Admiral of the South, hove to off Calais at around the same time as the army got there on land. The soldiers began to block off all roads and tracks running to and from the town, and a vast camp was set up on the dry ground around the church of St Peter where the roads from Boulogne and Ardres crossed. The camp was intended to be in position for the long term, and soon shops, armourers' tents, quarters for the nobility, butts for the archers, paddocks for the horses, and all the facilities of a large town were in place or being constructed. While the army was on the move, it could feed itself from the French countryside, but, now that it was static, the available food in the immediate area would soon be exhausted and provisions would have to be brought in.

It is sad but perhaps inevitable that interest in military history is centred on the battles and those who fought them, and that most soldiers would rather be out killing people than in barracks counting blankets. But the fact is that you can have the best soldiers in the world, superbly trained, highly motivated, brilliantly led and equipped with the best weapons that money can buy, but, if you cannot feed them, house them, resupply them, move them and tend them when they are sick or wounded, then you can do nothing. Administering an army is far more difficult than commanding it in battle. The real heroes of most of England's and Britain's successful wars are the logisticians, and they get precious little recognition for it. For the siege of Calais, government agents went out all over southern England to purchase foodstuffs and other supplies for the army. They had to be found, collected, paid for, moved to the ports, loaded on ships – which themselves had to be impressed – and delivered to the army. The French scored a minor success when a fleet of galleys from the Seine intercepted one of the first supply convoys and sank or burned most of the ships, killing the crews and dumping the cargoes. Future convoys would have men-at-arms or archers on board and the supply line was never broken again, but the need to put soldiers on the ships did increase the expense of the logistic effort.

While arrangements for the siege of Calais were being put in place, and the king's agents were scouring the southern and eastern counties for supplies, the Scots decided to take a hand. After Crécy, frantic messages had gone from the French to the twenty-two-year-old Scottish king David II, son of Robert Bruce, who had been married to Edward III's sister Joanna at the age of four and had returned from exile in France in 1341, pleading with him to do something to distract the English. Assuming that all the English soldiers were safely out of the way in France, David invaded England in early October 1346, a move generally popular with the Scottish magnates, who assumed that the north of England was ripe for the plucking. Storming down the Roman road and pillaging as they went, they took the castle of Liddel Strength, eight miles north of Carlisle, and beheaded its captain, Sir Walter de Selby. At this point, David's chief military adviser, Sir William Douglas, the thirty-six-year-old Lord of Liddesdale, advised that enough was enough, they had done what they promised the French they would do, and it was now time to return over the border before retribution arrived. David rejected this sound advice, claiming that there was no one to oppose them but 'wretched monks, lewd priests, swineherds, cobblers and skinners'.[22] The raid continued and included the despoiling of the priory of Lanercost, which presumably accounts for the Lanercost chronicler's obvious hatred of the Scots, claiming as he does that King David and his men made a habit of defecating in the fonts of churches that they passed.

Given that the Scots were almost as terrified of the wrath of God – as opposed to that of his earthly representatives – as everyone else, this charge seems unlikely.*

But David's assumption that England had nothing with which to reply to a Scottish incursion was very wrong. Edward had not arrayed any troops north of the River Trent, and the defence of the Scottish marches had been entrusted to the very capable hands of William de la Zouche, the fifty-two-year-old archbishop of York, Warden of the Marches and principal commissioner of array in the north, who mustered an army at Barnard Castle on 15 October before moving north to Bishop Auckland, south of Durham, the following day. The army numbered around 1,000 men-at-arms, 2,000 archers and 5,000 spearmen, against probably a similar or smaller number of Scots. The usual three divisions were commanded by the archbishop himself, Ralph, Lord Neville, and Henry, Lord Percy. The Scots army was encamped in the priory grounds of Beaurepaire (which still exists but is now Bearpark), a few miles north of Durham, when on the morning of 17 October 1346 a foraging party of around 400 men under Douglas ran into the archbishop's vanguard in a thick mist and got very much the worst of the encounter, with only Douglas and half his men getting back to raise the alarm.

The Battle of Neville's Cross which followed went on for most of the day.† The Scots came on in the same old way, and the English archers on the wings slaughtered them in the same old way. When the lines of infantry met, it was rapidly evident that the Scots could not hold and the officers and men on the Scots flanks began to flee the field, leaving the king and his immediate household to fight on. Lanercost probably exaggerates the speed of desertion, though he does say that Earl Patrick should have been named Earl 'Non Hic'.‡ In any event, the

---

* In Professor Maxwell's translation of Lanercost, published in 1913, he refuses to translate this accusation, presumably on the grounds that it was not suitable for the more tender ears of the time. He does make the point that the chronicler continually shows 'monkish spite' against all things Scots – but then, if your priory was plundered and burned every time the Scots crossed the border, you would feel quite spiteful.
† Neville's Cross is now a western suburb of Durham and the (refurbished) cross is still there, albeit that the area is now heavily built up.
‡ Probably Sir Patrick Dunbar, and for readers whose Latin may be rusty, *non hic* means 'not here'.

Scots king and Sir William Douglas were taken prisoner and carted off to the Tower, while the remnants of their army fled back to Scotland, not even stopping to defecate in fonts on the way. The captor of David received an annuity of £500 a year and promotion to banneret. Brave but foolhardy, David was said to have sustained two head wounds from arrows. The surgeons removed one, but the arrowhead of the second remained lodged in his head for many years, until it apparently popped out one day while he was at prayer.

Back at Calais, a brief attempt to bring down the walls by hurling rocks at them failed when the ground was too soft to allow a firm foundation for the trebuchets and petraries; an ingenious plan to assail the walls from boats fitted with scaling ladders was finally abandoned despite considerable expenditure in preparing the boats. And so the blockade went on. Although the town was well provisioned, its stores would not last forever, so the commander of the garrison, Jean de Vienne, an experienced and competent officer, decided to evict his useless mouths, expelling around 2,000 civilians – women, children, the old, the sick and the weak – into no-man's-land between the walls and the investing army. At first Edward would not allow them to pass through his lines and, as there was nothing for them to eat save what little they had managed to carry away with them, they soon began to die. Edward relented and the dispossessed were allowed passage through the siege lines. While no food could reach the garrison overland and attempts to run supplies in by sea were usually prevented by the English navy, the occasional blockade-runner did manage to reach the harbour, but the quantities that could be delivered by this means were small.

During the latter part of summer and autumn, life within the English camp was reasonably comfortable, but with the onset of winter conditions began to deteriorate. An army on the move could keep reasonably healthy, but, once it became static, disease inevitably followed. Edward's army of 1346 was no exception. Little attention was paid to the cleanliness of water sources, latrine arrangements were primitive, flies and rats abounded, and soon dysentery – 'the bloody flux' – began to take its toll. Dysentery is an infection of the gut and is passed on by contact with an infected person or by touching or eating something that has been handled by an infected person. Symptoms include watery diarrhoea, often with blood in the faeces, nausea and vomiting, stomach pains and fever. While medieval man was probably more resistant to it than we are today, it could still be fatal, and, even if it was not, a man's ability to do his duty was severely affected. Many of the spearmen and archers would have been infested with worms, and colds and influenza would have been common. Malaria was then endemic throughout Europe but was more of a summer affliction, there being a lot fewer mosquitoes around in the winter.

On top of the health hazards, manning siege lines was boring and gave few opportunities for acquiring glory or loot. Hence there was a steady trickle of desertion by archers and spearmen, while many of the knights found excuses to return to England to sort out a land dispute or see to a son's marriage. There was also a problem with the horses, which started to die off from the cold. Or so the chroniclers tell us, but, as horses grow a substantial winter coat and are very capable of surviving all but the most severe weather, it may have been an epidemic of strangles,* or perhaps starvation: hay would have been running out and barley and rye intended for the horses may have been eaten by the men.

In February 1347, commissions of array were issued for another 3,600 archers and the commissioners in Wales were instructed to provide more spearmen. These reinforcements were needed not only to make up the shortfall brought about by sickness, desertion and leave, but also to replace a contingent that had been sent off to Brittany with Sir Thomas Dagworth. This knight had served in Brittany in the previous year with a small mobile force which had not only managed to distract the French from their sieges of the English garrisons of Brest, Lesneven and La Roche-Derrien, but, in a series of battles where his tiny band of men-at-arms and archers had seen off far more numerous French soldiers, had also forced Charles of Blois to lift the sieges. Dagworth then joined the *chevauchée* to Crécy before being sent back to Brittany in January 1347.

Sir Thomas was typical of the professional soldiers who would make their reputations and fortunes out of this war. A younger son, born around 1306 of good but impoverished stock, he started life as estate manager for

---

* A highly infectious respiratory disease of horses caused by the bacterium *Streptococcus equi*. Often fatal even today, it spreads with incredible speed in large horse populations. Even if a horse recovers (unlikely in 1346/7), it can still be a carrier and never returns to its previous form.

the earl of Hereford and obviously impressed, for he married, far above his station, a grand-daughter of Edward I. He was knighted, possibly in recognition of service in the Scottish wars of the 1330s or perhaps as a result of the connections he made by his marriage. In 1345, he commanded a sub-unit under the earl of Northampton in Brittany, where he did well and was appointed commander of English forces there when the earl returned to England in January 1346. In the next four years, Dagworth would receive a large cash grant from Edward III, be ennobled, be called to Parliament and die fighting. A natural leader whose loyalty was unquestioned, he cared about his men, looked after them and made sure that any credit went to them – a hitherto unusual attitude to find in a commander but one that would become the norm as professionalism continued to permeate the English army.

The French had still not faced up to the implications of what they termed *la déconfiture de Crécy* (the collapse of Crécy), but Philip could not ignore the English army camped around Calais, where determined attempts to lift the siege by sea had proved futile. In early 1347, the French vassals were ordered to muster their troops at Amiens by Whitsuntide (28 May in 1347). The troops did arrive, eventually, but it was not until July that the army was ready to move, and, when they did, Edward was understandably concerned. Although the summer weather had improved the health of his army, there was still a large number on the sick list; long months in the siege lines had induced boredom and low morale; many soldiers had lost their physical fitness and fighting edge; and in June a reinforcement of the healthiest 100 men-at-arms and 400 archers had been sent off to Dagworth in Brittany. Although this detachment weakened the Calais army, it was a highly cost-effective investment. Charles of Blois had reinstituted the siege of La Roche-Derrien, hoping that by so doing he could lure the English army into trying to lift the siege, which might allow him to fight and win a battle on his own terms. Instead, it was the French who suffered a crushing defeat, for on 20 June 1347 Sir Thomas Dagworth led a night attack on the French army dispersed around its siege lines and defeated it piecemeal. Sir Thomas himself was wounded and captured, escaped, then captured and escaped again. When dawn broke on 21 June, nearly half the French men-at-arms had been killed, and those nobles not killed had been captured, including Charles of Blois himself, whom Sir Thomas sold to the king for £3,500. At a stroke the whole balance of power in Brittany had been reversed and the foundations laid for the eventual success of the Montfort faction in the Breton war of succession.

Meanwhile, within Calais the siege was biting ever more sharply. The garrison had eaten all the horses and was starting on the cats and dogs, so Jean de Vienne expelled another 400 citizens who were not contributing to the defence. This time Edward did not permit them to pass through his lines; he refused them food and water, and let them die. Not everyone in the English camp agreed with this, but most did. By allowing the previous expellees to pass without hindrance, the English had given de Vienne a pain-free way of extending the siege by reducing his ration strength, and there was also the question of spies and messengers being sent out in the guise of refugees. It was a harsh decision, but the right one in the circumstances.

With the approach of the French army from Amiens, summonses were sent to England to recall knights on furlough and those who had gone back to buy horses to replace those that had died during the winter. In any siege the investing army had not only to worry about sallies from the defenders, but also to guard against the risk of being attacked from behind by a relieving force. The French army got as far as Sangatte, saw that the English were apparently soundly entrenched and well able to withstand an attack (which they probably were, but not as well able as it appeared), issued a half-hearted challenge to come out and fight, and then withdrew. The news of La Roche-Derrien had reached the army, the men were not enthusiastic after Crécy the previous year, and many saw no point in continuing the war. As they scuttled back to Amiens, they were followed up by a mounted party led by the earls of Lancaster and Northampton, who gave them no chance to rest or recover their appetite for a fight. Philip now ordered his divisions to disband.

Inside Calais, Jean de Vienne had hung on in the hope of relief, and with the withdrawal of Philip's army that last chance was gone. A messenger was sent out offering to negotiate and Edward sent Sir Walter Manny in to parley. De Vienne said that he would surrender the town if the lives of the garrison and the property of the inhabitants were spared. Manny relayed the king's orders that, in accordance with the customs of war at the time, the lives of a garrison that held out during a siege were forfeit. Only unconditional surrender was acceptable and Edward would do with soldiers and civilians as he wished. This policy was not popular with Edward's own knights, who pointed out that to kill men for doing their duty could rebound on them in the future. The whole point of adhering to modern laws of armed conflict that protect prisoners of war is to ensure that the other side does the same, and Manny and the others were arguing that very same point. Eventually, the king gave way. It was relayed to de Vienne that the majority of the garrison and the civilians would be spared, but not their property, and six of the leading men of the town were to come to King Edward dressed only in their shirts and with nooses around their necks bearing the keys of the city.

On the morning of 3 August 1347, Calais surrendered, and what happened next became the stuff of the French legend-makers, desperate to produce some tale of heroism from the disastrous years of 1346 and 1347. The story goes that the six burgesses, led by Eustache de Saint-Pierre, who had supposedly volunteered for the task, came out of the city gates to find the whole English army drawn up on parade, with the king and his queen and senior officers seated on a platform. The emaciated party approached the platform and fell on their knees, and Saint-Pierre asked for mercy. Edward refused and ordered them to be beheaded. At once there began a murmuring among the senior officers – to execute the men at once was bad enough, to execute them unshriven would be disgraceful. Edward was unmoved, and only when the pregnant queen, Philippa of Hainault, pleaded piteously with him was he moved to spare their lives. The truth, though, is surely that this was a carefully prepared and rehearsed charade to show the world that Edward was capable of great mercy: a queen might well argue with her husband in private, but not in public; similarly, whatever advice the king's senior commanders might proffer in the council chamber, they would not cross him in the presence of a beaten enemy. As it was, Saint-Pierre and his companions were indeed spared.*

Jean de Vienne and the more prominent of the French knights were sent off to join the growing band of notables in the Tower, and all the

---

* Rodin's sculpture *The Burghers of Calais*, erected in 1889, still stands in Calais, while a copy is in Victoria Tower Gardens in London.

buildings of Calais and their contents were now to be the property of King Edward. Despite the insignificance of Calais as a trading port, it turned out to be stuffed with riches of all descriptions, largely as a result of many years of piracy, and, once the majority of the inhabitants had been expelled with little more than what they stood up in, the spoils of victory were collected and doled out. It was said that there was not a woman in England who did not wear something taken from Calais. It was Edward's intention to keep Calais, but rather than rule it as part of English France, it would become a colony, with English merchants and tradesmen encouraged to settle there permanently with the promise of free housing and land. Calais remained English for another 211 years, until it was lost through Tudor neglect and French guile in the reign of Mary Tudor.

Edward's initial intention was to follow up the victories of Crécy and Calais by another great *chevauchée*, which might end the war once and for all. However, the army was tired after over a year of constant campaigning and money was once again in short supply, so, when the inevitable approach for negotiations was made through the offices of the French cardinals, Edward was prepared to listen. For the French, a truce was imperative: they had suffered serious reverses in Normandy, Aquitaine, Flanders and Brittany, and, wealthy though their nation was, they were short of cash to pay the army. Messengers sped between Calais and Amiens to try to get agreement – almost any agreement – that would end the fighting. The English were, of course, in much the stronger position, and, when a nine-month truce was signed at the end of September 1347, it left them in possession of all that they had gained and held.

The return home of Edward and most of his army was greeted with acclaim. Parliament agreed that the money had been well spent and the king's personal position was enormously strengthened by his obvious prowess in battle. At the same time, the taking of Calais and its plantation by settlers were seen as providing England with an opportunity for trade and an entrance to Europe that did not depend upon Flemish support, which might not always be provided. On St George's Day, 23 April 1348, the king founded the Order of the Garter, a chivalric order which would comprise but twenty-six members and be a close companionship of those who had proved themselves in battle; it was also intended to promote King Edward's court as one just as glorious as any in Europe. The order was to be headed by the king and his successors, who would choose the membership, and there were only two stipulations: knights were not to fight each other and they could not leave the kingdom without the king's permission. Of the twenty-six original members, eighteen were definitely present at the Battle of Crécy and the others had distinguished themselves in various ways. The order would have its chapel in Windsor Castle and would support a chantry of twelve priests and twenty-six 'poor knights' – originally men who had been captured by the French and who had had to sell their estates to purchase their freedom.

The Garter was not the first such order of chivalry. There was already one in Hungary and another in Castile, but both are now long gone and in any case were not as exclusive. Much speculation surrounds the origin of the name, mostly centring around a garter supposedly dropped by the countess of Salisbury at a post-siege celebratory party at Calais and picked up by the king with the words '*Honi soit qui mal y pense*', which can be translated 'Evil to him who thinks evil'. There are, however, a number of candidates for the countess. It is unlikely to be Katherine Montagu, countess of Salisbury, as she would have been getting on for fifty in 1347; it just might be Joan, the daughter of the earl of Kent executed by Queen Isabella's Mortimer, who had a racy past;* and legend also cites a mysterious Alice of Salisbury, who by some accounts was a mistress of the king and by others a victim of rape by him. We shall never know, but a more likely, albeit mundane, explanation is that the badge of the order had to be something that could be worn over armour,

---

* Joan was known sarcastically at the time as the Virgin of Kent because she wasn't, and later prudery called her the Fair Maid of Kent. She married Sir Thomas Holland of Caen fame in 1340, when she was twelve. The marriage was clandestine but lawful and was consummated. When Sir Thomas went off with the Teutonic Knights in late 1340 to fight the heathens in what is now Prussia, her mother married her to William Montagu, son of the earl of Salisbury and later the second earl of Salisbury himself, which ceremony duly took place with much pomp. When Sir Thomas returned, he appears not to have mentioned that the girl had been married to him and became the Montagus' steward. Only after the 1346/7 *chevauchée*, when Holland had made his name and his fortune, did he begin proceedings in the papal court to get his wife back, which he eventually succeeded in doing in 1349. They had five children before Holland died in 1360, after which, still only thirty-three, she married the Black Prince and gave him a son, later Richard II. Quite a girl!

so the order might just as easily have been the Order of the Armband. (Similarly, the motto could equally well be translated 'Shame on him who thinks badly of it' – 'it' referring to Edward's claim to the French throne.) Now the Garter is the oldest order of chivalry in the world, and, while the twelve priests did not survive the Reformation, the twenty-six knights live on. Retired service officers, they are no longer necessarily poor, very few are knights and their appellation was changed by William IV to the Military Knights of Windsor.

At this time, Europe was struck by a catastrophe so appalling that it made any major military endeavour impossible until it had run its immediate course. Sometime in the winter of 1347, a terrible sickness arrived in Sicily, supposedly on a ship from either the Black Sea or the Middle East, and was carried on to Marseilles, from where it spread rapidly throughout Europe. While today we refer to it as bubonic plague, because of the buboes that appeared as symptoms, modern medical science still does not know exactly what it was, although it is believed that it was some form of virus spread by fleas that live on rats and mice. In the unhygienic conditions of the time it was almost impossible to prevent it spreading, particularly in towns where people lived close together and sanitation was poor, and the mortality rate was very high indeed. In August 1348, it arrived in England, either on a ship from Bordeaux carrying wine or on one from the supply run to Calais landing at Weymouth, from where it spread inexorably through Dorset, Somerset and Devon and then to London, where it was first reported in November. The symptoms were swellings (buboes) in the groin and armpits, black blotches on the skin, a fever and death within four days.

France, already reeling from military defeat and without a strong central administration, suffered appallingly. Crops went unharvested and fields untilled; fodder that would have gone to warhorses went to animals that were of greater agricultural value; and knights who found their incomes gone took to brigandage. As the population shrank, so did state revenues, and the currency was devalued. The court and government fled Paris, with Philip wandering around the borders of Normandy with a handful of clerks and personal servants. To many of the French, this was God's punishment, although witchcraft and sorcerers of various hues were also blamed. So, too, was the practice of blasphemy, which was now to be punished by the removal of the tongue for persistent offenders; and, inevitably, the Jews, who came in for even more persecution than usual.

In England the effects were less, but still serious. The death rate was particularly high among the clergy, who, if they were doing their job properly, were in constant contact with victims; in the dioceses of York and Lincoln 44 per cent of the beneficed clergy died, while in Exeter, Winchester, Norwich and Ely it was 50 per cent.[23] For long it has been generally accepted that up to a third of the population died in that first visitation, which by 1350 had largely run its course and was now in Scotland, but some modern authorities think that the figure may have been much higher. Dislocation was far less in England than in France, largely for the reason that the former had both a more efficient central government which controlled the whole country and a popular king, while the latter had to make do with various semi-independent feuding magnates and a failed and unpopular king. In England this first outbreak tended to hit the poor and undernourished, while the nobility, who lived in a (relatively) cleaner environment, were less severely affected – unlike their counterparts in France, where the queen, the duchess of Normandy and the Chancellor all died, as did many of the aristocracy.* With the reduction in the labour pool, English agricultural workers were no longer so closely tied to their lords and could demand higher wages. Various strictures emerged from Westminster exhorting labourers to claim no more than they had before the plague, and lords who paid over the odds were to be fined. (The French took a rather different view and there labourers who would not work for the old rates were branded.) While in France law and order and government did break down for a time, in England, despite rising crime and economic problems, the authorities never lost control. Recent excavation of a so-called plague pit in East Smithfield, London, has revealed that, far from being tipped higgledy-piggledy into a hole in the manner of Belsen, the bodies were buried in neat rows, each body in its own grave, albeit not in a coffin.

---

* Although Edward III's fifteen-year-old daughter Joan died of the plague in Bordeaux on her way to marry the heir to the throne of Castile.

While neither side could embark on any large-scale operations of war, the fighting did not die down completely. In 1349, there was an attempt to bribe a Genoese mercenary commander in Calais to leave the gate open and the drawbridge down one night to allow a French raiding party to recapture the town. The man took the money, agreed to betray the town on 31 December, and sent a fast galley to report the bribe to King Edward. The king crossed to France with personal retainers and archers and ambushed the raiders as they crept through the gate. The Genoese kept the bribe. Then Philip persuaded the Castilians, who since the death of Joan Plantagenet had thought better of their alliance with the English, to send a fleet into the Channel, presumably to disrupt the wine trade from Bordeaux, the supply convoys to Calais, or both. English intelligence gave early warning, and on 29 August 1350 off Winchelsea at the Battle of Les Espagnols sur Mer, the English fleet, with King Edward, the Prince of Wales and the ten-year-old John of Gaunt aboard, won a great victory over a smaller fleet but one composed of much higher (and thus more difficult to board) Spanish ships. Edward was now thirty-seven and this was the last time he engaged in hand-to-hand fighting, but by now his prestige was such that he did not have to.

Then, in August 1350, just as France was recovering from the Black Death, Philip VI died, to be succeeded by his thirty-one-year-old son, Jean II. Jean is known in French history as Jean le Bon – John the Good – the myth-makers having taken note of his undoubted personal courage and love of tournaments, while quietly ignoring that he was vicious, irrational, unjust, militarily incompetent and stupid (which, in the pantheon of French royalty, means that he was very stupid indeed). He is described as being handsome and with a fine red beard, although in his portrait in the Louvre it looks more like designer stubble that has got out of control. He too founded an order of chivalry, the Chevaliers de l'Étoile (Knights of the Star), whose members had to swear an oath never to leave a battle alive, which largely explains why the order no longer exists. What particularly annoyed the English, and reinforced the existing antipathy to the papacy that would eventually find expression in the Reformation, was the creation by the pope of twelve cardinals to mark the crowning of Jean II – eight Frenchmen, three Spaniards and an Italian, completely ignoring the English candidates.

Jean was, however, in no position to renew the war just yet, although he did start to gather the funds for it, largely by imposing even more oppressive taxes and debasing the currency – minting more of it while reducing the silver content. Despite the truce of Calais, the skirmishing in Aquitaine and Brittany had never died down, and in Brittany on 20 July 1350 the great Sir Thomas Dagworth was treacherously ambushed and killed, having fought furiously to the end. The following year, Henry of Lancaster led a short but devastating *chevauchée* through Artois and Picardy, and in Brittany the Battle of the Thirty was perhaps one of the last hurrahs of chivalric warfare. A French force commanded by Jean de Beaumanoir sallied out of the castle of Josselin and arrived outside the walls of Ploermel eight miles away. Rather than undergo a siege, the English garrison commander, Robert of Bamborough, agreed that thirty men-at-arms from each side would fight a decider on foot. Rules were agreed, stipulating which weapons could be used and when there would be breaks for refreshment and the dressing of wounds, and the location was to be midway between the two castles. On 13 March 1351, the encounter duly took place, and the English lost, although they accused the French of cheating.

Dagworth's successor as theatre commander in Brittany was Sir Walter Bentley, a hard professional from a Staffordshire family that had often in the past been in opposition to, and in trouble with, the king. Edward III was not, though, a man to hold grudges against those who could be useful to him and who were prepared to serve him loyally – the fact that he did not believe in the inheritance of the sins of the fathers is shown by the inclusion among his senior commanders of a Hugh Despenser and a Roger Mortimer, both sons of men whose execution Edward had ordered or been associated with.

On 14 August 1352, Bentley, with a small force of perhaps only 200 men-at-arms and 300 archers, beat a far larger French force at Mauron, midway between Rennes and Ploermel. In accordance with English tactical doctrine, he placed his men on a slope with a hedge in front, men-at-arms on foot and archers on the flanks. The French had learned a little from Crécy, and their commander, Guy de Nesle, ordered the majority of his men to dismount while several hundred mounted men were ordered to ride down the English archers. Had the attack been properly coordinated and commanded, it might have worked. As it was, the French mounted knights did disperse the archers on the English right, but, instead of then wheeling round and attacking the English line in rear, they carried on to plunder Bentley's (sparse) baggage convoy. On the English left the archers repulsed the cavalry, but in doing so they were unable to deliver the usual arrow storm on the advancing French infantry, and de Nesle did get his infantry line to close. However, after a march uphill in layers of clothing worn both under and over their armour, these men were in no shape for pitched hand-to-hand fighting and were seen off by the English men-at-arms. As usual, casualties are hugely over- or understated. According to the chronicle of Geoffrey le Baker, the French dead included ten great lords, 640 knights and noblemen, and a number of 'common people not counted', while 140 knights and nobles were taken prisoner.[24] A more recent source claims eighty nobles and 500 men-at-arms were killed and 160 knights taken prisoner.[25] The real figure is probably 200 or so French killed (many of whom were Knights of the Star), while the prisoner figure seems credible. Neither source makes any mention of English casualties, and yet there must have been some among the archers on the English right. Le Baker says that Bentley had twenty archers executed on the spot for running away when the French cavalry attacked, but this is most unlikely – although he may well have had one of the captains or vintenars executed as a warning to others.

Although England's economy had recovered more quickly from the plague than that of France (wages had gone up, but prices had too, so the lords could retain almost the same income as before), Edward was quite happy to negotiate while still preparing for a renewal of the war. Desultory negotiations had been going on since the capture of Calais, but always foundered on Philip VI's refusal to restore the English lands other than as fiefs of the Valois, which was quite unacceptable to the English. Things had changed by 1353, as not only had Philip been succeeded by Jean but also Pope Clement VI had died and Innocent VI was elected to replace him. Innocent was even more pro-French than his predecessor, but he did see the need to end the war in a Europe still trying to recover from the ravages of the plague.

Serious deliberations began in the castle of Guînes, five miles south of Calais, which had been taken, in breach of the truce, by a *coup de main* led by John Dancaster, a squire stationed in Calais. Bored by garrison duty there, he had collected a few soldiers, taken them over the Guînes wall by night with blackened faces, and seized the castle. The go-between, moving between Avignon, Paris and Guînes, was Cardinal Guy of Boulogne, and the result, arrived at in April 1354, was the Treaty of Guînes, by which, in return for giving up his claim to the French throne, Edward was to receive Aquitaine, Normandy, Touraine, Poitou and the town and surrounding area of Calais in full sovereignty. It would bring the war finally to an end, give the English what was rightfully theirs, and allow Jean to retain part of his kingdom rather than lose all of it. The treaty was to be ratified by the pope at Avignon. It did not happen. Jean thought better of it, his magnates were against it, and Guy of Boulogne was in any case out of favour. King Edward was angry and frustrated with the collapse of the negotiations, particularly as he had assured Parliament in Westminster that a permanent peace had been obtained and that there need no longer be increased taxation to support the war.

The French king must be made to see the error of his ways and this time there would be no compromise. The plan for 1355 was to attack France from three directions: the king himself would strike inland from Calais, Henry of Lancaster, now a duke, from Normandy, and the Black Prince (as the Prince of Wales was known after Crécy) from Aquitaine. There were problems with the weather and with finding enough soldiers, but in October 1355 Edward landed at Calais with perhaps 8,000 men and moved inland towards Amiens, where Jean of Valois had assembled a much greater French army. Then, bad news arrived from England: the Scots were on the rampage again, had invaded England on 6 November and were laying siege to Berwick Castle. They were perfectly accustomed to coping without a king (David was still a prisoner in England) and claimed that they were bound by treaty to attack England if France was invaded. When the Scots last invaded, in 1346, there had been sufficient troops in the north to deal with them, but the need to raise three armies in 1355 and the reduction in the population caused by the plague had forced the king to array men from the north, and there were very few left in the border counties. Edward had no choice but to reverse his progress into France, return to Calais and re-embark.

Lancaster's army never got to Brittany: constant bad weather and unseasonable winds kept blowing his fleet back to England's shores. The only English army that crossed the Channel and stayed was that of the Black Prince. Prince Edward landed in Bordeaux in September 1355 with perhaps 1,000 men-at-arms, 1,700 archers and a few hundred Welsh spearmen. Now twenty-five, he had proved his personal bravery at Crécy but had never previously been in independent command. His father had, however, provided him with seasoned and wise officers to assist him. The earls of Warwick, Suffolk and Salisbury had all served in the Scottish wars, at Crécy and at the siege of Calais. They would give advice when needed and curb any tendency to hot-headed adventurism.

At Bordeaux, the English were joined by their Gascon troops and, having unloaded his horses and allowed his men time to recover from sea sickness, the prince moved off on a *chevauchée* through Armagnac and Languedoc. He burned, he killed, he looted, he levelled, and by November he had reached the Golfe de Lion, having traversed 300 miles from coast to coast. So far, he had avoided fortified towns and castles. While tempted by Toulouse, he bypassed it, and when he came under a bombardment from French trebuchets at Narbonne – and it was apparent that the garrison was a strong one – he wisely withdrew, burning the suburbs as he went. Now it was time to turn about and return to friendly territory – the nights were drawing in, the rivers were rising and a large number of horses had been cast, having been ridden too hard on inadequate feed. French troops were also on the move, as were private adventurers who sniped at the baggage train, heavy with a month's worth of loot. To return to Aquitaine meant crossing a series of rivers, now swollen with the rains and their bridges broken down by the French, but to the amazement of the latter – the Ariège and the Garonne were supposed to be impossible to cross with horses – the English managed as much and struggled on westwards. Soon the pursuing French forces were only a day's march behind, and at night the English could see their enemy's camp fires. But the French too were held up by flooded rivers and dissension among their commanders, as they argued about what to do next, and on 28 November 1355 the Black Prince and his army crossed the border into Aquitaine.

In some ways, 1355 had been a disappointing year: the expected perpetual peace had not arrived, the three-pronged attack had not happened, and the Scots had once more invaded England. The latter threat was soon dealt with, however, and, while the Black Prince's mounted raid led to no great battles, it once again demonstrated the inability of the

French king to protect his subjects, put heart into the Gascons, reduced the taxes that could be raised from the raided areas, and liberated a great deal of valuable plate, cloth and wine, to say nothing of horses and prisoners for ransom. Edward's troops had good reason to be satisfied and they looked forward to similar success the following year. In that hope they were not to be disappointed, for 1356 would see the second of the great English victories on land of the Hundred Years War.

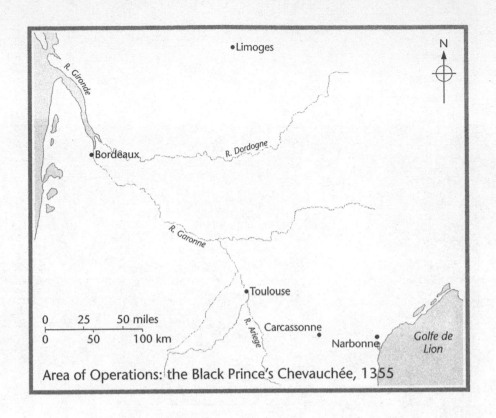

N

•Limoges

R. Gironde

•Bordeaux

R. Dordogne

R. Garonne

•Toulouse

R. Ariège

Carcassonne

0   25   50 miles
0   50   100 km

Narbonne

Golfe de Lion

Area of Operations: the Black Prince's Chevauchée, 1355

The tomb of Edward the Black Prince in Canterbury Cathedral. A highly competent military commander, his early death at the age of forty-six set back by forty years England's hopes of regaining her rights on the continent of Europe.

6

THE CAPTURE OF A KING

The Black Prince spent the winter of 1355 and spring of 1356 consolidating his position in Aquitaine and preparing for another *chevauchée*. Although no major operations were launched, there were constant but limited raids into French territory designed to recapture English possessions, and by the spring of 1356 thirty castles and towns had been recovered and garrisons installed. Orders were sent to England for the despatch of reinforcements and Sir Richard de Stafford was instructed to enlist 300 mounted archers. Two hundred were to be from Cheshire and the rest from wherever they could be found. They were to be arrayed, tested and equipped, and conveyed to Plymouth to take ship for Bordeaux without delay and in any case by Palm Sunday (15 March 1356). A resupply of weapons was also needed, so the prince sent one of his logisticians, Robert Pipot of Brookford, back to England to purchase 1,000 bows, 2,000 sheaves of arrows and 400 gross (57,600) of bowstrings. Clearly, the wastage rate of bowstrings was considerable. Pipot had problems in getting arrows, as all available stocks had already been bought up by the king and fletchers had to be hired to work night and day to make the quantities needed.

There was at least no problem in persuading soldiers to enlist, provided that they were available, for the depredations of the plague were of course still a major factor. Pay was reasonable and the rules for the division of plunder and ransom clearly spelled out. Wages were calculated by the day and there was usually a generous advance of pay on enlistment. In addition to their own pay, captains and leaders of companies were paid a bonus of 100 marks (about £66.66) per quarter for every thirty men they produced, and a leader who could produce 100 men (and there were some) could amass a lot of money in a reasonably short period of time – to say nothing of his cut of the loot and any ransoms paid for men captured by his company.

From the English point of view, it was increasingly important to meet the main French royal army and defeat it. Despite the successes of the 1355 campaign and the enormous plunder that had been realized from it, the English were still no nearer to forcing the French to recognize the legitimacy of English France. A decisive battle was needed, one which would end the war. Once again, the English plan was to coordinate attacks into central France from three directions: Henry of Lancaster from Normandy, King Edward from Calais and the Black Prince from Aquitaine. The prince would strike north for Paris, and, while we have no written evidence, he was almost certainly aiming to link up with Lancaster somewhere around the River Loire. The expense of such a plan – keeping three armies in the field, maintaining the various scattered garrisons and providing for the defence of Calais and Aquitaine – was enormous: around £100,000 in the financial year 1355/6 alone, about half of this for the Black Prince's forces. But England could afford it, partially from taxation but mainly from customs duties and profits accrued from the campaigns so far and the ransoms obtained.

Jean of France had huge problems. His policy of avoiding pitched battles until the English ran out of money and went home had failed completely; he had demonstrably failed to protect those whom he regarded as his subjects; his government was riven with dissent and still suffering from the dislocation caused by the plague; his son and heir was plotting against him with the king of Navarre; and he was very short of money with which to continue the war – so much so that he declared a moratorium on the payment of government debt, which ruined great man and humble tradesman alike. This last point was perhaps Prince Edward's major achievement of the previous year, for in a great swathe of territory from Bordeaux to the Mediterranean Sea the economy had been utterly ruined; it was calculated that by the destruction of Carcassonne and Limoux alone the French had been deprived of the funds to support 1,000 men-at-arms.[26] English propaganda made much of Jean's inability to prevent the English from going wherever they wanted and of his profligate frittering away of

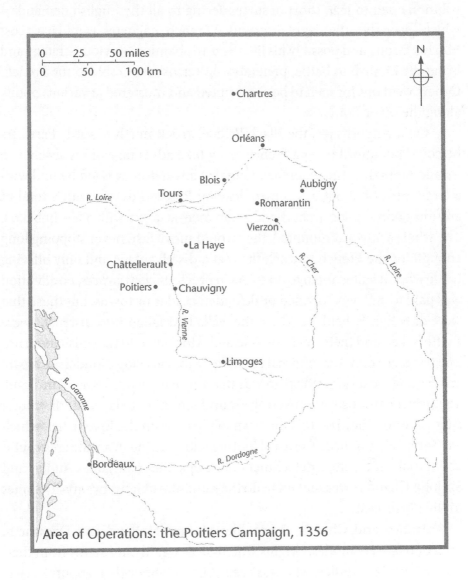

0 25 50 miles
0 50 100 km

N

•Chartres

Orléans
•

Blois •
Tours
R. Loire

Aubigny
•

•Romarantin

Vierzon
•

R. Cher

R. Loire

•La Haye

Châttellerault •

Poitiers • •Chauvigny

R. Vienne

•Limoges

R. Garonne

•Bordeaux

R. Dordogne

Area of Operations: the Poitiers Campaign, 1356

funds and oppressive taxation, stressing how much better life would be under the legitimate king of France – Edward III of England. The only solution open to Jean short of surrendering to all the English demands – which, given the attitudes of disgruntled French magnates, would have cost him his throne and possibly his life – was to abandon previous strategy and bring the English to battle, preferably on terms favourable to the French. Orders went out for men to be conscripted and mustered at various points along the River Loire.

On 4 August 1356, the Black Prince struck north towards Paris. As he could not afford to let a French army take advantage of his absence to invade Aquitaine, the seneschal, John de Chiverston, was left behind with a large force of about 2,000 men, leaving Prince Edward with a total of around 5,000 – 3,000 archers and 2,000 men-at-arms with a few hobelars. The whole army was mounted: they would move fast, never stopping long enough for the French to catch them at a disadvantage and only offering battle when it suited them to do so. As in previous *chevauchées*, no attention was paid to strongly fortified or defended castles or towns, but those that were only lightly held, or where the walls had fallen into disrepair, were swiftly taken and their stocks of food and wine taken to replenish the army. The baggage train was minimal and largely for carrying plunder and spare arrows and weapons – the plan was that the army would live off the land. The prince's troops were covering around ten miles a day until the end of August, when they reached the town of Vierzon on the River Cher, which was found abandoned. The usual looting and burning in a wide area round about took place, and a detachment of troops under Sir James Audley and Sir John Chandos was sent off to do the same at Aubigny, twenty-five miles to the north-east.

Audley and Chandos were, like Manny, Holland and Dagworth, men of relatively modest origins who rose in wealth and status from their prowess in war. Audley, who was aged thirty-eight or thereabouts in 1356, was the illegitimate son of an Oxfordshire knight and a knight's daughter and is first mentioned by the chroniclers as being in the retinue of Edward, Prince of Wales, during Edward III's expedition of 1346/7. He was present at Crécy and at the siege of Calais, and, while we do not know when he was knighted, he was one of the founder members of the Order of the Garter. John Chandos was a younger son of a Derbyshire knight, and, while his date of birth is unknown, he was probably much the same age as Audley, for they appear to have been great friends and comrades in arms. Chandos was knighted in 1339, largely as a result of favourable comment on his courage and ability in a single combat outside Cambrai. He fought at the sea-battle of Sluys and, like Audley, was in the Prince of Wales's retinue at Crécy. He was on board the prince's ship at Winchelsea in 1350 and, again like Audley, was a founder member of the Garter.

Audley and Chandos completed their work of destruction at Aubigny and on their way back ran into and routed a band of French freebooters commanded by one Phillip de Chambry, known to his friends as Gris Mouton – 'Grey Sheep' – presumably from his appearance. It was from prisoners captured in this skirmish that the Black Prince discovered that the French were not as far away as he had thought. By now, Jean of France had assembled an army and had moved the various contingents to Chartres, but he still had no definite idea where the English were. With the obvious clues of a fifty-mile-wide trail of devastation pointing towards Paris and hordes of refugees fleeing the invaders, Jean knew from which direction the Black Prince was advancing but had no real idea of exactly how far he had got. What was clear to the French was that once the English crossed the Loire – assuming they could cross it – then the advantage would swing towards the French. For the river was in spate and the French hoped to trap the English army against it, leaving them no escape route.

It was probably when he was in the vicinity of Vierzon that the Black Prince realized he must abandon any intention of joining up with the duke of Lancaster. The duke had presumably calculated that, if he continued in the direction of Tours, he was going to meet the French army before he could join with Prince Edward. As he had no intention of fighting a hopeless battle, he wisely withdrew, sending a message to the French king that he had no intention of fighting as the French hoped but would 'go where he liked and do as he wished'.[27] The Black Prince's expedition was not dependent on combining with Lancaster, but, now that this was no longer possible, he had to reappraise the situation. He was not afraid of a pitched battle with the French – indeed, he hoped for it – but to push further towards Paris without the addition of Lancaster's troops would be unwise. It was essential that, if a battle were to take place, it was on ground of the prince's choosing, where the English tactics could be best employed, rather than an opportunistic encounter dictated by the French. To move back the way he had come was not an option, as the territory had been laid waste and there would be no supplies or fodder for the horses to be found. He therefore decided to move west as far as Tours, from where he had the option of retiring south out of the devastated area and back to Bordeaux if no opportunity for a decisive battle presented itself.

Edward Plantagenet, Prince of Wales, the Black Prince, is in many ways an enigmatic figure. We are not even sure of the origin of the soubriquet. The Victorians thought it was because he wore black armour, and they painted his funerary monument in Canterbury Cathedral accordingly (it was later restored to its original steel and gilt); alternatively, it has been suggested that it was a French appellation, indicating how much they hated him. From contemporary descriptions and paintings and from the effigy on his tomb, he appears to have been tall, well built and handsome, with the long face of the Plantagenets, and like most sprigs of the nobility of the time he was fond of tournaments and jousting. From the age of thirteen he accompanied his father on campaign, and there can be no doubt that he was personally brave, as he showed at Crécy, and cognizant of the chivalric conduct of others, even of his enemies, as he demonstrated when he honoured the dead King John of Bohemia by taking his ostrich feather badge as his own personal insignia.* In matters of religion, he appears to have gone beyond the conventional display of faith and to have had a genuine and deep belief. We know from lists of allowances and gifts of armour and plate given to friends and to those who had served him well that he was generous and, at least in his earlier years, accrued little personal profit from ransoms, often distributing much of the monies to companions and attendants. As a military commander, once away from his father and in sole command, he was a sound tactician and a natural leader, while always prepared to listen to subordinates who had more experience than he. On the debit side, he had the reputation of being a stern landlord, and tenants and inhabitants of the lands that were his main sources of income – Wales, Cornwall, Cheshire and Aquitaine – often found themselves heavily taxed. This was mainly in order to pay for military campaigns, however, rather than to fund personal extravagance, as was alleged.

---

* Later, it became three feathers and has been the badge of Princes of Wales ever since.

To some, the prince appeared aloof and unapproachable, but this may simply have been the result of a preference for the company of those whom he knew and trusted. Politically, he could be naive: he was hopeless at intrigue and often settled for less than he might have got with more skilful negotiation. To modern eyes, his conduct on campaign – the burning, the levelling of towns, the destruction of crops – is nothing short of criminal, but it was the normal mode of behaviour in an enemy country at the time. It was intended not as wanton ruin *per se* but to entice the main enemy army to give battle, and to show the populace that he who claimed to be their ruler was unable to give them the protection that should have stemmed from allegiance. Overall, the verdict of history – British history at least – is that Edward was a great soldier, a great Englishman and a worthy occupant of the British pantheon.

It has to be said that on this occasion the young Edward showed a great deal of confidence in himself and his men, and very little sense of urgency, reinforcing the evidence that he wanted to provoke a battle. He calculated that his mounted army could easily outmarch the generally ponderous French military machine, so he moved along the River Cher to Romorantin, on the Loire, and laid siege to it. Not only could the Black Prince not afford to leave a hostile garrison in his rear, but there was also the hope that the French might try to relieve the town and thus give the prince his battle. If Jean did not take the bait, however, Edward was confident that he could take the town and be on his way long before the French could interfere. Romorantin took five days to subdue and was eventually forced to surrender when the walls were collapsed by mining and the central keep was set on fire, but there was no attempt by the French to raise the siege. More time was lost trying to find a crossing of the Loire in the Tours area, although the wait here may also have been dictated by a renewed hope that the duke of Lancaster might yet be able to rendezvous with the prince.

The French had destroyed all the bridges over the Loire from Tours north-east to Blois, so, having failed to find either the duke of Lancaster or a crossing point, the prince decided on 11 September to move south in the direction of the English base at Bordeaux, still at a leisurely pace. Whether this was due to overconfidence or because he wanted to entice the French into following him is still debated; all the evidence seems to point to the latter, but it may well have been a combination of the two. In fact, the French army was much closer than either the Black Prince or Jean of France knew, and soon they were marching parallel to each other as the English reached Châtellerault and the French La Haye, twelve miles to the north-east. Both commanders wanted a battle: the Black Prince because he needed to strike a decisive blow, being, as the chronicler le Baker avers, 'Anxious for battle for the sake of the peace which usually follows';[28] and Jean because he could no longer placate his own people by procrastination. Moving rather faster than anyone expected, on 15 September, the French reached the east bank of the River Vienne at Chauvigny, from where they intended to move west towards Poitiers and cut the English off from Bordeaux. Reports from the Black Prince's mounted reconnaissance patrols that the French were now to their south discomfited Edward not one whit. The French had now committed themselves to battle and Edward would oblige them. The English baggage train and its accumulated booty was moved off to the west so as not to hinder the movement of the army.

The first blows were struck on 17 September, when strong English mounted patrols under the Gascon knights d'Aubricourt and de Ghistelles intercepted the French rearguard, with the advantage going to the English. The lead scouts of the main bodies clashed briefly too, when the English tried to intercept the French as they crossed the Vienne, arriving too late to do so. The French army now took up position on the plateau south-east of Poitiers, with Jean himself in the town and the English army to the south. Before first light on the following day, Sunday, the English army was on the march south, in order to find a position suitable for battle, halting somewhere in the area of Nouaillé-Maupertuis, about four miles south-east of Poitiers.

The rest of the day was spent in negotiation on the instigation of the cardinal of Périgord, who scurried hither and thither trying to persuade each combatant to come to an arrangement that would avoid a battle. Eventually, Prince Edward agreed to talk and discussions began. On the French side were two archbishops, the count of Tancarville, who had been captured at Caen and ransomed for £6,000, and three other lords, while the English were represented by the earls of Warwick and Suffolk, senior commanders, and the trio of Audley, Chandos and Sir Bartholomew Burghersh. Burghersh was another who had made his name from war, although starting from rather more comfortable circumstances than most. He was the great-nephew of Lord Badlesmere, whose wife had refused Queen Isabella entry to Leeds Castle in 1322, the family losing their estates as a result, regaining them after Isabella and Mortimer's invasion, losing them briefly on Edward III's coup, and then finally re-establishing themselves in good standing. Burghersh's father, the first Lord Burghersh, had made a great deal of money (relatively honestly), but his son owed his position to being a first-class soldier who was present at most of Edward III's and the Black Prince's battles and was another founder member of the Order of the Garter.

It is difficult to see what either side thought could come out of these parleys. Indeed, it is unclear whether they seriously wanted them to succeed. Points at issue included the prisoners in English hands, and the obvious sticking points were the French demand that the English should provide hostages and the English insistence that any agreement arrived at must be ratified by Edward III. Neither condition was in the least acceptable, and, when the French suggested that the question might be settled by a combat between 100 knights on each side, the earl of Warwick refused, saying that the issue must depend upon a battle between two armies and nothing else. Even if the French could be trusted to keep their word, the English had no intention of abrogating their tactical mix of archers and dismounted men-at-arms, which they knew gave them an advantage, in favour of an equal contest which they might lose. Jean was still leaning towards compromise but was eventually dissuaded by the rhetoric of two men, William Douglas and the bishop of Challons. Douglas commanded a force of 200 Scottish soldiers in the French army. There is some confusion over exactly who this Douglas was – the Scots have lamentably few surnames and use but a handful of Christian names. He was not the William Douglas, Lord of Liddesdale, who was still languishing in the Tower, but he had certainly fought the English, and he now assured Jean that, whatever the Black Prince might appear to agree to, he would continue to lay waste French lands and it would be much better to deal with him now than to have to fight him later in less advantageous circumstances. The bishop meanwhile made an impassioned plea, citing the shame and disgrace that the English operations had brought upon the present French king and his father, and insisting that the English were short of supplies, cut off from their base and hugely outnumbered. The only thing the English – any English – understood was force. Now was the time to deal with them once and for all. Jean was convinced and negotiations were broken off, the departure of the cardinal of Périgord's entourage to fight for the French only serving to emphasize the existing English suspicion of papal peacemakers. One advantage to the French was that they had bought time for a reinforcement of another 1,000 men-at-arms to arrive – and perhaps buying time was the sole French intention in the first place.

While the negotiations were going on throughout the Sunday, the English were preparing their position. In conformity with what was now standard tactical practice, the three divisions would dismount and take position with two forward and one in rear, with archers on both flanks. We are told that the vanguard was commanded by the earls of Warwick and Oxford, the second division by the prince himself, and the rearguard by the earls of Salisbury and Suffolk. Confusingly, the prince took up position in rear, as was normal procedure for the overall commander, with the vanguard on the left and rearguard on the right covering the front. The command arrangements for the vanguard and rearguard are, on the face of it, unclear. Divided command is never a good idea and was a major factor in the series of defeats suffered by the French for most of the war. The chroniclers were not, of course, military men, and it may be that they simply tell us the senior magnates in each division, not meaning to imply that they exercised command jointly. While joint command might work in a static battle of attrition, it would be a recipe for chaos once any form of manoeuvre was required, and we may assume that divisions were commanded by the senior magnate in each – in this case, Warwick and Salisbury.

Not all historians agree the exact positions of the opposing armies, but the most likely location for the eventual English defensive position is on a low ridge running along an ancient track across a bend of the River Moisson, on the Plaine de Plumet west of the village of Les Bordes. The frontage is about 800 yards and the flanks are protected by steep drops to the river, while the rear is protected by the river itself. French accounts say the French army marched along a 'maupertuis' or 'bad road' from Poitiers to get there, and there is what is now a farm track running south-south-east from Gibauderie through Le Maupas and Brout de Chèvre to La Cadrousse, which

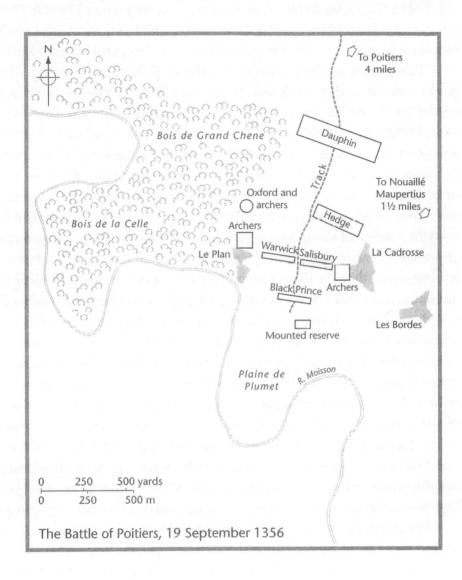

The Battle of Poitiers, 19 September 1356

is of considerable antiquity and may well be the road referred to. The two forward English battles would have been on the track, the right-flank archers south of La Cadrousse and those on the left somewhere around Le Plan. The reserve would have been placed some hundred yards to the rear, with a small mounted reserve of 200 knights under the Gascon lord, the Captal de Buch.

This was an excellent position for the English way of fighting. The flanks were secured by thick woods on one side and a steep escarpment on the other, and the frontal approach was crossed by sunken lanes and thick hedges. If the Anglo-Gascon army had around 2,000 men-at-arms and 3,000 archers, and the three divisions were of roughly equal size, then the frontage to be covered would dictate that the forward divisions fell in in no more than three ranks. Each division of archers would, as usual, have formed up in a square, lozenge or wedge shape. The Black Prince was not concerned about fighting a battle, even against a far larger force of probably around 3,000 crossbowmen and 16,000 men-at-arms, but he was concerned that the French might play for a stand-off until the meagre rations carried by the English ran out and the prince was forced to march off to find resupplies. Of course, the prince could decide to attack the French, but to do so against such superior numbers and where the English missile weapon could not be used to best advantage would be to invite disaster. It was imperative that the French be encouraged to attack, but they were unlikely to do so if they thought the English were well ensconced in their favourite defensive posture – the French had at least learned that from Crécy. The French would, however, be likely to attack if they thought they could catch the English on the line of march, or retreating, and it appears that the prince ordered his own division and that of Salisbury on the right flank to manoeuvre in order to give the impression that they were departing.

For all his many faults, Jean was inclined by now to listen to sound advice. Many of his senior commanders had faced the English, if not at Crécy, then in Normandy or Brittany, and Sir William Douglas had fought them in Scotland, and perhaps in France too. These men insisted that to send heavy cavalry against a dismounted English line was suicide: the only way to deal with English foot-soldiers whose flanks were secure was for the French to dismount too. They were also well aware of the slaughter that could be dealt out by English archers. The remedy was to attack them with cavalry, but only with men and horses that were covered in plate armour that arrows would not pierce. Mindful of this wise counsel, Jean had ordered 500 knights to equip their horses with armour that covered the animals' bodies, heads and necks completely. It would slow them down, but it would allow them to reach the hated archers and kill them. Apart from this mounted task force, split into two units, each commanded by one of the French marshals, the French army was divided into three battles or divisions. The vanguard was commanded, at least in name, by the dauphin, Jean's son;* the second division by Jean's brother, the duke of Orléans; and the third by Jean himself, with the bearer of the oriflamme – signifying no quarter or mercy – by his side. But, despite the French having three or four times as many men as the English, the Black Prince had chosen his ground well, and his numerical inferiority was partially nullified by the approach being restricted by marshes, streams and small ravines which limited the number of men that could advance at any one time.

The French plan, if they could not starve the Black Prince out, was to send the armoured cavalry against the archers and, having taken them out of the frame, to attack with the lead division on foot, supported by the next two divisions if they were needed – which they surely would not. The hedges and trees made it difficult to see exactly what the English were up to, but the commander of the right half of the anti-archer task force, Marshal Arnaud d'Audrehem, encouraged by William Douglas, and probably stationed around the east side of the Grand Chêne forest, was convinced that he could see movement of pennants and banners in the left-hand English division of the earl of Warwick – perhaps he could, for this may have been the Black Prince's planned encouragement – and without reference to anyone ordered his men to charge. Up the slope they came and at first the volleys of arrows had little effect, glancing off the plate armour of man and horse. This would have had very serious repercussions had not Warwick's second-in-command, the earl of Oxford, dismounted and run to the archers, ordering them to move further to the flank and to shoot at the horses' unarmoured legs. Now the tables were suddenly turned, as arrows sliced into horses' legs and bellies. Those

---

* Jean II's son, Charles, was the first to be styled 'dauphin', henceforth the title of the heirs to the French throne. It came from the territory Dauphiné, embodied into France by his grandfather, Philip of Valois.

animals not brought down but with arrows hanging off stifles and rumps became uncontrollable: they reared, whipped round and dumped even the most competent horsemen, before galloping back the way they had come and over unhorsed knights. D'Audrehem was captured and Douglas badly wounded, only evading capture (and probable execution) by being carted off the field by his personal retainers.

It was a terrible slaughter of the pride of France's equines, only equalled by that which befell Marshal Jean de Clermont and the other mounted task force. He had not been fooled by the appearance of waving guidons, but, when his brother marshal went charging off against the English left, he had little choice but to follow suit against the right. Clermont was even more restricted than Audrehem, for he came up against a thick hedge with only one carter's gap in it, wide enough for perhaps four horses abreast. Having run the gauntlet of the arrows, he then came up against infantry at the gap. He too could make no progress, and the survivors fled, picking their way through downed horses and men. The first phase of the battle had gone in favour of the English, but their officers now had to ensure that their men stayed in position and resisted the temptation to chase and take prisoners.

Now it was the turn of the French dismounted men-at-arms. The first division, led by the eighteen-year-old dauphin, who made up in personal courage what he lacked in common sense, advanced along the *maupertuis* preceded by a screen of crossbowmen. With a strength of around 5,000 men and covering an initial frontage of 1,000 yards or so, they would presumably have been in four or even five ranks. They had to climb the slope and negotiate the hedges before they could get to grips with the English infantry, and soon the inevitable arrow storm began to strike home, disposing of the crossbowmen and forcing the men-at-arms to crowd together towards the centre and causing death and destruction to such an extent that one chronicler says that the division was destroyed by arrow fire.[29] While this was an exaggeration, the effort of trudging uphill for 800 yards or so in plate armour (and the French knights were always more heavily armoured than their English equivalents) and then coming under attack from something like 30,000 arrows each minute for the last 300 yards or so meant that, when the dauphin's men managed to force their way through the hedge and meet their opponents, they were ill prepared for the physically punishing business of hand-to-hand fighting. They had shortened their lances, normally ten to fourteen feet in length and intended to be used on horseback, to a far more manageable five feet, which allowed them to compete on more even terms with the English wielders of pole arms, but it mattered little. Once two lines of men-at-arms closed, it was a question of who could thump the hardest: a sword would probably not go through plate armour or chain mail – although a halberd point might penetrate the former and certainly would the latter – and the aim was to knock one's opponent off his feet, whereupon he could be despatched by a dagger though crevices in the armour or the visor slits, or be persuaded to yield on the promise of ransom. Try as they might, the men of the dauphin's division could not break the English line, and, as casualties were mounting, either the dauphin or, more probably, one of his professional advisers ordered a withdrawal.

Even in modern armies, a withdrawal in contact with the enemy is one of the most difficult manoeuvres to carry out successfully. With inexperienced or undisciplined troops it can too often turn into a rout, and this is what happened here. The dauphin himself was hastened off the field by his personal retainers – a French heir was far too valuable a prize to risk capture – while those of his defeated troops who could still move fell back upon the next division in a disorderly panic. The commander of the second division, Jean's brother, the duke of Orléans, saw the dauphin being removed from the stage and decided that he should depart as well, which he did, taking his two nephews, the dukes of Artois and Normandy, with him. The men of Orléans's division, seeing themselves deserted by their commander, not unnaturally saw no point in staying and in moments they too were transformed into a disorderly rabble. Some called for their horses to be brought forward to effect their escape, others ran into the woods, and others fell back upon Jean's third division, the only part of the army to stand its ground.

Jean did not run, nor did his division, which was augmented by those of the first two divisions who had not fled the field and the crossbowmen who had survived the first French attack. Altogether this final French formation probably now numbered around 7,000 men, mostly men-at-arms – considerably more, in other words, than the Black Prince could muster. Furthermore, the men of Jean's division were mostly fresh, whereas the Anglo-Gascons had been in their battle positions for over twenty-four hours; they were exhausted, short of food and water, and had taken casualties. Jean ordered his reserve to dismount and join the line, and the advance began with the French moving towards the by now depleted English lines with a screen of crossbowmen in front. The archers were by this time running very short of arrows: the Knighton chronicle tells us that they ran out into no-man's-land to pull arrows from corpses and the wounded to be used again, and that the real pessimists among them armed themselves with stones to throw at the advancing enemy.

The Black Prince was well aware that, while so far the fortunes of battle had been with him, the tide could easily turn and he could still suffer a massive defeat. He ordered the Gascon Captal de Buch to take his mounted reserve and a party of mounted archers (perhaps fifty or sixty) to work his way round to the flank and attack the French from the rear. Meanwhile, the French crossbowmen and the English archers began a long-range duel, which was won by the archers, despite their shortage of ammunition. The crossbowmen disposed of, the archers turned to the advancing infantry, but, while the high-angle arrow storm wreaked its usual savage carnage in the French rear, those in the front two ranks were relatively unscathed as they advanced behind their shields, which were interlocked and angled upwards. The Captal and his party now began to move back prior to working their way round to the French rear, and this seemed to some of Edward's troops as if it were the beginning of a retreat. Some murmuring began and the prince, fearful that panic might set in and infect the whole of his division, immediately ordered 'Banners – Advance'.

While this stilled any notion of a withdrawal, it was a very risky move. Standing on the defensive with hedges and other obstacles to their front and with archers on the flanks, the English were in a reasonably secure posture, whereas to advance gave up the advantage of ground and gave the French the ability to use their superiority in numbers. The prince's division moved forward, at first level with and on the left of Warwick's division, and then ahead of it until the two lines of infantry met with a mighty roar of 'Saint-Denis!' and 'Beate Martin!' from the French* and 'God and St George!' from the English.† This was the crunch for the Black Prince: the

---

* It is said that the English Cockney slang expression 'All my eye and Betty Martin', meaning incomprehensible rubbish, comes from what the English thought the French 'Aidez moi, beate Martin' to be.
† Although, if the Black Prince's soldiers were anything like their modern descendants, they were probably shouting something very different.

French line lapped around his, the English missile weapon could not be used, and it now came down to bloody brute strength, with the archers picking up discarded lances and swords from the first French assaults and joining in where they could. The French pushed the English back: Poitiers was going to be a French victory after all. And then, just as suddenly, the tide turned again. The earl of Salisbury turned his troops to their right and led them north, advancing them into line and falling upon the French left flank. At the same time, the Captal de Buch's archers, having worked round to the west, appeared on the *maupertuis* and began to shoot arrows into the backs of the French men-at-arms, only pausing to let the Captal and his mounted followers hammer into the French rear.

Disciplined infantry in line can withstand cavalry if their flanks are secure, but not if that attack is preceded by an arrow storm, not if it comes from a totally unexpected direction, and not if they are already being assaulted from two other directions at the same time. Faced with the Black Prince in front, Warwick's very nasty infantry to their left, and archers and cavalry to their rear, Jean's division began to fall apart. Formations broke, banners began to fall, and men were running out of the line to escape or find their horses, to be promptly cut down by lightly armed archers hovering on the flanks. In minutes, the battle was over and the slaughter of those not worth holding for ransom began. Those who could fled towards what they thought would be the safety of the city of Poitiers, but they found the gates closed against them and many were killed by the pursuing Captal and his mounted knights. Jean II was captured with his youngest son Philip, as were four royal princes (including the count of Tancarville, who was by now making a habit of being captured by the English), eight counts, around 2,000 lesser nobility, the archbishop of Sens and twenty senior clergy. These latter were yet more evidence, thought the English, of papal bias, for as the contemporary satirical verse had it:

Now is the Pope a Frenchman born
And Christ an Englishman
And the world shall see what the Pope can do
More than his saviour can.[30]

Those French slain included two dukes, one marshal, one constable of France, several pages from the French equivalent of *Burke's Peerage*, the bearer of the oriflamme and the bishop of Challons, the most vociferous exponent of fighting a battle on that day.[31] Altogether the French probably lost around 2,500 dead, and, although a total of perhaps 5,000 casualties may not seem very much, it was who they were that was significant, for at a stroke the government and the administration of the French nation had been rendered impotent – dead or prisoners of war. Not only was it a massive tactical victory for the English, but it was a huge strategic victory too, one that might well bring the war to an end. English losses were slight, perhaps surprisingly, and were probably no more than a few hundred dead and wounded, although among the latter was Sir James Audley, who was carried in on a shield, stripped of his armour and laid on a bed in Edward's tent. While in attendance on the prince when Edward's division was in rear, Audley had asked permission to join the battle and dashed off into the thick of the fighting. It was thoroughly irresponsible, but the sort of behaviour that appealed to the Black Prince (and indeed to well-bred society generally), and as a result Audley was granted an annual pension of £300 (around sixteen years' salary for a man-at-arms).

The capture of Jean was, of course, a tremendous coup, and there was much argument about who had captured him, for, while he would have to become the Black Prince's prisoner, his actual captor would be well rewarded. It seems that Jean, realizing that the game was up, had looked around the field to see where the Black Prince was, as it was to him that a king should surrender. Edward was not in the vicinity and it may have been a renegade French knight in the English service to whom Jean yielded. In any event, it was not until the arrival of the earl of Warwick that the unseemly argument going on around Jean was stilled, and Warwick took charge of the royal prisoner and delivered him to the prince.

The chronicles are generally silent about the fate of the wounded at Poitiers, as indeed they are for most medieval battles. We do not know how many eventually died days or weeks later from loss of blood, infection or botched surgery, but it must have been a significant number. Military surgeons of the time were not unskilled, but they suffered from a lack of an effective counter to what they termed 'spasm' (probably tetanus) as a post-operative complication, a lack of sterile conditions in which to operate, and a tendency to amputate a damaged limb (with the risk of shock leading to a sudden lowering of blood pressure and death) rather than attempting to repair or splint it. There were numerous medical manuals available, describing various ways of treating wounds, the most commonly used probably being Roger of Salerno's *Practica chirurgiae*, which first appeared in 1180. Well regarded in England, it was still in use as an authority in the early fifteenth century.

There were many theories about the best way to deal with a wound caused by an arrow or a crossbow bolt – increasingly common as the Hundred Years War went on. If the offending metal had lodged in flesh, there were those who advocated pushing it on through until it exited; others recommended applying poultices to the wound to make it easier to pull out the foreign body; while others still advised doing nothing until the wound became so full of pus that the flesh was soft enough to allow the arrowhead to be extracted. Far more difficult was the removal of an arrowhead that had lodged in bone, as it had in the jaw of the young prince Henry (the future Henry V) at the Battle of Shrewsbury. In all cases, once the bolt or arrowhead had been removed, the wound was to be sealed by molten lard or boiling oil, and cauterized with a red-hot branding iron. Surgeons of the time were aware of the danger of nerve damage and local paralysis as the result of a cutting wound, and frequent massage of the affected area was encouraged. In an age before anaesthetics, having a wound treated would have been a long and often agonizing process.

As it was, the Anglo-Gascon army camped that night in the Forest of Nouailles to the east of the field of battle. The baggage train was called forward and tents erected for the prince and his immediate retinue, where he entertained Jean, his son and the senior French prisoners to supper – the food sequestered from the French stores, as the English had none. Gentlemen may fight each other, but they do not have to hate each other, and the Black Prince assured Jean that his father, Edward III, would treat him as befitted his high-born status (although continuing to refer to him as 'the usurper'). It was not until the next day that the English could count the French dead, many of whom had already been robbed and stripped by the locals. The bodies of around 150 of the highest born were taken away by the clergy of Poitiers and buried in the Dominican church or the Franciscan cemetery, while the rest were left where they lay, to be eventually loaded on carts and dumped in grave pits near the church.

It was now time for Edward and his army to head back to the safety of Aquitaine, and, while the prince had inflicted a massive defeat on the French, he could not assume that he was safe from them. Poitiers contained a large garrison and was far too well fortified to fall quickly; the dauphin was still on the loose and might act as a rallying point; and the division of the duke of Orléans, though it had fled the field, had done so without casualties and was probably still somewhere in the vicinity. Given stout leadership, the French might yet block the route to Bordeaux and pluck a victory of sorts from the ashes of defeat. Speed was of the essence, but movement would be slowed in any case by the baggage train, where the booty had been hugely increased by the rich arms and robes acquired from the battle. Add to this the huge flock of prisoners, most of them on foot, and the chances of getting to Bordeaux without interference were sharply reduced. The solution was to use captured horses to carry baggage and to release all but the most important of the prisoners, having first made them promise to report to Bordeaux and pay their agreed ransoms 'by Christmas'.

The Black Prince's army marched straight to Bordeaux, a distance of 125 miles as the crow flies but not as the soldier marches. They averaged around fourteen miles a day and arrived at Bordeaux on 2 October 1356. Messengers were sent to England to give the good news to the king and the people; it was immediately ordered that it should be announced from all pulpits in the kingdom and read out at market crosses. Coupled to this was more good news from Brittany, where the duke of Lancaster was supporting John de Montfort in gobbling up towns loyal to Charles of Blois, who, released from prison on parole pending payment of an enormous ransom of around £60,000 and thus unable to take up arms, could only watch as more and more of Brittany fell to the English. Eventually, Charles fled to Paris to join the dauphin in the Louvre.

In Bordeaux, Prince Edward and his men settled down to see the winter out until the spring weather would allow safe passage for the army to return to England. Some of the French noblemen who had promised to turn up with their ransom money defaulted, but even so the money raised, along with the plunder acquired in the *chevauchée*, paid for the cost of the campaign many times over. The ransom for the archbishop of Sens was paid – £8,000 – and King Edward bought a batch of nobles for £66,000, an outlay he would recoup with a handsome profit to boot. In London there was jubilation, in Paris dismay that turned swiftly to anger. The French armies had been defeated, their king captured, and his brother and sons had run away. Knights who had escaped the slaughter dared not show their faces in Paris, and many could not even return home for fear of being blamed for the disgrace and physically attacked.

Negotiations now began from Bordeaux, before Jean and his court were taken to England, but, while Jean was prepared to concede almost anything for his freedom, the Estates General, consisting of nobility, clergy and bourgeoisie, nominally headed by the dauphin and trying to govern a kingdom that was rapidly falling apart, did not regard the return of their king as their first priority. Rather, they wanted to find a way to end the war, either by raising an army big enough to expel the English, or by coming to terms with them. King Edward, too, was in no hurry to release Jean, viewing him as a useful pawn in arriving at a permanent settlement, and his secret instructions to the Prince of Wales in Bordeaux were to enter into negotiations but to stall and to agree to nothing except perhaps a temporary and short truce, which was in any case to exclude Normandy and Brittany.

In Paris, the dauphin suspended the Estates General and attempted to raise money by a further devaluation of the coinage. When this aroused massive civil disobedience and when no help could be obtained from the Francophile Holy Roman Emperor at a conference in Metz, the dauphin's clique had no option but to recall the Estates and to concede to their demands for a root-and-branch reform of the administration. This was to include the dismissal and imprisonment of many of the dauphin's and his father's advisers, the withdrawal of the new, devalued coinage, an insistence that the dauphin could only rule with the advice of a council nominated by the Estates, and a levy of new taxes to support a continuance of the war. No mention was made of raising money to release Jean. The dauphin agreed to all the demands – being without a sou in his empty treasury, he had no alternative. When the news percolated down to Bordeaux, Jean decided to take matters into his own hands and issued letters to be taken to Paris and read out at street corners repudiating the new administration and cancelling the levy. This resulted in even more chaos and a counter-repudiation from the dauphin, and, when Jean entered into negotiations with the Prince of Wales, nothing could be decided except for a two-year truce to run until Easter 1359.

In the spring, ships arrived from England to bring the army home, and on 24 May 1357 the Black Prince and his army made a triumphant entry into London to the cheers of the populace. Jean rode on a smart grey charger, while the Black Prince rode a modest pony – no doubt to make the point that, for all the French bombast and show, it could avail nothing against English skill at arms. Jean was lodged in the Palace of Savoy, built by Henry of Lancaster with the proceeds of French ransoms and near what is now the Savoy Hotel in the Strand, and began a luxurious detention while negotiations continued for his ransom. Edward III took a liking to his captive and took him hunting at Windsor, and occasionally paraded him along with that other captive king, David II of Scotland, who was now in his eleventh year in the Tower.

In June 1357, the French deputation arrived at Westminster to attend what would be a long-drawn-out conference to decide upon terms to bring the war to an end. It was headed by Cardinals Périgord, who was regarded with great suspicion by the English, and Cappoci, an Italian who was considered to be relatively unbiased. With them was a plethora of lawyers, civil servants, advisers, royal councillors and general hangers-on, all with their own servants, who had to be accommodated and fed. Parallel to these talks were discussions with the Scots, who had finally realized the hopelessness of continuing hostility to England when their backers, the French, were in such dire straits. At a meeting in Edinburgh, they agreed to pay a ransom of £67,000 – a huge sum for an impoverished country with a small population and no raw materials – to be paid over ten years, during which time the Scots agreed not to take up arms against England and to provide hostages against their good behaviour. King David was brought up to Berwick to attend the signing in October and was then released, although he now had little authority over the quarrelling factions in his country. Meanwhile, after much discussion and argument over the agenda, a draft treaty between England and France was at last agreed in December 1357. It allowed for almost a third of French territory, including Calais and the pale around it, to be ceded to Edward III in full sovereignty and a ransom of £650,000 with £100,000 down, after which Jean would be released on parole subject to hostages being delivered. In return, Edward would give up his claim to the throne of France.

The English parliament was summoned to meet at Westminster in February 1358 to agree the terms of the treaty. The members were in no hurry to come to a conclusion. England was now safe from invasion but there were vested interests keen to continue the war: the professional soldiers, civil servants who would administer conquered areas, owners of troop-ships hired by the government, manufacturers of arms and armour, bowyers and fletchers, and, presumably, the breeders of flocks of geese. Parliament decided that a solution to other long-standing matters could be tacked onto the treaty, particularly matters of papal authority. The pope was known to want peace between England and France, so concessions could be squeezed from him in order to get it. Specific matters were the taxation of English clergy by the pope, which meant English money going to Avignon in France, and appointments by the pope to English ecclesiastic posts, which most Englishmen felt should be a matter for them and not for some foreigner across the seas.* (Similar grievances would eventually lead to a final break with the Roman church less than two centuries later.) An embassy to Avignon would mean sending at least one senior bishop, lawyers, civil servants, clerks and escorts and would take a very long time, while armies would continue to be paid and arms manufacturers to thrive. King Edward drew the line at this, and, while he agreed that emissaries could be sent to Avignon, they could be reduced to a couple of knights and a clerk or two and thus conclude their business promptly. At the same time, Jean, knowing that the terms of the treaty might not find universal favour in France, despatched a group of his advisers to explain the finer points to government and people.

The difficulty for Jean was that France was effectively in a state of civil war. The Estates, trying to govern without their king, attempted to collect the increased taxes, but with the death or capture of so many magnates, normally the enforcers of good order and discipline, lawlessness spread. Demobilized soldiers and deserters, mainly English and Gascon but some

---

* At this pre-schism stage, the Avignon pope was regarded as legitimate by all Christian countries.

Frenchmen too, formed themselves into 'free companies', or *routiers*, and roamed the countryside working for whomsoever could pay them. If no paymaster could be found, they simply appropriated a suitable castle or fortified town and set themselves up as district robber barons, levying tolls on all who moved and taxes on those who did not. The king of Navarre, who had been imprisoned by Jean for plotting against him, escaped from prison and, arriving in Paris, 'persuaded' the dauphin to pardon him. In Paris, the third estate, that of the bourgeoisie, was increasing in influence just as the nobility – defeated and disgraced at Poitiers – lost their authority, and their leader, Étienne Marcel, a prosperous cloth merchant, considered at one point making Charles of Navarre (who was, after all, a Capet) king of France. Navarre, who was quite happy to claim the crown when the time was ripe but was far too clever to have it given to him by acclamation of the mob, left Paris at speed. He was followed in March 1358 by the dauphin, who felt (rightly) that government had broken down to such an extent that even his life was in danger – a fact that was finally corroborated when agents of Étienne Marcel broke into the dauphin's chambers and murdered two high-ranking officials lodging with him. The Parisians were now in control of the capital and they were against any treaty with England.

In the French countryside, those magnates who were still in control of their estates and had to raise money either for their own ransoms or for those of their relatives, and for the eventual ransom of Jean II, began to put even more pressure on their tenants and peasants, who were already taxed almost to extinction. Finally, the worm turned. It began in the Beauvaisis – now the *département* of Oise – in 1358 when the peasants, exploited beyond endurance, rose up and attacked their masters with whatever weapons they could find. It appears to have been a spontaneous rising, and in savagery it presaged the French Revolution over four centuries later, but unlike the latter it did not have a corps of the middle class and educated to lead it, at least not at first. Horrific bloodshed and disruption were caused by the *Jacquerie*,* mainly directed against the nobility, the clergy and any owners of property. Lynchings and burnings spread, and, as the movement expanded into Champagne and Picardy, the reports of the doings of the disaffected became more and more lurid. One tale circulating

---

* Jacques was then the commonest French Christian name among the peasantry.

told of a lady being gang-raped and then forced to eat the roasted flesh of her husband (at least they roasted him first). In the past, there had been regular outbreaks of defiance of authority in rural France, sometimes with violence, but they had usually fizzled out in a few days with little harm done. Here, however, the peasants themselves appear to have been so shocked by the excesses of what they had done that they had no option but to keep going, even attracting the support of some townsmen and minor nobles – who no doubt thought that they could thereby preserve their own lives and property. Étienne Marcel tried to make common cause with them, which did him no good in the end. And when a deputation of the *Jacquerie* tried to enlist the support of Charles of Navarre, he turned his soldiers on them and slaughtered the lot.

While the *Jacquerie* were neither encouraged nor supported by Edward III – peasants massacring their betters were not to be approved of, even if the betters were French – their activities served his purpose in that the uprising concentrated the minds of the French government and encouraged them to find a means of ending the war so that they could concentrate on restoring order internally. France was now in a state of complete and utter confusion, with the *routiers*, the *Jacquerie*, the Navarrese, the dauphin and the citizens of Paris all in arms and all out for what they could get. What was increasingly clear was that the *Jacquerie* was a threat to any sort of established order, and, when Charles of Navarre and noblemen whose castles had not been stormed began to organize themselves, the armies of peasants could not stand against them. Although the destruction was immense – eighty castles and manors destroyed between Soissons and Paris alone[32] – by mid-June the rebellion was over and retribution began, with the vengeful nobility meting out punishment every bit as unpleasant as that inflicted by the rebellious peasants and finding novel ways to execute their leaders. The result of the rising, which was seen as threatening everyone's way of life (except, of course, that of the downtrodden peasantry), was an upsurge of loyalty to the crown in the shape of the dauphin, a trickling away of Charles of Navarre's supporters, and second thoughts among the citizens of Paris. The latter were beginning to turn against their erstwhile leader, Étienne Marcel, who had made common cause with Charles against the dauphin and had allowed the detachments of the army of Navarre, mainly composed of English mercenaries, into the city. On 31 July, the mob rose, in the name of the dauphin, and murdered Étienne and his principal lieutenants. On 2 August, the dauphin entered Paris and Charles of Navarre withdrew his army from its encampment at Saint-Denis, looted the abbey and then marched off to Mantes to plot his next moves.

Despite the pleadings of Jean's advisers, the terms of the treaty agreed at the Westminster conference were not agreed by the dauphin and his government, whose confidence had been restored by the departure of Navarre and the end of the Parisians' attempt to gain their independence. King Edward received their refusals and decided that only another military campaign would bring the French to their senses. Accordingly, more claims were attached to those already in the treaty, including a restatement of the claim to the French crown, and an army, numbering (according to the Chandos Herald) 10,000 men but more likely 6,000, evenly split between men-at-arms and archers, landed at Calais on 28 October 1358. It then advanced through Artois and Champagne, burning, looting and levelling in the usual manner, as far as Rheims. One of the men-at-arms was the poet Geoffrey Chaucer, whose experiences led him to write later: 'There is ful many a man that crieth "Werre! Werre!" that wot ful litel what werre amounteth.'* The army stayed at Rheims from December 1358 until January 1359, in appalling winter conditions, and, having failed to force a surrender of that heavily fortified city, moved off to Paris. In accordance with the now standard English military practice, King Edward took up a defensive position and tried very hard to persuade the dauphin to come out of the city and attack him. He even sent Sir Walter Manny up to the walls to shout insults at the craven French, some of whom were beginning to learn of the inadvisability of attacking an English army in a position of their choosing and wisely resisted the offer. The only small crumb of comfort for the French at this time was a raid on Winchelsea in March 1360, when a few French ships hove to offshore and landed men who burned the town, stayed there for one night and left again. The English had grown complacent; no such raid had happened in twenty years and the infliction on them of the sort of terror they had been imposing on the French for many years caused short-lived panic and long-lived indignation.

---

* 'There are many men who cry for war without knowing what war amounts to.'

King Edward now moved off to Chartres and began to lay waste the area round about. It was the realization that the English could continue to wander all over France dealing out death and destruction at their leisure for as long as they liked, provided they avoided fortified cities, that brought the dauphin and his advisers to their senses. Negotiations began at Brétigny, near Chartres, in May, and in a week agreement was reached. The terms were very much the same as those in the December 1357 document, except that the ransom for Jean was reduced to £600,000. The agreement was signed at Calais in October 1360, by the dauphin for his father and – King Edward having returned to England – by the Black Prince for his. King Edward was to have Aquitaine, Ponthieu and Calais in full sovereignty and would drop his claim to the French throne. Once two-thirds of the ransom had been paid, raised by swingeing taxes on salt, wine, cloth and most movable goods and by the betrothal of Jean's eleven-year-old daughter to the son of the duke of Milan, Jean was allowed to return to France, leaving his three younger sons behind. When John, duke of Anjou, broke his parole, returned to France and refused to come back, Jean went back to England in his son's stead and was so well looked after that he died, still only in his mid-forties, in the Savoy Palace in April 1364. Meanwhile, the territory had been exchanged and the Black Prince, now duke of Aquitaine, had been installed as the ruler of English France. It seemed a very satisfactory outcome.

Sir John Hawkwood. Painting by artist *Paolo Uccello* created in 1436, currently displayed at the Duomo in Florence, Italy. A highly competent military commander made redundant by Edward III after the Treaty of Brétigny in 1360, he took mercenary service in Europe and died in service of Florence in 1394 aged about 75. The stirrup leathers are so long as to be no more than an aid for mounting.

7

THE FRENCH REVIVAL

The Treaty of Brétigny marked the culmination of Edward III's twenty-four years of campaigning in France and the end of the first phase of the Hundred Years War. The king had stated his claim to the French crown aged twenty-four and he was now forty-seven. Poitiers was a great victory and told the world, if the world needed telling, that the English had moved from being backward amateurs in the waging of war to being the foremost practitioners of it. The combination of professional soldiers fighting on foot with archers on the flanks was unbeatable, and the mobility of English armies meant that the French could neither trap them, nor fight them other than on ground which favoured the English, nor starve them out – although sometimes the latter was a close-run thing. Certainly, the Black Prince had been unable to take Rheims or Paris in 1356, but he had accepted that fact rather than become bogged down in a lengthy siege which would have forced him to remain in one place long enough for the French to concentrate against him. Given their inability to defeat the English militarily, the French had little option but to sue for what terms they could get: the economy was in ruins, the government had broken down, the fields could not be tilled, the population yearned for peace at any price, and Jean would promise virtually anything to gain his freedom. From the English point of view, the gains were enormous: it was true that the claim to the French throne had been abandoned, but a third of the kingdom definitely assured was better than the whole of the kingdom as a possibility. No one, French or English, could have predicted that in a mere fifteen years almost all the English gains would be lost.

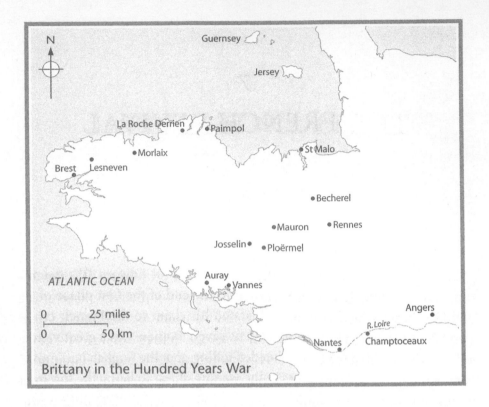

Brittany in the Hundred Years War

The Treaty of Brétigny did not stop war by surrogacy from continuing. In Brittany, the struggle between the Blois and Montfort factions was finally settled with the death of Charles of Blois at the Battle of Auray in September 1364, when the English army was commanded by Sir John Chandos with Sir Hugh Calveley as his second-in-command. One of the prisoners taken at Auray was to make a habit of being captured by the English and subsequently ransomed, in this case the sum agreed being paid by the French king. He was Bertrand du Guesclin, a Breton born of impoverished gentlefolk who was the exception to the rule of French social immobility. He had come to the attention of the dauphin during the earlier fighting in the Breton wars, and eventually – although with no great ability as a general – he would become a great French hero in a land badly needing heroes, be made constable of France and prove a constant thorn in the side of the English. On the English side, Calveley was yet another who had risen to prominence on the strength of his ability as a soldier. A native of Cheshire, he first fought under Sir Thomas Dagworth in Brittany, and in the guerrilla war that followed he was twice captured and ransomed, once at the Battle of the Thirty in 1351 and again as the captain of the garrison of Bécherel. He was a captain of archers at Poitiers and subsequently commanded a mixed force of men-at-arms and archers which became in effect a free company after the Treaty of Brétigny. Calveley and his company served in Spain as mercenaries in the army of the king of Castile, who was an ally of Edward III's, before returning to Brittany. At some stage, Calveley was knighted and success at Auray brought him the grateful thanks of John de Montfort, now duke of Brittany, and a large annual pension.

In 1361, the Black Prince, now thirty, married his childhood friend Joan, countess of Kent and widow of Sir Thomas Holland, described by the Chandos Herald as a 'lady of great worth' despite the fact that until recently she had been stony broke. This was in many ways an extraordinary match. No heir to the throne had taken an English bride since the Norman Conquest. Dynastic marriages with members of foreign royal families were major diplomatic instruments in the hands of English kings, and not only did Joan have a racy past, as we have seen, but she was also the same age as the prince and already had four living children, two sons and two daughters (a fifth, a daughter, had died in infancy). It seems, nonetheless, to have been a genuine love match, and, surprisingly perhaps, to have been approved of by King Edward, for he instigated a petition to the pope for a dispensation to allow the marriage (the couple were cousins).

That same year, the plague returned, and, while (as in its first visitation) it had a less destructive effect in England than in France, it nevertheless slowed down the complex and inevitably bureaucratic process of transferring lands to English rule. In England, the first outbreak of the pestilence had hit the aristocracy less severely than the common people, probably because of the cleaner living conditions and better food of the former. This time, the mortality rate was reversed. Overall, the death rate was lower: in Bishop's Waltham, fifty-three tenants died this time compared to 264 in 1348/9, although there were, of course, fewer tenants to start with in 1361. In Yorkshire, 'only' 14 per cent of priests died this time, whereas 22 per cent of tenants-in-chief and 24 per cent of the lords of Parliament were taken.[33] It has been suggested that the class disparity in the mortality rate points to the 1361 outbreak being of a different disease to the previous epidemic, but the contemporary chronicles all say that the symptoms in 1361 were identical to those of the earlier plague. Rather, it may be that the lower orders had acquired some immunity, which could have been passed on to their children but was denied to their betters, who had not been in contact with the disease on its first appearance.

In July 1362, the Black Prince was confirmed as the ruler of Aquitaine, in return for an annual payment to the king of one ounce of gold. Prince Edward, Joan and Joan's four Holland children all moved to Bordeaux. While English officials and garrison commanders were appointed to the more senior posts, there was little interference with the local administration at the grass roots. It was hoped that the duchy could be entirely self-supporting, and, given that a long period of peace was now expected and that the wine trade, already lucrative, would presumably become more so, this was a reasonable assumption to make. It had not taken into account the intentions of the dauphin.

The cause of the death of Jean II in London in 1364 is unknown. It may have been a last flicker of the plague, although rich food and an abundance of alcohol may have had something to do with it. In any event, Jean was only in his forties and his reign could not in any sense have been described as successful. The dauphin now ascended the French throne as Charles V. Known to the French chroniclers as Carolus Sapiens (Charles the Wise) in tribute to his library of over 1,000 books in the Louvre, he was sickly, of insignificant appearance and no soldier, but he was no fool either. He had no intention of accepting the new status of the English in France, but was too much of a lawyer to attempt to oppose it openly. Rather, he would whittle away at English possessions and try to undermine their government rather than attempt to confront them militarily, which he was experienced enough to know he could not do – at least not yet. He was a far greater threat to the English than either of his Valois predecessors. The problems facing Charles were reduced when Duke John of Brittany, now put in place by the English, accepted that he held that duchy as a fief of the king of France (as in law he did) and paid homage to Charles for it. In Brittany, at least, there would be relative stability. That left the problems of Charles of Navarre (who had by now acquired the soubriquet 'the Bad'), the *routiers* (free companies) and the shortage of funds in the national treasury.

Charles of Navarre was a constant threat because he held lands near Paris and could block the routes into and out of that city. He had vacillated between opposing Charles when he was dauphin and making alliances with him, and was very much a man who looked to the main chance, whatever the rights or wrongs might be. Infuriated by Charles V's bestowal of the duchy of Burgundy on his son Philip and insisting that his claim was much stronger than that of the Valois, Charles of Navarre raised a largely mercenary army, consisting of *routiers*, Navarrese, renegade Frenchmen and the Captal de Buch and his Gascons, and marched on Paris, only to be roundly defeated by the king's forces and forced to retreat back into Normandy. He had no option but to sue for peace in 1365 and had to surrender all his lands near Paris to get it.

The *routiers* were a far greater problem. Owing loyalty only to themselves, they were well organized, well led and well equipped, and preyed on vast tracts of the French hinterland. To the French, they were all 'English – the scourge of God', whereas their companies were in fact made up of Spaniards and Germans and occasional Bretons and Normans as well as Englishmen, and the majority in their ranks were Gascons. Nonetheless, most companies were commanded by officers who had held commands in the English army and were now demobilized – men like Sir Hugh Calveley, Sir Robert Knollys, who was of Cheshire yeoman stock and had started his military career as an archer under Calveley, and Sir John Hawkwood, the son of a London tanner and another ex-archer. The *routiers* had strict rules on the division of spoils, a proper chain of command and in most cases a uniform. They had become accustomed to life as soldiers and to being able to burn and plunder as they liked, and saw no reason to stop doing so just because there was now peace between England and France.

As far as Edward of England was concerned, provided the *routiers* did not profess to act in his name, he was perfectly happy that they should exist – and, given that they did exist, it was better that they should ply their unpleasant trade in France than in England. Although each of the many *routiers* was nominally independent, they did occasionally combine into 'great companies', sometimes numbering several thousand, which allowed them to indulge in undertakings even more ambitious than mere large-scale brigandage. At one time, a great company under Sir Robert Knollys advanced on Avignon and menaced the pope, while another carried out a *chevauchée* around Lyons. Charles V's France was in no state to put them down by force and more often than not local dignitaries and city authorities simply bought them off. Then a recurrence of the war by proxy gave Charles V his chance to rid France of the *routiers*.

The Iberian peninsula in the 1360s was divided into the kingdom of Portugal, with borders more or less where they are today, Castile and Leon covering central and northern Spain, Aragon south of the Pyrenees and east to the Mediterranean, Navarre bordering on Aquitaine to the north and sandwiched between Castile and Aragon, and the last Moorish kingdom, Granada, in the south. The king of Castile, Pedro the Cruel, was in dispute with his half-brother, Enrique of Trastamara, who claimed the throne, a dispute that escalated into civil war. Enrique appealed to Charles V for help, and Charles, seeing a chance of striking a blow at the pro-English Pedro and getting rid of his own troublesome *routiers* at the same time, ordered Bertrand du Guesclin to gather together the greatest company he could and take them into Spain to fight for Enrique. Bertrand did just that. He assembled perhaps 10,000 men, a mixture of English, Gascon and Navarrese free companies, French men-at-arms and mercenary crossbowmen, and crossed into Castile, where he collected Castilian supporters of Enrique, deposed Pedro and placed Enrique on the throne. Up to this point, the Black Prince was not overly concerned: Pedro was generally regarded as a nasty piece of work and the prince did nothing to stop the free companies and his own Gascons from marching off to join du Guesclin. In England, King Edward took a different view. However unpleasant a character Pedro might be, it was not in England's interest to have a French client state controlling the north of Spain: Castilian galleys had menaced the English coast and the routes for the Bordeaux wine trade in the past and might well do so again. When Pedro invoked the treaty of alliance with the English, signed in 1362, King Edward ordered his son to put Pedro back on his throne. The Black Prince began to collect an army which would consist

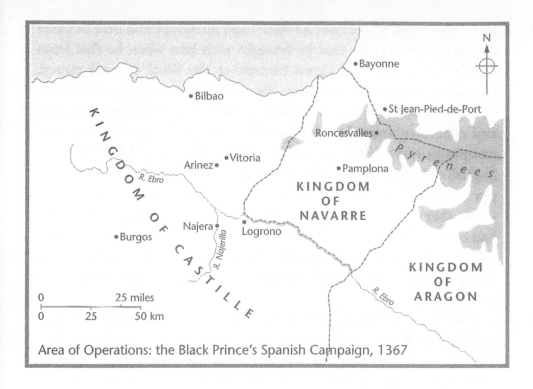

Area of Operations: the Black Prince's Spanish Campaign, 1367

of his own retinue of professional English soldiers, Gascons lately in the pay of du Guesclin and Enrique, and a contingent from England, mainly archers, commanded by the Black Prince's younger brother, the twenty-seven-year-old John of Gaunt, duke of Lancaster since 1362.*

If the English were to support Pedro with an army from Aquitaine, then they would need to cross the Pyrenees, and that meant getting Charles of Navarre, who controlled the mountain passes and could easily close them, on their side. This was achieved by Pedro promising him Castilian territory that would allow Navarre an outlet to the sea

---

* John of Gaunt had married Blanche, daughter of Henry of Grosmont, cousin of Edward III and the first duke of Lancaster – and only the second duke to be created in England, after the Black Prince (who was duke of Cornwall, a title borne by all Princes of Wales ever since). When Henry died without male issue in 1361 (probably of the plague, which had returned to England after the Treaty of Brétigny), Edward III made John duke of Lancaster in 1362.

and a cash grant of £20,000. As Pedro had no money and little of value save the crown jewels that he brought with him when he fled from Castile to Bayonne and threw himself on the Black Prince's mercy, the money was lent to him from the coffers of Aquitaine. In Castile, Enrique, now that he was on the throne, saw no need to retain the huge and expensive army that had put him there, so he paid off the free companies except for du Guesclin's Bretons and a force of around 400 English archers commanded by Sir Hugh Calveley. With their severance pay in their knapsacks, the companies either returned to Aquitaine, where they promptly took service with the Black Prince's army – they had been well paid to put Enrique on the throne and were quite happy to be well paid to knock him off it – or headed east into Aragon, where there was employment in guarding the frontier area against Castilian incursions.

When Enrique heard from French spies that the Black Prince was marshalling an army to come against him, he realized that neither Calveley nor his archers would fight against the Black Prince. But if he could prevent the English from getting into Spain, he would be safe, so, at some time around Christmas 1366, he approached Charles of Navarre, who was persuaded to turn his coat by Enrique's promise to match everything that Pedro would give him, with the added bonus of the fortress town of Logrono and £11,000 in cash. Satisfied that the invasion would not now take place, Enrique paid off Calveley, which was sensible, but also du Guesclin's Bretons, which was not. Once the Black Prince heard the news that Navarre was now in Enrique's pocket, his immediate reaction was to send messengers to Sir Hugh Calveley, who was in northern Castile on his way back to Aquitaine, ordering him to invade Navarre from the south. This put the wind up Charles of Navarre to the extent that he personally hastened to meet the Black Prince to explain that it had all been a most unfortunate misunderstanding and that he would of course support the cause of Pedro and supply a contingent of 400 men-at-arms.* Once Enrique realized that the passes would not,

---

* In the event, having sold himself to both sides, Charles arranged a bogus kidnapping so that he would not have to go on campaign himself. Both sides saw it for what it was and the whole caper only served to make Charles the laughing stock of Europe.

after all, be closed to the English, he hastily recalled du Guesclin and any mercenary troops that he could contact.

In mid-February 1367, the prince's army of around 8,000 men started its march up the traditional invasion route from Saint-Jean-Pied-de-Port through the pass of Roncesvalles. Roncesvalles can be treacherous even in summer, and now it was the middle of winter, with thick snow, temperatures well below freezing, and not a blade of grass for the horses nor an ear of corn for the men to be found. It says a very great deal for the logistic arrangements of the army that they traversed the pass and reached the plains north of Pamplona in good order. We do not know the names of the quartermasters who worked out how much fodder and rations needed to be carried, and who hired the mules and the carts to transport it, but, with experienced men like Sir John Chandos, Sir Robert Knollys and Sir William Felton,* it was an army well accustomed to campaigning in difficult terrain and in foul weather. From Pamplona, the Black Prince's objective was Burgos, the capital of Castile which sat on the main communication routes north and south. Enrique did his best to block the river crossings, but by March the English had reached the plains before Vitoria.

The Black Prince hoped for a decisive battle at Vitoria. The army was arrayed in battle formation and various challenges were sent out, but, if Enrique had not fought the English in France,† du Guesclin and his French officers certainly had and their advice was bolstered by a letter from Charles V of France, who advised Enrique that he should on no account be tempted into a set-piece battle, which the English would win, but rather that he should delay until the English ran out of food and fodder and had to retreat. What the Castilians could do was fall upon patrols and scouts, and it was in one of these minor skirmishes that Sir William Felton was killed. He was in command of a foraging party of around 300 mounted men-at-arms and archers west of Vitoria when he was surprised by a much larger French force. Taking up a position on a knoll near the village of Arinez, Felton's little group held off all comers

---

* Felton was the son of a soldier and part of the vanguard commanded by John of Gaunt. He was probably there to look after the duke of Lancaster on his first serious military campaign.

† Some sources suggest that he had.

until Felton was killed and the archers ran out of arrows, whereupon they had to surrender. For centuries afterwards, the knoll was known as *Inglesamendi* – the Hill of the English.*

The advice to Enrique not to force a battle was sound, and sure enough, in mid-March, the Black Prince had to move, heading south-east and then south-west to approach Burgos from the east, reaching Logrono on 1 April 1367. But politics forced Enrique's hand. Towns and fortresses on the English approach route were declaring for Pedro; there were mutterings in the ranks of the army, from the Castilians who thought Enrique was behaving in a cowardly fashion, and from the French and the mercenaries who wanted a battle so that they could be paid. Against all his better judgement and against du Guesclin's strongly worded urgings, Enrique decided to fight, for, if he did not, he would forfeit his throne by default as the population increasingly turned to Pedro.

The Trastamaran army took up a blocking position east of the village of Najera on the main road to Burgos. In front of them was a tributary of the River Najerilla, which flows into the Ebro to the north, while behind them was the Najerilla itself and then the village. There was one narrow bridge over the Najerilla, and to the west of the village there was (and is) a line of sandstone cliffs, difficult to scale without weapons and armour, impossible with them, and lacking any route for a horse. It may be that Enrique, or more probably du Guesclin, chose the position for the very reason that the army would thus find it difficult to run away. It was in any event a good defensive position for an army that was probably outnumbered by that of the Black Prince, who would have to attack – and thus reduce the effect of the archers – if he wanted to force the road to Burgos. But the prince had no intention of doing what his enemy wanted. Well before first light, the army left Logrono and made a wide flank march to form up on the north (left) flank of the Franco-Castilian line. The first indication the troops of Enrique had that the English were anywhere in the vicinity was when they saw banners and pennants fluttering away a few hundred yards on their left.

---

* It is still there and was the centre of the French General Gazan's position at the Battle of Vitoria in 1813 when Wellington destroyed the last major French army in Spain.

Du Guesclin desperately issued orders to the whole army to swing round to face north, while the English dismounted and formed their usual line of men-at-arms with the archers on the wings. The left-hand French division managed to wheel round reasonably quickly, but in the rest of the army panic set in, with the second division dissolving into a mass of men running for the village, while some of the Castilian light cavalry decided to desert to the English. Du Guesclin realized that he had no option but to abandon any idea of standing on the defensive: his only chance was to attack the English and hope that his men could run the gauntlet of the arrow storm. They could not. The Castilian heavy cavalry refused to dismount and paid the penalty in dead, wounded and maddened horses, while the light infantry could not stand. The whole thing was over in a matter of minutes, with fleeing Frenchmen and Castilians trying to get across the one bridge over the Najerilla and trampling and crushing each other in the process. The English rearguard slaughtered them as they were trapped by the river or struggled to reach the bridge, which was now blocked by the bodies of their own men. It was a complete rout, with du Guesclin and nearly all the senior commanders captured. The next morning, the heralds claimed to have counted over 5,000 bodies of Enrique of Trastamara's men. English losses were negligible.

Now began the accounting for prisoners and the calculation of ransoms. Many of the prisoners, du Guesclin and Marshal Arnaud d'Audrehem among them, had been captured by the English before and had not paid the ransoms promised then, and some heated discussion ensued. Enrique himself had not been captured – although unhorsed, he had fled on a horse taken from one of his knights, and eventually crossed the border into Aragon and got away into France. For Pedro the matter of who owned which prisoner was academic – he wanted to slaughter the lot as being the sure way to prevent any further trouble from them. The Black Prince demurred: the prisoners belonged to those who had captured them, who were in turn entitled to the ransoms, and in any case the knightly code prevented the killing of prisoners – or at any rate the killing of rich prisoners.

The Spanish campaign culminating at Najera was a spectacular success militarily: a professional English army had crossed inhospitable terrain in the depths of winter and once again had defeated a French-sponsored enemy with few casualties of its own. Politically and economically, however, it was a disaster. Pedro began to renege on all that he had promised; he failed to hand over the Basque country around Bilbao, he was unable or unwilling to pay for the cost of the campaign, as he had agreed, and he could not even repay the loan made to him to buy off Charles of Navarre. Most of the Castilian knights had no intention of paying the ransoms promised, and in some cases legal arguments in the courts of Castile and Aragon went on for years. In the event, Pedro's Spanish practices did him no good at all, for only two years later he was again dethroned and murdered, stabbed to death by Enrique of Trastamara himself, who was helped by those whom Pedro had failed to have executed after Najera. From 1369, Castile with its navy was therefore firmly in the French camp.

If Pedro was not going to keep his word and pay for the campaign that restored him, then the Black Prince would have to raise the money from Aquitaine, where there were already grumblings about the expense of maintaining what was seen as his lavish court in Bordeaux. As even higher hearth taxes (roughly equivalent to rates or a form of poll tax) were announced, some in the population began to wonder whether being protected from French occupation was worth the cost. Some of the Gascon magnates decided, rather shrewdly, to appeal to the French king Charles V against the hearth tax. To allow such appeals was entirely contrary to the Treaty of Brétigny, so for the moment Charles simply collected the appeals without doing anything about them. In the meantime, he was restocking the French treasury – the extra taxes imposed to raise the ransom for his father were retained – and building up an army.

By January 1369, Charles was ready to make his move: he announced that he was going to hear appeals against Edward's taxation policies, and, when challenged that this contravened Brétigny, he replied that France had never ratified the renunciation of sovereignty over Aquitaine. King Edward, more politically aware than his son, advised the prince to drop the hearth tax, but Prince Edward could see no other way of restoring his finances. When in June 1369 war broke out once more and Charles announced that he had 'confiscated' Aquitaine, the Black Prince was both furious and caught by surprise. He was in any case incapable of taking the field personally, as he had contracted some sort of disease – possibly dysentery, possibly malaria, possibly both and possibly while campaigning in Spain – which had led to further complications and necessitated him being carried everywhere in a litter.

Charles V had taken note of the lessons of Crécy and Poitiers, and well understood that to fight the English in open battle was to lose. Rather, he instructed his commanders, including Bertrand du Guesclin, whom he appointed constable of France in 1370, to whittle away at English power by selective targeting and what in modern parlance would be called guerrilla warfare. Towns with only a small English garrison could be attacked, foraging parties ambushed, supply convoys destroyed, and inhabitants persuaded, bribed or coerced into changing sides. The English did not have the manpower to put garrisons large enough to hold out in every town, and the only answer was to resort to the *chevauchée*. Sir John Chandos was recalled from his estates in Normandy but was killed in January 1370 in a skirmish at Lussac-les-Châteaux. He was wearing a long surcoat and slipped on the frozen ground. He was either not wearing a helmet or, if he was, had the visor up, and a French esquire stabbed him in the face. His was a serious loss as not only was he a highly competent military commander and strategist, but he was also well liked in Aquitaine and noted for his diplomacy. John of Gaunt led an expedition through Normandy, but, while he created a great swathe of destruction, he met no French armies. Sir Robert Knollys burned and plundered his way to the very gates of Paris, but still Charles avoided battle and Knollys could only retire.

In the same year, 1370, the citizens of Limoges transferred their allegiance to the French, a move that particularly incensed Prince Edward, as their leader, the bishop of Limoges, was godfather to the prince's son and had always been considered a personal friend. Such betrayal could not be tolerated and the Black Prince's army of over 5,000 men (according to Froissart, but probably nearer 3,000) laid siege to Limoges. After a month of mining and counter-mining, the English collapsed the walls and the soldiers poured in. The prince from his wheeled litter ordered a massacre of the population. As the contemporary chronicler puts it:

Men, women and children flung themselves on their knees before the prince crying 'have mercy on us gentle sir'. But he was so inflamed with anger that he would not listen. Neither man nor woman was heeded but all who could be found were put to the sword including many who were in no way to blame. I do not understand how they could have failed to take pity on people who were too unimportant to have committed treason. Yet they paid for it, and paid more dearly than the leaders who had committed it... more than three thousand people were dragged out to have their throats cut.[34]

They had indeed paid more dearly than their leaders,* for many of the nobles who had instigated the change of allegiance were allowed to surrender and were subsequently ransomed, while the bishop of Limoges, who should in all conscience have suffered a traitor's death, was handed over to the (French) pope. The numbers of the slain may, of course, have been wildly exaggerated, but, if the slaughter did happen, it lends weight to the theory that it was the French who coined the nickname 'the Black Prince'.

But, although Limoges had been recovered, at least for the time being, English France was falling fast. In 1371, the Black Prince, now crippled by his illness, returned to England, leaving John of Gaunt as ruler of Aquitaine and the other English territories, but he could not stop the rot either, and, as the husband of the daughter of Pedro the Cruel, he was particularly disliked in Castile by the ruling Trastamara faction. In 1372, du Guesclin marched into Poitiers when the citizens threw open the gates in defiance of the English garrison commander, and La Rochelle fell when blockaded by the Castilian fleet and attacked on land by du Guesclin. The last real opportunity to recover the situation came when King Edward mustered an army of 4,000 men-at-arms and 10,000 archers to be transported to France in 400 ships from Sandwich in August 1372. Although Edward was

---

* Although Richard Barber, in his *Dictionary of National Biography* entry on the Black Prince, quotes local historians in Limoges as saying that only the garrison, and not civilians, were put to death.

old, ailing and in the grip of a greedy mistress,* he himself embarked, as did the Black Prince, who was carried on board on a stretcher, but the weather conspired against them. The fleet spent weeks being buffeted to and fro and was never able to make landfall until eventually, after the ships had been blown back to England yet again, the adventure was called off, at enormous cost.

The following year, John of Gaunt mounted another *chevauchée* from Calais, and, although he created a great band of devastation through central France as far as Bordeaux, he lost most of his horses through hard riding and lack of fodder without meeting a single French army, du Guesclin contenting himself with cutting out foraging parties, stragglers and small patrols. By the end of 1373, most of Aquitaine had gone, with only the county of Guienne, around Bordeaux, and the coastal strip as far as Bayonne holding out. The French had overrun most of Brittany, whose duke had taken refuge in England, although they could not take Brest, which remained firmly in English hands, while in the north only Calais and a few garrisons in Normandy remained of the great holdings confirmed as a result of the Battle of Poitiers. The French tactic of guerrilla war and piecemeal reduction was working, but the task of invading Guienne was formidable and, despite increasing French and Castilian strength in the Channel, Calais, supplied by English ships, could hold out for far longer than Charles V wanted to spend on a siege. In 1375, negotiations for a truce began.

On Trinity Sunday, 7 June 1376, the Black Prince died in England at the age of forty-six. Had he escaped the illness that killed him, he would surely have been as great a king as his father, who followed his son to the grave a year and two weeks later. By the time of his death, Edward III was sixty-five years old and senile, cantankerous and losing much of his earlier popularity. Nevertheless, he was a great king, perhaps one of our greatest: he had dealt with Scotland, recovered English lands in Europe, presided over a genuine revolution in military affairs, renewed faith in government after the unstable years of his father and then of his mother

---

* Edward's mistress, Alice Perrers, is variously described as a sorceress, a wanton and the daughter of a thatcher. She was more probably of perfectly decent origins and certainly a lady-in-waiting to Queen Philippa when she came to Edward's attention.

and Mortimer, stabilized the currency, expanded English trade, and made England a power to be feared and respected. That it all began to fall apart in his later years does not detract from his essential greatness.

England has always been at her weakest when there is a disputed succession, an incompetent monarch or a child king. The successor to Edward III was the ten-year-old second son of the Black Prince (the older son, another Edward, had died in 1369 aged six), Richard of Bordeaux, who would reign as Richard II. The real power was to be exercised by a council, chosen from Lords, Commons and Clergy, until Richard came of age, with the whole edifice supervised by the king's uncles, John of Gaunt and the younger earls Edmund of Cambridge and Thomas of Buckingham. Gaunt was frequently suspected – then and later – of harbouring ambitions for the throne himself, and, had primogeniture for the English succession not been firmly established by then, he would surely have succeeded. All the evidence, however, shows that he was a genuine supporter of royal legitimacy and of his nephew, whose magnificent coronation he arranged, at enormous expense.

Despite the wishes both of the ruling council of England and of the French king Charles V for some form of truce, there were too many vested interests in mayhem and murder for fighting to stop completely. While there were no great battles for the next few years, raids, sieges and encounters at sea went on, and, although the English no longer got the best of all these skirmishes, the seemingly unstoppable French advance was slowed and then halted. The efforts of those wishing a permanent peace suffered a setback when the French pope Gregory XI died in 1378 and the conclave of cardinals elected an Italian, Bartolomeo Prignano, as Urban VI. The French refused to accept his election and put forward their own candidate, Cardinal Robert of Geneva, who, although Swiss by birth, had spent most of his time in France, and acclaimed him as Pope Clement VII. Thus began the Great Western Schism, with Urban in Rome recognized by England and Clement in Avignon supported by France and Scotland. Previously, while the popes were regarded with great suspicion by the English, they did at least provide a forum for peace negotiations, but now with the schism that option was gone and there was no professedly disinterested single body to act as a go-between.

Richard II was in many ways a tragic figure. As the younger son, he would not have been raised to be king, and, although his mother had considerable (and generally beneficial) influence on his early education and subsequent development, he had little contact with his father, who was frequently away on campaign, and his senior uncle, Gaunt, was unpopular in the country. This unpopularity was, of course, partly engendered through envy: the dukedom of Lancaster was immensely rich and in many aspects was independent of the central government. But Gaunt's frequent quarrels with various bishops (usually over the question of sanctuary in churches),* his obvious disdain for public opinion, and his lack of charisma (perhaps surprising given his genes) as a military commander did not help his reputation.

It was an unfortunate start to the reign that the truce negotiated in 1375 ran out only a few days after Richard's accession. It was even more unfortunate that the French had used the brief peace to prepare for war, by embarking on a major ship-building programme based in Rouen, while the English, short of money, had been much less energetic. In the summer of 1377, French fleets, aided by the Castilian galleys of Enrique, raided the English Channel ports from Rye as far as Plymouth. They would land, loot what they could, set fire to anything that looked as if it might burn and set sail again. They landed on the Isle of Wight and extracted a ransom before departing; attacked Southampton, where they were bloodily repulsed by local forces under Sir John Arundel, a younger son of the third earl of Arundel; raided Poole; and tried (and failed) to effect a landing in Folkestone. On the continent, the French admiral Jean de Vienne blockaded Calais by sea while the duke of Burgundy laid siege on land. Fortunately for the Calais garrison, commanded by Sir Hugh Calveley, although some of the outer defences fell, bad weather and heavy rains made mining and the movement of siege engines impossible and the French withdrew, giving Sir Hugh an opportunity to sally out, attack Étaples further down the coast, and remove the large quantities of wine stored there. Meanwhile, in the Dordogne, the duke of Anjou was steadily reducing English-held

---

* In 1379, Gaunt managed to have it agreed that 'fraudulent debtors' had no right of sanctuary.

towns. He captured the seneschal of Aquitaine, Sir Thomas Felton, father of the Sir William who had been killed in Spain, and threatened Bordeaux, only to have to turn back when he found pro-English forces in his rear. Brest was under siege, but was reinforced from England in January 1378, although English attempts to capture Saint-Malo and to initiate a campaign in Normandy failed.

Then, later in the year 1378, an opportunity to hit back at the French by proxy presented itself when Charles of Navarre re-entered the frame. Charles had once again fallen out with Charles V of France, for much the same reasons as Edward III had with French monarchs over Aquitaine: Charles of Navarre was a king in his own right, but also held Navarre as a vassal of the French king, and, when Charles of France declared Navarre forfeit, Charles of Navarre appealed to England. The council was very happy to support Charles of Navarre on the grounds that any enemy of France was a friend of England, and contracted to send 1,000 men for a period of four months, in exchange for the port of Cherbourg. This was agreed and the English duly occupied Cherbourg.

By the time the English army arrived in Navarre, however, delayed by bad weather and shortage of shipping, the situation had been resolved. Enrique of Castile had invaded Navarre on behalf of his French ally, but, when he heard that an English army had landed in Aquitaine and was on its way, he wisely withdrew. As the English troops, under Sir Thomas Trevet, who was at this time only in his late twenties but had fought for the Black Prince at Najera, were no longer required to defend Navarre, they embarked on a foray through Castile, reducing numerous Castilian towns, damaging Enrique's reputation considerably and acquiring large quantities of booty before returning to England. Charles of Navarre, meanwhile, made his peace with the French, who retained the Navarrese lands in Normandy. While the tactical achievements of Trevet's expedition were minor, the acquisition of Cherbourg was a major strategic gain: along with Brest, Bayonne, Bordeaux and Calais, England now had an outpost line of strongly fortified ports with which to counter French naval ambitions and which could serve as springboards for invasions of France.

Charles of France, having at least gained the Normandy possessions of Navarre, decided to try the same ploy in Brittany, and in 1379 declared that he was confiscating that duchy. This time he went too far and the Bretons, touchy about their independence and with no wish to be part of France, took up arms and demanded the return of Duke John from England. Having secured a promise of English military support, John returned to Brittany, where he was welcomed with acclamation at Saint-Malo. The English army to support him had been agreed at 2,000 men-at-arms supported by the same number of archers for four and a half months from 1 August, but, when the English council discovered that they could not afford to pay and transport so many, the size of the contingent was reduced to 650 of each arm.* They were to be under the overall command of Sir John Arundel, the defender of Southampton, who had been part of the relieving force sent to Brest in 1377 and was in Cherbourg in 1378.

The troops duly mustered at Southampton, but the weather and problems in finding troop transports delayed their departure and Sir John is said to have billeted his immediate retinue in a convent, dismissing the mother superior's protests that the presence of such a large number of young men might lead to 'an unforgivable sin which would bring shame and disgrace to the nunnery'.[35] The unforgivable sin duly occurred. Arundel did nothing to stop it (commanders of other units in the area managed to keep their men under control), and it extended to the soldiery looting the silver from a local church and generally behaving like their modern successors on a Saturday night in a garrison town. When ships were finally found, Arundel's men took some of the nuns along with them, no doubt to sew on buttons during the journey, and divine retribution caught up with them when a violent storm raged in the Channel. Most of the ships carrying horses sank, either off the coast of Cornwall or off Ireland, and in an effort to lighten the troop-ships the men are said to have thrown most of the nuns overboard. When that had no effect, the ladies were followed by the accumulated plunder of Hampshire. Arundel's own vessel ran aground off Ireland in December and he was drowned. Sir Hugh Calveley and

---

* Froissart says only 600 altogether (400 men-at-arms and 200 archers), but, given the number of senior commanders in the force, including Sir Hugh Calveley and Sir Thomas Trevet, this seems for once to be too low.

most of the other captains survived.

While the French assault on what was left of English France had been halted, lack of coordination between the various expeditionary forces on land and at sea meant that much of the expenditure on men, ships and weapons was to no great purpose. When Edward III was alive, there was a strong king who made decisions, supported by an administration that could carry them out. Now rule was by committee, never a recipe for strong government, and, although decisions were made in the king's name, they were too often a distillation of conflicting opinions resulting in weak compromise. Dissatisfaction with the way the war was being conducted and the tax burden imposed to pay for it eventually boiled over in 1381.

The catalyst was the decision in June 1380 to send another expedition to help the duke of Brittany. The king's uncle, the twenty-six-year-old duke of Buckingham, would be in command with around 5,000 soldiers, probably 3,000 men-at-arms and 2,000 archers, all to be mounted Given the difficulty of finding enough ships and the ever-present threat of storms in the Channel, the troops would be ferried by the most direct route from Dover and Sandwich to Calais, from where they would make a *chevauchée* to link up with Duke John at Rennes. On 24 June, the army marched from Calais, creating the usual swathe of destruction as it went across the Somme, to Rheims, south of Paris, and then to Rennes, but without meeting a single French army, Charles V having instructed his commanders that on no account were they to offer battle. Buckingham was now running short of money, and a request was sent back to England asking for sufficient funds to maintain the army throughout the winter and to continue campaigning in the spring. At home, the treasury was empty and, after much argument, it was decided by Parliament that the government's demand for £150,000 – to cover the expenses of Buckingham's army and the maintenance of the fortress ports (where the garrisons had not been paid for months), with possibly a little to be secreted for John of Gaunt's ambitions in Spain and Portugal (he intended to pursue a claim to the throne of Castile by reason of being married to Pedro the Cruel's daughter) – was too much. They would agree to find £100,000: two-thirds from the laity and one-third from the church. And then Charles V died, Duke John came to terms with his successor, and Buckingham's army was left high and dry with no option but to go home. It was to be the last major English expedition of the fourteenth century.

In England, the imposition of yet another poll tax caused widespread discontent. It had last been levied in 1377, when the amount was graded according to rank and ability to pay, with the basic rate being one groat or four pence. Now it was to be a flat rate of one shilling – three times as much and with no concessions according to income. Since the death of Edward III, there had been a number of levies but with very little to show for them: English possessions in France were being whittled away, the seas were no longer safe, and, despite the huge reduction in population caused by the various outbreaks of plague, many magnates were insisting on the imposition of manorial rights and duties that were no longer relevant nor seen to be fair. When the time came to collect the tax, there was widespread avoidance, evasion and fraud, with householders hiding their wives and children or taking to the woods to avoid the commissioners or simply refusing to pay. In May, a commissioner was set upon in Essex, and, when the Chief Justice of Common Pleas was sent to investigate, he too was set upon. By the end of the month, widespread rioting had broken out in Essex and in early June it had spread to Kent. There had often been outbreaks of local indiscipline in the past, but they had always been contained; this time it was serious, the most serious attack on authority in England of the fourteenth century. As usual the rebels were blaming the king's evil counsellors and, under the watchword 'King Richard and the True Commons', they demanded the heads of those they called traitors. With the army still away in France or on the Scottish borders, it was a good time to stage a revolt, and the government was slow to react.

Although these events are known to history as the Peasants' Revolt, the name is misleading. While many of those who embarked on widespread hooliganism were indeed peasants – probably the majority – a great number were tenant farmers, small-holders, owners of land in their own right and local government officials – jurors, reeves, bailiffs and constables. There must also have been large numbers of demobilized archers in their ranks. The fact that the various rebel groupings were able to communicate with each other and were reasonably well disciplined would indicate that there were enough men of education and accustomed to leadership to provide a cadre of officers of sorts.

As disorder and rebellion spread, the king, the royal family and the king's counsellors took refuge in the Tower. One of the party was the king's cousin, Henry Bolingbroke, son of John of Gaunt, who was the same age as the king and who would eventually supplant him and rule as Henry IV. The king was persuaded to meet the rebels, who were now in the London suburbs with the gates of the city closed against them, and on 13 June the king left the Tower by barge and was rowed downriver to Rotherhithe. There he addressed the rebels from the boat, his advisers having considered that it was too dangerous for him to disembark. The demands of the rebels were presented to the king: the heads of John of Gaunt, the Chancellor (the archbishop of Canterbury), the Chief Justice and the Treasurer – to which the king gave the diplomatic reply that they should have whatever heads they liked subject to the law, whereupon he was rowed back to the Tower.

The rebels were now running out of supplies and the obvious place for them to get them was London. Moving along south of the river, they looted the archbishop's palace at Lambeth and released the occupants of Southwark prison. Then, despite the orders of Lord Mayor Walworth, somebody lowered the drawbridge over London Bridge and opened the gate. The rebels poured in and – their movements clearly organized – looted John of Gaunt's Savoy Palace and the lawyers' offices at the Temple, released prisoners from the Fleet and Newgate, and, almost inevitably, slaughtered any foreigners (mainly Flemings) who could be found. The king could only watch form the Tower as the plumes of smoke rose over the city. By this time, the acknowledged leader of the revolt was Walter the Tiler, or Wat Tyler, whose origins are obscure. He may have been from Kent or from Essex, his home may have been in Maidstone or in Colchester, and he was probably indeed a tiler, although there are suggestions that he may have been of the Kentish gentry.

The king agreed to meet the rebels again, at Mile End on 14 June, and now their demands went way beyond just the heads of those whom they disliked. There were political issues too: the abolition of serfdom and villeinage, a fixed rent of fourpence an acre for land, equality of all men below the king (abolition of the lords and knights) and an amnesty for all involved in the revolt. The king announced that he would grant all the demands and returned to the Tower, to discover that during his absence another group of rebels had forced entrance, dragged out the Chancellor, Archbishop Sudbury, and the Treasurer, Sir Robert Hales, and beheaded them both on Tower Hill. Henry Bolingbroke was fortunate not to have suffered the same fate. Whether the murders were at the instigation of Tyler, who may or may not have been present at Mile End, we do not know. Most of the rebels now dispersed and began to make their way home, satisfied that the king had granted their demands, but a hard core including Tyler remained, and the king agreed to meet them the next day at Smithfield.

On Sunday, 15 June, the king rode out from the Tower, escorted by 200 mounted men-at-arms, some of his household and the Lord Mayor. At Smithfield, the king's party lined up at one end of the field and the rebels at the other. Tyler was summoned to speak to the king and rode across the field on horseback. What happened then is disputed and depends on which chronicler you believe. Tyler may or may not have got off his horse. He may have seized the king's hand, called him 'brother' and failed to remove his hat. He may have added to the previous day's demands the disestablishment of the church and the abolition of the offence of outlawry, and he may have demanded a flagon of wine to quench his thirst. He may have drawn a dagger and threatened the Lord Mayor, or he may have been accused of being a thief and a knave by a squire of the king's household. Alternatively, it may have been the intention all along to arrest or kill Tyler, a plan to which the king may or may not have been privy. What is not in dispute, though, is that Tyler was stabbed, probably by Mayor Walworth, and fell to the ground. Some of his men, former army archers, seeing their leader felled, strung their bows, whereupon the young king, showing considerable courage (or perhaps, given he was a spoilt child, it never occurred to him that he might be in danger and he simply had no fear), cantered over to them, drew his sword, and invited them to look upon him as their captain and to follow him to Clerkenwell, where he would grant them all that they had asked. The rebels set off to Clerkenwell and the king and his escort made their own way, while Mayor Walworth may or may not have galloped back to the city and called out any available soldiers, knights and citizens accustomed to bearing arms.

The resulting group, numbering 1,000 according to Walsingham but probably several hundred, set out for Clerkenwell, where they may or may not have surrounded the rebels and forced them to drop their weapons, or the rebels may have simply been persuaded to go home and escorted to the city gates by knights of the king's household. What is not in doubt is that the dying Tyler was rushed to Tyburn and hanged under the auspices of the Lord Mayor.

With the death of Tyler and the dispersal of the rebel armies that had converged on London, the revolt collapsed, although mopping up took a little longer. Initially, it was the government's intention to promote reconciliation. There were few executions and, as a result of legal arguments over what exactly defined treason, those that were carried out were mainly for felony, until there was a renewed flaring up in Essex. This time, there would be no mercy and anyone remotely suspected of rebellion was tried and hanged or beheaded. The king did not, of course, keep any of his promises to the rebels, and the lesson of successful deceit was not lost on him, nor did he fail to notice the rebels' touching faith in him personally. Although the king avoided having to grant concessions on this occasion, later in his reign there was some reform of the administration, forced upon him by the members of Parliament and the money-granting power that they and they alone had, one which they guarded jealously.

In France, too, there was revolt caused by excessive taxation, but ruthless and immediate action by the duke of Burgundy put it down. However much some elements in both countries wanted to continue the war, neither could afford to do more than engage in inconclusive skirmishes at sea, and a threatened French invasion of England in 1386 was called off because of bad weather and an exaggerated French view of the reception that they might get.* While a continuance of the war by England would undoubtedly have been attractive to her soldiers, who saw it as the only way to make a name and a fortune, it had cost the treasury dear: shipments of wool or wine could now only be carried in armed convoys, which

---

* As most of the army had gone off to Spain with John of Gaunt, the reception might not have been very fierce, and there was certainly panic around the ports on the English south coast.

made them hideously expensive, and the pay of the garrisons in English France was reduced to an extent that the men had to rely on ransoms and extortion to survive. That ransoms and extortion were a good source of income is evidenced by the fact that desertions and mutinies as a result of the reduction in pay were very few.

Richard II was now growing up and increasingly resenting the control exercised by the various councils established to govern the realm. When his uncle Gloucester and the earl of Arundel demanded the sacking of the chancellor Richard de la Pole, earl of Suffolk, because of his disastrous foreign policy – one which had failed to prevent the French gaining control of Flanders and had lost England the support of John of Brittany – the king arrogantly said that he would not dismiss a scullion from his kitchen on their say-so. When Gloucester reminded the king that monarchs had been deposed before and pointed to the case of his own grandfather, Edward II, Richard then overreached himself by saying that his subjects were in rebellion against him and he would ask his brother the king of France to aid him. But, rather than instigate outright opposition, Richard now backtracked; Suffolk was dismissed and impeached, and a new council with Gloucester and Arundel as leading members was installed. Nonetheless, Richard's insistence on the appointment of court favourites to lucrative offices and his failure to prosecute the conflict with France very nearly led to civil war, with Gloucester, Arundel and their associates and armed retinues on one side and the king and soldiers paid by him personally on the other.

The Lords Appellant,* as the opposition termed themselves, won the only battle, at Radcot Bridge in December 1387, and the following year the so-called Merciless Parliament sentenced five of the king's friends to suffer the death of traitors, with the full panoply of drawing, hanging and quartering. However much they may have deserved it, theirs was judicial murder all the same and the king would have his revenge – but not just yet. His first move came the following year, 1389, when he announced that henceforth he would reign in his own right, which, at the age of twenty-two, he was fully entitled to do. He was crafty enough not to change many of the court appointments that the Lords

---

* 'To appeal' then meant 'to accuse', so these were the 'Lords Accusing'.

Appellant had forced upon him, nor to upset the lords themselves. With the national coffers empty, the crown jewels pawned, large loans due to be called in and Scottish raids on the increase, Richard desperately needed to bring the war with France to a close. He needed peace and genuinely seems to have wanted it, and this view was shared on the other side of the Channel. So, in 1389, a temporary truce was agreed while negotiations for something more permanent could take place. England gave up Cherbourg and Brest, which brought murmurings from the Lords Appellant but did not disturb a sort of peace that endured for the next few years. During this time, Richard made his court as glorious – and as expensive to finance – as any in Europe and quietly began to recruit soldiers, mainly from Cheshire, who wore his livery of the white hart badge rather than the accepted English cross of St George.

In 1396, Richard married for the second time (his first wife, Anne of Bohemia, whom he married in 1382, had died in 1394). The bride was Isabel, the nine-year-old daughter of Charles VI of France, and during the marriage ceremony at Calais Richard made a statement repugnant to all levels of English society. He promised that he would work with the French to depose Pope Urban and have Pope Clement at Avignon recognized as the only legitimate heir to the keys of St Peter. In England, there was outrage, not only among the clergy, who saw themselves abandoned by their king, but also among the laity, who saw it as playing into French hands. Richard cared not a jot. His dowry from the French on marriage was £170,000, enough for him to recruit even more soldiers and take the next step to avenge the deaths of his friends nine years previously. In July 1397, he ordered the arrest of Gloucester, Arundel and Warwick, the senior members of the Lords Appellant. Gloucester was conveyed to Calais and quietly murdered, probably by smothering – he was, after all, the son of a king – while Arundel, Warwick and their adherents were tried before Richard's equivalent of the Merciless Parliament, with John of Gaunt presiding. In September, Arundel was sentenced to death and executed, while Warwick was awarded life imprisonment. Henry Bolingbroke, Gaunt's son, had at one stage joined the Lords Appellant, but, although he had been pardoned on the grounds that he had moderated their demands, he was now seen as a potential threat and exiled, banished for ten years.

Opposition grew as Richard's rule descended into a tyranny of disregard for the laws and customs of the realm and the raising of forced loans to fund ever more extravagance at court. The king insisted that he ruled by God's will and not by leave of the people and adopted the title 'majesty' – never before used by an English king. John of Gaunt had himself raised no objection to the fate of his brother Gloucester, nor to the exile of his son, at least not in public, and, as far as we can tell, he remained a loyal supporter of the crown to the end – although what he might have told his son and how he may have advised him can only be supposition. Then, in 1398, Richard at last got what he wanted and needed in his foreign relations, when a twenty-eight-year truce was agreed with France. But, after John of Gaunt's death the next year, the king finally went too far: he extended Henry Bolingbroke's banishment from ten years to life and confiscated the duchy of Lancaster with all its castles, lands and titles. This was the final straw for the magnates, for, if the king could do this to the duchy of Lancaster, whose lands might be next? Unaware, or uncaring, of the reaction in the country to his arbitrary actions, Richard set off for Ireland – that unhappy country was once more in a state of unrest – and Henry Bolingbroke saw his chance. He had spent much of his exile in Paris, and elements of the French nobility were more than ready to help and support him. With only about fifty personal retainers, fellow exiles and men-at-arms, Henry took ship at Boulogne sometime in June 1399, having given out that he was off on a pilgrimage to the Holy Land, and landed somewhere in the Humber estuary at the end of the month.

As Henry moved through Yorkshire, knights and magnates declared their support for him and joined him with their retinues. At this stage, he does not seem to have had any intention of deposing Richard, only of regaining his Lancastrian heritage and removing Richard's 'evil counsellors'. Once the earl of Northumberland and his son, Henry Percy or 'Hotspur', came over to him, Henry was assured of the support of the north. With the defection of Edmund, duke of York – the king's uncle and regent during his absence in Ireland – and the submission of the Ricardian stronghold of Chester without a fight, Richard's spies knew that the situation was serious. In Ireland, the king was indecisive, and even when ships were found to embark his army, he changed his mind about the port of departure, and the unloading and then loading of men and horses wasted more time. Eventually, Richard landed in Wales and his soldiers began slipping away. With a few trusted advisers he took refuge in Conway Castle, and, when the earl of Northumberland arrived as Henry's emissary, the king was persuaded to give himself up and was taken to London and lodged in the Tower.

At some stage, probably when the duke of York had gone over to him, Henry elected to aim for the throne itself, rather than just regaining what he considered to be his rightful due. Knowing how duplicitous Richard could be, he presumably decided that he could not risk leaving Richard on the throne plotting revenge, but the question was how to assume the crown in a manner that could be portrayed as legal. The deposition of Edward II was not a true precedent, as he had been replaced by the next in line, his son Edward III. Richard's immediate heir was not Henry but another cousin, the eight-year-old Edmund Mortimer, fifth earl of March, whose mother Philippa was a daughter of Lionel of Antwerp, Edward III's second son, whereas Henry was the son of the third son. As the English claim to the French throne was based on inheritance through the female line, Edmund's claim could not be dismissed on those grounds, and the justices strongly advised Henry against claiming the throne by right of conquest, this being quite the wrong message to send to other potential usurpers. Eventually, on 29 September 1399, Richard's twenty-two-year reign came to an end when he was persuaded to relinquish the crown to Henry, although there was much legal fudge to justify it. Henry was acclaimed by Parliament and duly crowned on 13 October – he would reign as Henry IV. Richard was despatched to the Lancastrian stronghold of Pontefract.

Sometime in December, a conspiracy to restore Richard was discovered. Of the chief plotters, Salisbury was lynched by a mob in Gloucester, Despenser murdered in Bristol, and Huntingdon caught and beheaded in Essex. As long as Richard lived, he was bound to be the focus for those who opposed the new regime, and, like Edward II's, his demise would be convenient, and the sooner the better. Only one chronicle suggests that Richard was murdered, by being hacked into pieces; others variously claim that he was starved to death by his jailers, that he deliberately starved himself or that he died of grief. His corpse was removed from Pontefract to London, and, as there were regular stops on the way so that it could be exhibited to the public, the hacked-into-pieces theory can be discounted. Nobody actually dies of grief and, as death by starvation, whether forced or self-inflicted, can take an inconveniently long time, we may reasonably suppose that Richard II was done to death in the usual way when the body of a high-born personage must be exhibited – by suffocation. And, as it was in Henry IV's interests that Richard should die, we may suppose that he ordered it.

The death of Richard II ended a period of vacillation and weak government which precluded any serious resumption of the campaign to realize the cause of English France. On the face of it, Henry IV – young, healthy, outgoing and popular – was just the man to revive it, but events were to take a different turn and it would be another generation who reignited the flame of English conquest.

King Henry IV from his tomb in Canterbury Cathedral. In a (presumably unintended) touch of irony it is opposite that of the Black Prince, for the death of whose son (Richard II) Henry was almost certainly responsible.

8

REVOLTS
AND RETRIBUTION

Henry Bolingbroke had a peripatetic existence as a child: his mother died of plague when he was only a year old; he was lucky to survive the Peasants' Revolt; he was looked after by a variety of guardians and tutors while his father was away campaigning; and he lived in the households of both his father's second and third wives. In spite of all this, he seems to have grown into a normal and well-adjusted adult. There can be little doubt that as a young man he exhibited all the qualities of kingship that his cousin Richard, the rightful king, did not have. A champion jouster and an experienced soldier who served with his father in Spain and with the Teutonic knights in Lithuania, he had travelled throughout Europe and the Mediterranean, and he had gone on pilgrimage to Jerusalem and visited the holy sites. He had learned sufficient guile to side with the Lords Appellant when they seemed to be winning, and to abandon them when it was apparent that they were not. His usurpation of the throne was generally welcomed by the population and most of the great magnates supported his accession. On the face of it, he should have been a popular and effective king. The problem of a disputed or not entirely legal succession, however, is that it leaves the way open for objectors to the regime, for whatever reason, to claim that it is illegitimate and that the usurper cannot therefore levy taxes, wage war, make land grants, treat with foreign powers or undertake any of the other myriad duties of royal government. Throughout his fourteen-year reign, Henry was plagued by shortage of money, unruly magnates, the Scots, the French, the Welsh and, finally, an uncooperative son.

A shortage of money was something that all English kings had to face most of the time, but it had not escaped the notice of Henry's subjects that he had inherited not only the vast wealth of the duchy of Lancaster but also that of his wife, Mary de Bohun, co-heiress to the earl of Hereford. Mary gave Henry four sons – the eldest would become Henry V – and two daughters before dying giving birth to Philippa in 1394, with her wealth passing to her widower. All that, added to the income of the crown, should, it was not unreasonably supposed, have been more than sufficient to fund the court and run the country. However, Henry had made large grants of land and money to buy the loyalty of Richard II's adherents and to reward his own followers, had rather unwisely given the impression that he did not intend to tax harshly (which many took to mean not at all) and, as he had little or no experience of government, was not able administratively to control court expenditure. While Parliament did grant him the customs duties on wool, exports of wool were down significantly and so therefore was revenue from that source. Henry was never able to live within his means, and, as one of his rallying cries had been the repudiation of Richard's policy of making peace, a resumption of the war with France would entail even more expense.

In France itself, the removal of Richard and his replacement by Henry was regarded with horror. While quite prepared to discommode the English by supporting Henry in his attempt to recover his Lancastrian inheritance, the French court drew the line at his becoming king. They claimed to object to the deposing of a rightful king, but in reality the French were worried that Henry might reject the truce agreed by Richard and that war would follow. France, in any case, was in turmoil. In 1392, Charles VI, the Valois king, had gone barking (literally) mad, the first manifestation being his setting on and slaying members of his entourage, this followed by his wandering around the palace howling like a dog and forming the conviction that he was made of glass. While casual killing and the occasional bark might not matter overmuch, a belief that one is made of glass rather militates against taking the field in battle, or indeed doing anything very much, in case of becoming a breakage. Charles did have periods of lucidity, but these were to become fewer and shorter as time went on. While government theoretically remained in the king's hands, the real power was exercised by his uncle, Philip, duke of Burgundy, when the king was mad, and by his brother, Louis, duke of Orléans, when he was sane. The two did not get on. Burgundy, who also ruled Flanders, was prepared to come to terms with the English in order to pursue his own interests in France and to protect Flemish trade, whereas Orléans coveted Aquitaine and also had ambitions in Italy (his wife was Italian). Burgundy supported the pope in Rome (as did England and most Flemings), while Orléans supported the Avignon claimant.

Although Henry IV sent emissaries to the French court assuring them that he stood by Richard's truce – an action that did not find favour with the war party in England – Charles VI and Orléans refused to recognize him as king and were particularly incensed by his refusal to send Richard's child queen, Isabel, back to France. Eventually, in 1400, she was repatriated but without her dowry, which Henry retained on the grounds that the ransom for Charles's father, Jean II, had not been paid in full. In fact, Henry could not have refunded the dowry as there was nothing to refund it with. Calais cost a huge amount to run, particularly with piracy in the Channel once more rife, and, when the garrison mutinied because they had not been paid, Henry had to buy them off with cash borrowed from Italian moneylenders. And then, that same year, 1400, trouble flared up once more in Wales.

A land dispute involving a Welsh squire, Owain Glyn Dŵr, and an Anglo-Welsh Marcher Lord, Sir Reynold Grey of Ruthin, a great friend of Henry IV and a member of his council, had not been resolved to Glyn Dŵr's satisfaction. Glyn Dŵr's family was of impeccably Welsh origins, being descended from a variety of tribal chiefs, but had regularly married into English or Anglo-Welsh families – his own wife was a Hanmer, from a family that is still to this day influential in the Welsh Marches. Glyn Dŵr had studied law at Westminster and may have accompanied English armies on at least one punitive expedition to Scotland. But the failure of Parliament to support Glyn Dŵr was the catalyst for the most serious uprising in Wales since the conquest by Edward I in 1283. It was the result of long-held and simmering resentment of the harsh taxation policies of both the Marcher Lords and the central government, the preference given to English settlers and the Anglo-Welsh, the lack of career opportunities for local churchmen and administrators, and the unhappiness of local civil servants who had to implement policies with which they did not agree. In a very short space of time, the rebels had gathered an army of sorts, declared Wales independent and Glyn Dŵr Prince of Wales, and demanded the deposition of Henry of Lancaster and the abolition of the English language in Wales. They invaded the border towns, began the usual burning and looting, and occupied those English castles which had been only lightly garrisoned. The rebellion would drag on for another fifteen years and, while never a serious threat to the throne, it did distract the king and divert troops that might have been more profitably employed in France.

Meanwhile, despite the fact that Richard's body had been displayed in public to show that he really was dead, there were those who believed, or purported to believe, that the ex-king was still alive, and who were prepared to foment trouble in his name or use the possibility that he was still alive as justification for insurrection. Henry faced a number of rebellions or potential rebellions during his reign, but the most serious was that of the Percy family in 1403. Henry Percy, earl of Northumberland, had been Henry Bolingbroke's ally in the deposition of Richard II and, with his son Henry 'Hotspur', was responsible for guarding the northern Marches against the Scots. On 14 September 1402, Percy had trapped a Scottish army under Archibald Douglas returning from a raid into England and laden with plunder at Homildon Hill, about forty miles north of Newcastle. The Scots took up a defensive position on the hill in schiltrons – a form of massed phalanx which had been very effective in the days when the English would attack on horseback. The English, true to the now accepted tactical doctrine, stood back and opened the battle with the archers shooting into the schiltrons at a range of 200 yards. They could not miss and there was bloody carnage. Douglas realized that, as his own archers were outnumbered and ineffective, standing still would simply invite wholesale slaughter, so he ordered both his infantry and his mounted cavalry to charge the English. Down the hill they came, but they never met the English infantry. The English archers withdrew at a measured pace, stopping every few yards to loose another volley of arrows. The Scottish schiltrons faltered and then broke, pursued by the English. The numbers engaged on each side and the casualties are obscure, but very large numbers of Scots knights and squires were captured, including Douglas himself, who was blinded in one eye by an arrow.

It was after Homildon Hill that the Percy allegiance began to waver. There had already been arguments about the cost of policing the Marches and how much was paid or not paid to the Percys, and it was said that Hotspur had not been reimbursed for his campaigns against the rebels in Wales. Now there was a major dispute over who should receive the ransom of the Scottish prisoners. In the spring of the following year, the impetuous Hotspur was moving south, ostensibly to join the king in another campaign against the Welsh rebels, when he reached Chester on 9 July and proclaimed that Richard II was alive and that Henry IV was a usurper. Swelled by the enlistment of a party of the famed Cheshire archers, the army now adopted the white hart badge of King Richard. As Hotspur knew perfectly well that Richard was dead, he could not keep up the pretence that he was alive for long, and, as the ranks of the rebel army were being swelled by adherents coming in from the areas around Chester, Hotspur announced that he had discovered that King Richard was in fact dead, murdered by Henry of Lancaster, and that the rightful heir was Edmund Mortimer, earl of March, who was then twelve years old.

Edmund's claim was derived from his mother, Philippa, who was a daughter of Edward III's second son Lionel, formerly of Antwerp but since 1362 duke of Clarence. Lionel was, of course, older than his brother John of Gaunt, from whom Henry's claim devolved, and, although it was weakened by being in the female line, it was a plausible claim nevertheless.* As well as the accusations against Henry of usurpation and murder, the usual complaints of unjust taxation, public funds being diverted to private use, corruption in high places and evil counsellors were given another airing. At some stage, Hotspur had put out feelers to Owain Glyn Dŵr, and had he been able to join forces with the Welsh – for whom the French had already announced support – then Henry IV's position would have become precarious indeed. As it was, the sixteen-year-old Henry of Monmouth,

---

* Descent through the female line could not be cited as an objection to Edmund's claim, as it was the basis of the English claim to the French throne.

the Prince of Wales and future King Henry V, was in Shrewsbury as the commander, in name at least, of operations against the Welsh rebels. He and Hotspur had been friends, campaigning together in Wales, and the prince had learned a great deal from the scion of the Percys. Also on the prince's staff in Shrewsbury was Hotspur's uncle, Sir Thomas Percy, earl of Worcester, who on hearing the news promptly took off to join the rebels. If Hotspur's army was to link up with Glyn Dŵr, they had to get across the River Severn and so headed for Shrewsbury, intending to cross using the two bridges there.

When the king heard that the younger Percy was in rebellion against the crown, he was at Derby, ironically taking an army north to aid the Percys on the Scottish border. Knowing well that he had to get to Shrewsbury and the Severn bridges before Hotspur, to say nothing of preventing the Prince of Wales being taken hostage, the king marched on Shrewsbury. On 20 July, after a forced march of thirty-two miles – a considerable feat even for a largely mounted army – he reached Shrewsbury just before Hotspur's rebels, who were now faced with only two options: stand and fight, or give up the struggle. Three miles north of Shrewsbury at Hallescote is a low ridge running east to west and about 800 yards long, and it was on that ridge that Hotspur decided to make his stand. As usual, the chroniclers all differ over the size of the rebel army and all almost certainly exaggerate. If we assume the men-at-arms and infantry were in four ranks, then there may have been 2,400 of them, and if there were the same number of archers, or slightly more – by now a standard establishment in English armies – then Hotspur may have had around 5,000 troops altogether. The king probably had slightly more.

On the morning of Sunday, 21 July 1403, the royal army marched out from Shrewsbury and formed up on the flat plain south of the ridge and probably around 400 or 500 yards from it. It is not entirely clear how the king deployed his troops. The normal formation would have had three battles, or divisions, with two forward and one, commanded by the king, in reserve. It seems certain that the Prince of Wales commanded the left forward division, but, in view of what happened later, it seems that the king may have commanded the right forward battle. Perhaps there were only two battles after all, or there may have been three but with no reserve. The ground now is a mixture of private gardens and grassland, but in 1403 it was mostly planted with peas, which grew on canes put into the ground and thus both hindered movement and made it difficult to see much farther than about twenty yards. Today, the remains of fishponds can be seen, but these may date from a later period.

Now began a long process of negotiation intended to resolve the dispute without a battle. For most of the day, Thomas Westbury, abbot of Shrewsbury, accompanied by a royal clerk, scampered back and forth bringing offer and counter-offer. The king offered pardon if the rebels submitted, while Hotspur proposed all sorts of constitutional changes that could not possibly have been accepted by the king. It is difficult to see how either side could have compromised, and late in the afternoon the king came to the conclusion that Hotspur was deliberately prolonging negotiations in the hope of buying time for reinforcements from Wales to arrive. In fact, although Hotspur did not know it, Owain Glyn Dŵr was at that time a hundred miles away, consulting a fortune-teller at Carmarthen,* and in any case the Welsh valleys were flooded and would have made any reinforcement from that direction very difficult.

In short, the battle could not be avoided and it was opened by the rebel archers. This was the first time that two English armies using the same tactical doctrine had faced each other, and at first it seemed that the rebel bowmen would overcome those of the king. Hotspur's men were on the high ground and could see their target; the royal army had tramped through the peas to get within range and its own archers found it difficult to identify what they were shooting at. A contemporary account says that under the rain of rebel arrows the king's soldiers were like 'leaves that fall in the cold weather after frost' and that, when the royal archers replied, 'on both sides men fell in great numbers, just as the apples fall in autumn when shaken by the south wind'.[36] It seems that at this point a portion of the royal army broke, presumably the rear rank of infantry, fearing that the king had been killed by an arrow. This was partially compensated for by the desertion to the king of a contingent of the rebel army led by its commander, one Richard Ramkyn, but the

---

* Glyn Dŵr was believed by many of his followers to have been a magician with the ability to make himself invisible. This is probably untrue.

actual process cannot have been as tidy as the simple statement makes it seem. Men moving down the hill towards the royal army would have been assumed to be attackers, not deserters, and, as the royal ranks apparently opened to receive them, we may suspect that at some stage during the pre-battle negotiations Ramkyn had let the royalists know of his intention to change sides.[37]

For all his impetuous nature, Henry Percy was an experienced soldier and must have known that the best plan in his situation would have been to stay on the defensive and let the royal army attack him. This is how the English had been winning battles for the past sixty years and, given that Hotspur held the high ground and that he commanded the best archers in England, that would surely have been a winning ploy. That the rebel army now advanced downhill towards the king may not have been Hotspur's intention – it may have been forced upon him. Most of the chroniclers agree that in the front rank of the rebel army was a contingent of Scottish knights, commanded by the now visually impaired Archibald Douglas. These men had all been captured at Homildon Hill and had agreed to fight for Hotspur in return for their release free of ransom. The sight of the king's banner, with the king himself clad in plate armour covered in a richly embellished jupon, may have so inflamed Douglas that he cast common sense to the winds and rushed off, followed by his Scots, and Hotspur may have felt that he had no option but to support. In any event, the rebel infantry, led by Douglas, tramped down the hill and, despite suffering casualties from the royal archers, fell upon the king's battle. The royal standard-bearer was cut down and fighting was fierce. King Henry apparently had three or possibly four knights wearing identical armour and royal accoutrements to act as decoys,* and at least two of them were killed. The fate of England hung in the balance.

It was the young Prince of Wales who saved the day for his father. The chroniclers are, as ever, infuriatingly vague over the details of the battle, but what seems to have happened is that the rebels crowded towards the king – after all, if they could kill or capture him, then the

---

* Including Sir Walter Blount, ancestor of the English pop singer and ex-officer of the Household Cavalry James Blunt (Blount).

battle was over and victory was theirs – with a much lesser press of Hotspur's men facing the left of the royal army. Some accounts say that the Prince of Wales advanced his battle, broke through the rebel line, turned his battle about and attacked the rebels from the rear. This may, however, be crediting the prince with a higher degree of command and control and ability to manoeuvre than was possible in a chaotic situation where commands passed on by drum, trumpet and banner signals would be difficult to hear and even more difficult to obey. It seems more likely that the prince swung his division round ninety degrees to his right and attacked the rebels in flank. However he achieved it, the prince showed great personal bravery – at some stage, presumably when the armies were at a distance from one another, he had been hit in the face by an arrow but refused to leave the field* – and considerable tactical acumen. The advantage had now swung to the royalists and, attacked on two sides and outnumbered, the rebel army began to disintegrate. When Hotspur was killed in the fighting, it was all over bar the slaughter. Those who were able to extricate themselves tried to get to the horse lines and safety, while those who stood their ground, before long in ever smaller groups, were left with no course open save surrender or death.

The victory was to King Henry, and the mopping up and pursuit of the fleeing rebels went on until midnight, whereupon the exhausted victors set about licking their wounds, cleaning their weapons and finding somewhere to sleep. The shaft of the arrow that had hit the Prince of Wales had been broken off but the head was still lodged in his upper jaw, so the king's surgeon, John Bradmore, was summoned to extract it. He already had, or had a farrier make, a tool to extract it. First he enlarged the wound by pushing into it a series of wooden dowels coated in honey, which has antiseptic properties; once the hole was large enough, he inserted his extractor into the socket of the arrowhead, screwed up the tongs of the instrument so that they gripped, and finally removed the iron.[38] In an age without anaesthetics, it must have been a long and incredibly painful

---

* Presumably an arrow that had bounced off someone else's armour, as a direct hit would surely have killed him. And it presumably struck him on the right side of his face, as his most famous right-facing portrait – and one that is thought to be most life-like – shows no scar.

process, but with a poultice of barley and honey all infection had gone within three weeks.*

We do not know the exact numbers of dead and wounded on both sides, but they were considerable and would perhaps have been even more had the royal army had to attack the rebels in their hill-top defensive position.† Archibald Douglas was captured, yet again, and, having lost an eye at Homildon Hill, lost a testicle this time. Also in the considerable bag was Sir Thomas Percy, earl of Worcester. With the rebel army defeated, the reckoning was severe. Thomas Percy could expect no mercy: he had been a trusted adviser to the Prince of Wales and had deserted him. He was beheaded in Shrewsbury the day after the battle, along with the Shropshire knights Sir Richard Vernon and Sir Richard Venables. Hotspur's body was initially buried, then disinterred and quartered, with Chester, Bristol, Newcastle and London each receiving one quarter, while his head went to be exhibited in York. Other rebels were dealt with summarily or after hasty trials. In York, the head of the Percy family, Henry, earl of Northumberland, submitted to the king and asked forgiveness, blaming the whole sorry business on his son, now conveniently dead. While Henry could perfectly reasonably have had the earl executed there and then, he decided to send him before Parliament, which decided that the earl's behaviour fell just short of treason. The old survivor, having got away with a large fine and the redistribution of his castles and lands to more loyal subjects, might be supposed to have learned his lesson.

The dead from the battle that could be found were buried in a mass grave on the battlefield, just off the Whitchurch road. In 1406, King Henry issued a licence for the building of a chantry chapel on the site, which is still there, with a statue of the king on the gable end. Inside the chapel is a (modern) list of the knights known to have fought on each side, with depictions of their coats of arms. Looking at it, one is immediately struck by the number of families who had a soldier on each side of the conflict. There were Calveleys, de Burghs, Masseys, Stanleys, Browes, de Cokes and

---

* The prince was fortunate that the archer had not adopted a common practice of dipping his arrowhead in human faeces before shooting it, which would have poisoned the wound.

† The best assessment of the dead and wounded is probably in Appendix 4 to Ian Mortimer's *The Fears of Henry IV* but even he can only make a very rough approximation.

Greys on both sides. The most important thing for any medieval noble family was to retain its land and, as being on the wrong side in a civil war meant losing that land, it would have made sense to back both runners in a two-horse race.

Although the king's victory at Shrewsbury put an end to the most serious rebellion of his reign, it was not the end of his troubles. French piracy was still rife in the Channel and there was little recourse except to encourage English sea captains to follow suit against French shipping. The seemingly interminable Welsh war was dragging on and attracting French raids in support of anything that would weaken England. And Richard II imposters sprang up in all sorts of likely and unlikely places, including one in Scotland whom the English could not catch. As was usually the case, money was short. The Parliament of 1404 insisted that the king had quite enough revenue of his own without further taxation and suggested that he might like to reduce the many grants and pensions that he had awarded since his assumption of the throne. As these grants had been made to benefit those who had supported his bid for the throne, they could not easily be reduced, and attempts by the court to reduce its costs by moving into castles that were less expensive to run met with little success. There was no money to pay for supplies for the army and the king's purveyors had to resort to requisition; and, when there was no money to pay the troops, the officers were told to carry on at their own expense.

Despite the lack of money and a hostile parliament, the king survived. He had learned from the example of Richard II, who had defied Parliament and the magnates and had paid the price: Henry swallowed his pride and compromised. A small crumb of comfort was gratefully received in 1405 when the French captured the English town of Marck, three miles east of Calais. One of the officers of the Calais garrison, Sir Richard Aston, decided that enough was enough and took a detachment of 500 men-at-arms and light infantry, supported by 200 archers with twelve carts of arrows, to win it back. The ammunition carried in those carts must have been more than sufficient, as the result was a very pleasing slaughter, with fifteen French knights killed and several hundred prisoners taken. The commander, the count of St Pol, a notorious raider of southern English seaports, fled, divesting himself of his armour as he ran to find his horse. Elsewhere, French raids on the Isle of Wight and Dartmouth were robustly driven off, but the fact that they happened at all did nothing to portray the king as a staunch defender of the realm, however hard he tried.

Despite keeping his head and many of his estates in 1403, Henry Percy the elder, earl of Northumberland, had clearly not learned his lesson, for in 1405 he was once more involved in rebellion. This time, he entered into what was termed the 'Tripartite Indenture', an agreement between himself, Sir Edmund Mortimer, father of the Mortimer claimant to the throne, and Owain Glyn Dŵr, whereby they would depose Henry IV and divide England and Wales between them: Glyn Dŵr would take Wales and the Marches, Northumberland the north, and Mortimer the rest. Whether any of them seriously thought this would actually work, or whether it was just weasel wording to try to cement the alliance, can be debated, but in any event the rising was never going to be successful, if only because there was no central coordination and little idea of what to do once armies of sorts had been assembled.

One of the principal supporters of the rising was the fifty-five-year-old archbishop of York, Richard Scrope. Scrope had been promoted to the See of York by Richard II and owed his position more to his father's success as a soldier and loyal servant of the monarchy rather than to any great theological acumen – although, being reckoned to be skilled in canon law, he had led the deputation that accepted Richard II's supposedly voluntary abdication of the throne. He supported Henry IV's accession and was one of the prelates who led him to the throne at his coronation. That being so, one can only assume that his involvement in the 1405 rebellion was the result of pressure from the local lord – Northumberland – although Scrope had preached against taxation of the clergy, would have been broadly sympathetic to the merchants' dislike of taxation in any form, and may have been the author, or at least the editor, of the manifesto issued by the rebels. This latter repeated the usual gripes about oppressive rule and unjust taxation but also maintained that Henry had broken his oath not to depose Richard II.

The nub of the rebellion was swiftly eliminated when Ralph Neville, earl of Westmorland, a loyalist and long-term enemy of the Percys, and the king's youngest son, John of Lancaster, marched against the rebels and defeated Scrope's hastily assembled and ill-armed troops, mainly citizens of York. Scrope was arrested, as was the nineteen-year-old Sir Thomas Mowbray, son of the first duke of Norfolk, previously Earl Marshal of England, who had died in exile having fallen out with Richard II. Northumberland abandoned his erstwhile allies and fled to Scotland. The king intended to show no mercy: last time, he had forgiven the prime movers; now he would make it very clear that rebellion would not be tolerated. Rather than hand Scrope over to papal authority as he had done before in similar circumstances, only to find treasonous bishops were given a mere slap on the wrist, Henry decided that he would go on trial with the other captured nobles. The order went to London to send a team of justices to conduct the trial, and, when the country's other senior cleric, Thomas Arundel, archbishop of Canterbury and a close personal friend of the king, heard that his fellow prelate was to be put on trial before a secular court, he rode all day and all night to Bishopthorpe in north Yorkshire, where the king was – no mean feat at the time for a fifty-one-year-old.*

Arundel reached Bishopthorpe on 7 June 1405 and pleaded with the king not to execute Scrope, reminding him of the last occasion a king named Henry had been responsible for the killing of an archbishop (Henry II and Becket). The king fobbed his old friend off, sent him to bed, put Scrope on trial that night, and had him beheaded with two others the next day. It was the first judicial execution of an archbishop and caused horror throughout England and Europe. Even if the death sentence was justified, which it surely was, to kill an ordained cleric, never mind an archbishop, was seen as shocking and allowed Henry's enemies to claim that he had not only murdered an anointed king but one of God's chosen servants as well. The pope in Rome was said to be appalled and to have laid curses on all involved, but his opposition was short-lived and probably mollified by a monetary payment, while an outbreak of miracle-working at Scrope's tomb in York Minster did not last much longer. Eventually, in 1408, Pope Gregory XII officially

---

* The distance is around 130 miles and he would have changed horses every twenty miles or so. At a trot and canter, he would probably have been able to do around ten miles an hour on the roads as they then were.

exonerated Henry in return for a promise to found three religious houses. Shortly after the execution, Henry fell ill with what some alleged was leprosy. We know now, from examination of Henry's skeleton, that he did not suffer from that most horrible of diseases to which there was then no cure, but it suited his opponents to put it about that he was being visited by divine punishment for his treatment of Scrope. Whatever it was that ailed the king, his health became progressively worse from 1408 onwards and eventually necessitated government being carried on by a council headed by Henry, Prince of Wales. It was a state of affairs that led to disagreements between father and son and King Henry to suspect his eldest son of plotting rebellion against him.

Northumberland was not to be allowed to get away with yet more treason; he had forced the king to divert his planned expedition to Wales to go north and deal with him, and Henry now began systematically to reduce those northern towns sympathetic to the rebellion. Northumberland tried to rally support in Wales, but there the uprising was beginning to collapse, and his brief trip to France achieved nothing, the French having quite enough internal troubles of their own. In desperation, Henry Percy decided to risk all on one final gamble and invaded England from Scotland in 1408. His army was tiny – probably no more than a few hundred, perhaps a thousand men at most. In addition to those soldiers he had raised in Scotland, he included retainers from his own lands in the north and the adherents of the bishop of Bangor and the abbot of Hayles. The invasion was short-lived. Before King Henry got anywhere near the area, the high sheriff of Yorkshire, Sir Thomas Rokeby, with a hastily raised force of loyalist retinues and arrayed archers, met Northumberland's men near Knaresborough and chased them twelve miles south to Tadcaster, where they were unable to make a stand and retreated four miles west to Bramham Moor, south of Wetherby. Percy found a defensive position and awaited Rokeby, who arrived in the early afternoon of 14 February 1408, won the missile fight with his archers, and attacked Northumberland with his infantry. The result was never in doubt: the rebel army was smashed and very few got away back to Scotland. Henry Percy himself was killed fighting furiously in a rearguard action; he was decapitated and quartered, with his head exhibited on London Bridge. King Henry duly came north and meted out retribution from York, assisted by a crowd of informers anxious to prove their own loyalty and no doubt seizing the opportunity to settle old scores. Among those executed was the abbot of Hayles, but of the fate of the bishop of Bangor the chronicles are silent. Henry Percy's titles and estates were forfeited by act of attainder.*

Meanwhile, in France, the descent into civil war had prevented effective action to capitalize on Henry of England's problems. Had France been united, then, given Henry's financial problems, the French might easily have taken Aquitaine, but, with the ever more frequent outbreaks of Charles VI's insanity, power was increasingly being garnered by the dukes of Burgundy and Orléans, who, as we have seen, had very different agendas. Their enmity came to a very public head when, on the night of 23 November 1407, only a few days after a supposed reconciliation between the two, the duke of Orléans was set upon in a Paris street and bludgeoned to death, his hand having first been cut off to prevent it casting spells on the attackers. The assassination was widely believed to have been at the instigation of the duke of Burgundy, and he is said to have admitted it some days later.

France now split into two armed camps. The cause of the late duke of Orléans was taken up by his son's father-in-law, the count of Armagnac, who gave his name to the Orléanist faction. This group controlled, in broad terms, most of France south of the River Loire, less of course English Aquitaine, while the Burgundians held the north – including, crucially, Paris – Flanders and most of the Low Countries. Brittany was generally neutral and Normandy too, with divided loyalties, managed to avoid taking sides. The duke of Burgundy had already signed a trade agreement with Henry IV, and the threat to Calais from Flanders was now lessened, the English wool trade picked up, and the English treasury began to look a little healthier.

---

* An act, or bill, of attainder was often resorted to when the government did not want to risk a trial. It was the passing by Parliament of a law declaring the accused, or in this case the late accused, to be guilty of whatever he was charged with. The titles and lands were restored to Hotspur's son by Henry V, and the present head of the Percy family is the twelfth duke of Northumberland.

In 1411, Paris was under siege by an Armagnac army and the duke of Burgundy appealed to Henry IV for help. At this stage, the Prince of Wales was leader of the king's council during his father's illness, and in September an English army of 800 men-at-arms and 2,000 archers, under the command of the thirty-year-old Thomas Fitzalan, earl of Arundel and nephew of the archbishop of Canterbury, landed at Calais. They then marched to Arras, joined with the Burgundian relieving army, and headed for Paris. On 9 November 1411, Arundel stormed the besiegers at the Paris suburb of Saint-Cloud and, having lifted the siege, marched back to Calais and sailed to England.

The following year, with the king recovered and the prince sidelined, English support went instead to the Armagnacs, who promised in return for military assistance against the Burgundians to support the annexation of Aquitaine to England (as opposed to it being a separate overseas province) – something which had already been enacted by the English parliament. Four thousand men were despatched under Thomas of Lancaster, King Henry's second son and recently created earl of Aumale and duke of Clarence, who landed at La Hougue in Normandy. The landing was opposed by what the Brut Chronicle describes as 7,000 men-at-arms, but was probably a great deal less, under a Lord Hambe, and, having defeated them and taken prisoners for ransom, the English moved south to link up with the Armagnacs in Poitou. By the time they got there, the two French dukes, young Orléans and Burgundy, had come to uneasy and temporary terms, so Clarence led his army on a burning and looting spree through southern France to English Bordeaux, and only agreed to go home when he was bought off by the Armagnacs. The short peace between the two opposing French factions brought the professed agreement by both to the English annexation of Aquitaine, but, as neither Armagnac nor Burgundian could speak for the Valois king nor for the French *parlement*, the agreement was illegal and worthless. In any case, the peace was soon shattered when in 1413 Burgundians in Paris fell upon Armagnac supporters and began to slaughter them and set fire to their houses and buildings. Rioting was widespread and only quelled by the arrival of an Armagnac army and the nine-year-old dauphin Charles. Burgundy was forced to yield Paris to the Armagnacs and flee to Flanders, where he began negotiations for English support to regain his power.

Then, on 20 March 1413, Henry IV of England died, aged forty-seven. His tomb in Canterbury Cathedral is opposite that of the Black Prince, whose son Henry had put to death – a touch of irony presumably not intended at the time. His effigy shows a face old and bloated, and indeed it is almost as if Henry were two different people. Vigorous, an accomplished jouster, well educated, articulate and sociable as Henry Bolingbroke, he had been supported by the vast majority of those who mattered in his unseating of Richard II, and admired, as the Brut Chronicle puts it, 'for his worthy manhood that often times had been found in him'. Once king, however, he faced uncooperative parliaments and at least eight rebellions during his fourteen-year reign. Increasingly suspicious and dogged by ill health, he survived by compromise and thus allowed much royal prerogative to be subsumed by Parliament – powers that it would be reluctant to give back. Although Henry maintained the English claim to the French throne – which Richard would have given up – he did little to advance it, and the war during his reign was one of raids, piracy and blockade. Militarily, Henry's main preoccupation was the Welsh rising of Owain Glyn Dŵr, and with that and the need to quell rebellion elsewhere there was no money for major expeditions to Europe. Henry did little to change the organization and tactical deployment of English armies – there was no need – but he did promote the development of cannon, which, while present in most armies since the middle of the fourteenth century, had had little effect so far on the outcome of a battle.

Although the Welsh troubles rumbled on until after Henry's death, even before Northumberland's last rebellion they were in decline. Owain Glyn Dŵr had the support of many, perhaps most, of the native Welsh princes, but not of the common people nor of the Anglo-Welsh and the English settlers, and he controlled only limited areas of the country. The English commanded the seas and, with the exception of a few minor French landings, no reinforcement could come by that means. Most castles held out, and those few that did fall to the rebels were relatively swiftly recovered. The English fortified the Marches, hemming the rebels in and preventing sympathizers from England reaching them, and, while the Welsh could and did mount raids over the border into Shropshire, detachments of English mounted troops were on standby to pursue them. English supply routes into and out of Wales were secured, while English soldiers severed those of the Welsh. Many of Glyn Dŵr's own family, including his wife, were taken prisoner and lodged in the Tower, and at least one of his sons was killed, as were increasing numbers of his senior commanders. Above all other factors, perhaps, there was that of finance. As the English exchequer grew healthier, English soldiers could be paid and supplies purchased, while Glyn Dŵr had to rely on ransom money and, when that ran out, on looting his own countrymen – not a policy guaranteed to maintain support for his cause. That the rebellion lasted as long as it did was due to the very sensible Welsh policy of not being drawn into a conventional battle, but to harry, ambush, snipe and raid and then fade away into the hills. But guerrillas cannot win a war all by themselves, and in the end a dogged English policy of attrition, control of the coastline, defence of the Marches and ensuring that even in times of financial difficulties sufficient money was always found to continue the campaign was bound to win in the end, and that it did was very much to the credit of Henry IV. Glyn Dŵr's own fate remains a mystery. He was never captured and is thought to have died sometime in 1415, but by what cause and where his body lies is unknown.

Nor was Scotland to be a problem once Northumberland's last foray from there was defeated. It was good intelligence and skilled seamanship in March 1406 that allowed the English navy to capture the heir to the throne of Scotland, James Stewart (later James I of Scotland), off Flamborough Head on his way to school in France; and it was good luck that his father Robert III died a month later, allowing the English to install yet another king of Scotland in the Tower. James was well treated but remained a prisoner for eighteen years, thus ensuring that England's back door was reasonably secure.

Henry IV may not have been able to pursue the French war, but his son and successor certainly would. By the time he came to the throne, Henry of Monmouth had already proved himself as a soldier – at Shrewsbury, where he may have been following the guidance of more experienced commanders but where he nevertheless showed great courage and understanding of battle management; and subsequently in the Welsh wars, where, as his father's health declined, the defeat of the insurrection was more and more left to him. He learned how to keep an army in the field in an underdeveloped country and how to conduct sieges, and he fully understood the importance of mobility and sound logistics, all of which would stand him in good stead for his future campaigning. He is generally considered to have been something of a lad during his apprenticeship – to have been rather fond of wine, women, song and dubious companions – and he certainly fell out with his father on numerous occasions, sometimes over foreign policy, more often when his father was concerned that young Henry was building an alternative court. But by the time his father died, he seems to have put such misbehaviour behind him.

In twenty-first-century Britain, the queen is head of the Church of England, but in truth religion no longer has a major influence, either in government or in most people's daily lives. That was not the case in the medieval world, and any consideration of government and kingship then must take account of the position of the church. It is not easy in this secular, cynical, sceptical age of ours to fully comprehend the influence of religion on our medieval ancestors. Religion was a powerful instrument of social control.* In medieval England, an instruction from the king was persuasive; that it was also an instruction from God made it doubly so. There were, of course, men who engaged in something approaching what we would today call the scientific method – nobody with any education thought the world was flat – but witchcraft and sorcery were largely tolerated until well into the sixteenth century. (The Inquisition, which equated witchcraft with heresy and burned practitioners at the stake, was never allowed into England – as much because it was foreign as for any theological reason.) The common man was, however, intensely superstitious. He believed that when he died he would either go to heaven, provided that he had prayed hard enough and had obeyed the dictums of the church, or otherwise would go to

---

* In some parts of the world it still is: India would have gone communist decades ago were it not for the Hindu religion, which preaches a stoic acceptance of one's position in the social order in the hope that good behaviour in this life will ensure reincarnation to a higher degree in the next.

a very unpleasant eternity in hell, something that he was continually reminded of every time he glanced at the tympana above the churches' doors. Things that were unexplained – a sudden storm, an earthquake, disease – were either expressions of God's displeasure or the work of the devil.

The uneducated and the untravelled in any age are superstitious and religious fundamentalism thrives among the ignorant, but whether the great men of the realm similarly believed in the reality of a personal god and heaven and hell is more difficult to answer. They certainly said they did, and the number of chantries founded, benefices subsidized and donations to religious orders made by the nobility would seem to indicate that they did, as would the number of recorded death-bed statements of belief – although many donations and declarations may have been made in the hope of a favourable mention in the history books. While we might question whether some aspects of religious belief were more than skin-deep, at least among the wealthy and the educated, there is no doubting the power and influence of the church. Although it no longer had a monopoly of education – and there was an increasing demand for men who could read, write and do sums for the civil service of an increasingly complex government administration – the church had a finger in most royal and state pies. Archbishops were chancellors, bishops could lead armies, local government in the shires often went with religious appointments, and the church was one of the great landowners of the realm as well as being fabulously wealthy. Unlike in our present day, when the origin of most British bishops is lower middle class, bishops then were members of great families and would have had standing and influence in the church or out of it. Much international diplomacy was carried out by clerics, while the pope, whether in Avignon or Rome, had huge transnational influence.

It was, of course, in the interests of the church to maintain the status quo, and in the interests of the secular power – the king – to keep the support of the spiritual arm, hence the fear of heresy and the enthusiasm shown in its suppression.* Clearly, some esoteric arguments contrary to accepted teachings could be tolerated, and much energy was expended on arguing about how many angels could dance on the head of a pin,† or about the relative poverty of Jesus Christ, but anything that struck at the church's power and influence had to be stamped on hard.

Ever since the first outbreak of the plague, strange cults and odd beliefs had been springing up, and one of the most prevalent English heresies of the time was Lollardy, which claimed to follow the teachings of John Wyclif, an academic born around 1330. Wyclif questioned the authority of the pope, produced a written English translation of the Bible, and objected to the doctrine of transubstantiation. Opposing the pope was something that many Englishmen and not a few English clergy would have had sympathy with, but translating the Bible into the vernacular was a different matter altogether. If the common people could read the Bible for themselves, then not only would priests – who were there to interpret, in all senses, the Latin of the Bible – be out of a job, but also people would see the inconsistencies inherent in the scriptures and perhaps question their whole validity. The doctrine of transubstantiation, meanwhile, taught that the bread and wine consumed in the mass turned into the actual flesh and blood of Christ once the supplicant had eaten them. While the validity of this could be debated and rests on faith rather than medical science, it was widely believed then and is still believed, or at least taught, by some Christian churches today.‡ Wyclif said that the change into flesh and blood was symbolic, not actual, and in doing so he was questioning a basic tenet of the church's teaching. Eventually, he was condemned by the pope, but he

---

* Heresy might be defined as a belief that is in opposition to the orthodox teachings of the church, but to avoid confusing reform with heresy the definition used by Michael Lambert, the authority on medieval cults, is convenient: 'Heresy is whatever was explicitly or implicitly condemned by the papacy.' See Lambert, *Medieval Heresy* (2nd edn), Blackwell, Oxford, 1992.
† This was not as daft an argument as it sounds. It was all about how often something could be divided and whether there was a basic particle which could not be reduced further. It was in a sense the forerunner of atomic theory.
‡ There are a number of belief systems in which eating the body, or parts of the body, of a dead hero, a dead enemy or a dead animal such as a lion allows the consumer to absorb the qualities of that person or animal, so the mass may be a vestige of ritual cannibalism.

survived to die in his bed in 1384, partly through the protection of John of Gaunt and partly through reluctance on the part of the University of Oxford to admit that its doctors could be disciplined by the church.

The Lollards – so called from the mumbling sound of their prayers – went a little further than Wyclif might have wished. They opposed the pope's practice of taxing the English clergy – and here they simply echoed the views of most Englishmen including Edward III – and they railed against corruption in the church and against the authority of the pope. Had they stopped there, they might have got away with it, but, when they extended their manifesto to declaring the pope the anti-Christ, calling for the abolition of the hierarchy of the church and, from around 1380, sending unlicensed preachers around the countryside with their English Bibles to spread their views, they became a direct threat to the established order and were declared heretics. Wyclif himself would not have supported the Peasants' Revolt, but many of his followers did; and, although most would have done so anyway, whether Lollards or not, they were now seen as seditious as well as heretical.

Up to this point, heresy was not a civil crime but a clerical one, to be tried in clerical courts which could impose fines but not the death penalty or imprisonment. In 1401, however, Archbishop Arundel persuaded the recently crowned Henry IV to make heresy a secular crime, which meant that a man found guilty by a clerical court could be handed over to the civil power and executed – by the rather unpleasant method of burning. Only two Lollards were actually burned during Henry IV's reign – it was only obdurate heresy that got a person burned: recantation brought a pardon, and many accused did recant at the last moment, sensible fellows that they were. One of these executions, of one John Badby, who was due to be burned to death in a barrel if contemporary artists are to be believed, was attended by Henry of Monmouth when Prince of Wales. The fire was lit, the victim began to scream. Henry ordered the fire to be put out and the man taken out of the barrel, and offered him a pardon and a pension for life if he would recant. The man refused, so Henry ordered him back in the barrel and the fire to be relit. The obdurate heretic duly burned to death.

While all kings expressed support for the church, even if they might be opposed to some of its practitioners from time to time, all the contemporary accounts of Henry V stress his religious piety as king. Partly this may be sycophantic, but, as Henry's faith is mentioned more frequently than that of his predecessors or successors, we may assume that it played a significant part in his thinking. At this distance, it is impossible to tell whether his frequent insistence that he was under the protection of God was what he genuinely believed, or mere propaganda to reinforce his claims and encourage a population and army which did believe, but throughout his reign Henry remained a strong supporter of religious orthodoxy – indeed, to some he was a religious fanatic. Fanatics do not, however, command a mass following, at least not in England, and on balance it is likely that, while Henry was certainly a believer, he was an astute enough politician to realize the importance of not alienating so powerful a bastion of the establishment as the church.

Otherwise, Henry of Monmouth was described as being tall, slim and well muscled, with hazel eyes and thick brown hair; in character he was said to be single-minded – and, if he was to pursue the English claims in France, he would have to be. Unusually for the time, he had no mistresses as king, although there is no suggestion that his sexual proclivities were anything but normal. Henry V was crowned at Westminster on Passion Sunday, 9 April 1413, and the day marked by an unseasonal fall of heavy snow, seen by many as an omen, but of what no one was quite sure. Henry's first task was to assure Parliament and the magnates that he intended to govern justly and to heal divisions. While he brought some of his own followers into government – chiefly Thomas Fitzalan, Thomas Beauchamp, the earl of Warwick, and as chancellor his half-uncle, Bishop Beaufort, the son of John of Gaunt out of his third wife and ex-mistress, Katherine Swynford – he retained many of his father's officials, although he did dismiss the Chief Justice of the King's Bench, Sir William Gascoigne.* In seeking to heal old sores, he released the earl of March, the Ricardian candidate for the throne, from house arrest and had Richard II's body exhumed from King's Langley and

---

* It has been suggested that this was because Gascoigne had committed Henry as Prince of Wales to prison for interfering in the trial of one of his servants, but, as there is no evidence whatsoever that this incident ever took place, it is much more likely that Gascoigne, having refused to try Archbishop Scrope in 1405, was dismissed because he was of too independent a mind.

reburied with much reverence, pomp and ceremony in the tomb that Richard himself had commissioned in Westminster Abbey.

Almost immediately, however, the new king became embroiled with the Lollard heresy in the shape of Sir John Oldcastle and his followers. Oldcastle, who was thirty-five in 1413, had been a loyal crown servant and was an experienced soldier who had served in the Scottish wars, in France with the English army sent to aid the duke of Burgundy in 1411, and against the Welsh rebels under Henry V when he was Prince of Wales. He had been summoned to Parliament as a knight of the shires and had served as sheriff of Herefordshire. It is probable that Oldcastle had long held unorthodox views – Herefordshire was notorious for religious radicalism – but it was only after the accession of Henry V that Archbishop Arundel felt able to challenge him openly, and Oldcastle was the first eminent layman to be tried for the Lollard heresy.* Condemned out of his own mouth when he launched into a tirade against the pope and his prelates, he was handed over to the civil authority which, at the behest of the king, who had no wish to see an old friend brought low, sent him to the Tower to give him an opportunity to recant. He then escaped, went on the run and attempted to organize a revolt with the aim of kidnapping the king. It was hardly a revolt; indeed, far from being a serious attempt to overthrow the existing secular and religious establishment, it was more the desperate reaction of a man who sought revenge for the way he had been treated. The active participants – no more than a few hundred – were asked to rendezvous at St Giles's Fields, outside London, on the night of 9/10 January 1414 in preparation for a march on London and the arrest of the king. However, the plot was betrayed to the authorities and, when the rebels arrived, they ran into an ambush. Oldcastle escaped, but most of his followers were rounded up. Over forty were executed and another seven, who were Lollards, were burned as heretics. Although his revolt died in the St Giles's Fields trap, despite several offers of pardon Oldcastle would not give himself up, and while a number of those who sheltered him were punished, and in at least one case executed, he himself would not be captured until

---

* It was well known that a number of nobles held Lollard sympathies, while falling well short of potential rebellion.

November 1417, after which he was executed by burning on 15 December of that year. It was the last serious internal threat to Henry V, who, having restored order within the kingdom, pacified Wales and defused doubts over the legitimacy of the Lancastrian succession, could now devote all his considerable energies to restoring English rights in France.

King Henry V. This is generally said to be the most lifelike portrait of the king, but as it was painted at least 150 years after his death it could only be so if the artist had access to earlier portraits now lost.

9

ONCE MORE
UNTO THE BREACH . . .

King at twenty-five, slaughterer of the French nobility at twenty-seven, regent and acknowledged heir to the throne of France at thirty-two and dead at thirty four: if Henry V had lived, the history of Europe might have been very different. There cannot be many Englishmen, even today, who do not feel a frisson of pride when they think of Henry V; he shaped English history and what he did and who he was affects Anglo-French relations to this day. He was a king who deliberately fostered a feeling of Englishness, the first to write his letters in English and to prefer conversing in that language rather than in Norman French; a natural and charismatic leader who, if he did not invent English nationalism, certainly encouraged it and, along with it, a pride in nation and in race. While he was a master of propaganda and knew how to use the tricks of oratory, his repeated declaration that his chief concern was for the well-being and good governance of his realm and its people was genuinely meant. Of course, despite his oft-noted piety, he was not always a paragon of Christian virtue. He could be cruel and inflexible, ruthless, brutal, devious, short-tempered, frequently unreasonable and always convinced that he was under the personal protection of God, but nice men do not win wars and withal Henry V must rank as one of our great kings, if not our greatest.

Well before he became king, Henry was determined to revive the English claims in France and to pursue them. Once he was king, embassies were sent to France and French embassies came to England. Initially, he asked only for recognition of Aquitaine as English in full sovereignty, but, as each request was turned down, the demands became stronger: everything agreed by the Treaty of Brétigny in 1360 was added, then the payment of the rest of Jean II's ransom, then the duchy of Normandy, until by March 1415, in the requirements placed before the dauphin, Henry was stipulating the return of all the French lands lost by King John 200 years before, the hand of one of Charles VI's daughters in marriage and the revival of the English claim to the French throne. Throughout, Henry emphasized that he only wanted what was his by right, but no French government, of whatever hue, could possibly agree to a restoration of King John's Angevin empire. Although negotiations were allowed to drag on, Henry had already realized by the spring of 1414 that the French were merely playing for time and had no intention of even coming to an acceptable compromise. It is probable that, whatever the French might have offered, Henry would have wanted more: he had long since determined that he would take an army to France and the negotiations can only have been window-dressing.

From early 1414, Henry began to prepare for war. Ships were impressed and purveyors travelled all over the kingdom buying up stores and equipment while captains and individuals were arrayed and indentured. By now, the system was that captains and leaders of retinues contracted either with a magnate or directly with the crown to provide a certain number of men of a certain type (archers, men-at-arms, gunners, artisans) at an agreed rate of daily pay. This had not changed in fifty years: thirteen shillings and fourpence for a duke; six shillings and eight pence for an earl; four shillings for a knight banneret; two shillings for a knight; one shilling for an untitled man-at-arms; and sixpence for an archer. As the shilling-a-day man-at-arms did exactly the same job as a two-shilling knight – stand in line with the infantry – there was a powerful incentive to do well and get knighted. For the first six months of a campaign, the rule was that the captain was paid half the total sum for his contingent on sealing the indenture – a piece of parchment on which the agreement was written twice and then torn across, with the captain keeping one part and the employer the other. Subsequent disagreements or accusations of forgery could be resolved by matching up the tears. It would then be agreed how subsequent six-month periods would be funded. In this campaign, indentures were for one year to begin with, which indicates that Henry expected a long war, but in 1414 the crown did not have the funds for more than a few months, never mind the initial six months; and even when in

November 1414 Parliament granted the king a double subsidy – in effect, agreeing that the country would go to war – some of the leaders of retinues and captains were given jewels from the royal treasury as security, while the soldiers were paid from the contingent commander's own pocket. Presumably, Henry was hoping for an early victory, or at least enough loot and ransom money to redeem his jewels and fund the campaign beyond the first six months – a considerable gamble by the ruler of around three million going to war against sixteen million. But then Henry had right, and God, on his side.

Although neither Richard II nor Henry IV had changed the basic structure of English armies, the proportion of archers to men-at-arms had steadily increased since Crécy in 1346. Archers had shown their worth. They were flexible and could act as light infantry if necessary, while, when mounted, they could act as light cavalry and reconnaissance troops – and they were, of course, considerably cheaper than men-at-arms. By now, the accepted order of battle was three archers to one man-at-arms, and, although not every retinue or contingent was composed of soldiers in that proportion, the king's officials ensured that overall the mix was the right one. Altogether, there were around 250 persons who contracted to provide a retinue of troops, varying in size from those of the great magnates such as the dukes of Clarence and Gloucester, brothers of the king, who were to produce 960 and 800 respectively, down to the more humble gentry, who might provide ten men or less, and in some cases just the contractee himself and one archer.

In addition to the retinues – themselves far more numerous than in any previous English army – there were large numbers of men, mainly archers, who enlisted directly with the crown, rather than joining a retinue. These men would, of course, have to be formed into sub-units under selected commanders and would have to train together and be instructed in the army's standard operating procedures. The assembly area for the army was laid down as being Southampton, and ships for the voyage were collected there and in other southern English ports, while the retinue commanders held their own musters and then marched to Southampton when ordered. Originally, the king had intended to concentrate the army by 1 July 1415, but inevitably things took longer than hoped. The duke of Gloucester held his muster near Romsey on 16 July and took under command 190 men-at-arms and 610 archers from fifty-six sub-retinues, while the duke of Clarence in the New Forest enlisted his 800 from sixty-nine separate units.[39] Altogether, there were probably around 12,000 soldiers – 9,000 archers and 3,000 men-at-arms – ready to embark for France, the largest English army assembled since the time of Edward III, but the total number would have been much greater than just the combat troops. Henry had also enlisted a company of 120 miners from the Forest of Dean, and there were seventy-five artillerymen, numerous bowyers, fletchers, farriers, blacksmiths, armourers, bakers, butchers, and a plethora of servants, grooms, clerks and pages, to say nothing of churchmen and surgeons.

The chroniclers generally say that 1,500 ships were needed to transport the force, although some historians consider that to be yet another exaggeration. Altogether, the number of men to be embarked may have been in the region of 14,000, not counting the ships' crews, and in addition there were horses, baggage carts, stores, rations for both men and horses, siege engines, cannon, ammunition for the guns and resupplies of arrows for the archers. Stores included large numbers of tents, and rations included salted meat and fish, ale, flour for bread, and beef on the hoof, along with their drovers. Given the number of men, horses, cattle and all the accompanying baggage to be transported, a huge number of ships would indeed be needed; and, given also that both Thomas of Walsingham, generally recognized to be one of the most accurate of contemporary historians, and the anonymous writer of *Gesta Henrici Quinti*,[40] who accompanied the expedition, give a figure of 1,500, there seems no reason to doubt it, particularly as the vagaries of wind and weather would preclude any idea of shuttling the force to France using fewer ships.

With such huge numbers of men, animals and ships being concentrated, it was impossible to hide that these were warlike preparations, and the French embassies that were still coming and going almost to the last moment were fully aware of what was going on and reporting everything back to their masters. If Henry could not hide the fact that he was assembling an invasion force, then he had to conceal its destination. Apart from a very few trusted senior commanders and one or two ships' captains, nobody knew where the invasion force was headed. Most observers and participants, French and English, assumed that the landing would be at

Calais, which was strongly held by the English and represented the shortest way across the Channel; others thought the king might repeat the route of Edward III's expedition of 1346 and land somewhere on the Cotentin peninsula in Normandy, or that of the Black Prince in 1356 and launch the invasion from Bordeaux. It was not until very late in the day that ships' crews were informed of their destination, and that only when all troops and stores were on board.

Meanwhile, the last opposition to the Lancastrian inheritance was snuffed out. When the king was at Portchester, supervising the final arrangements for the expedition, the young earl of March sought an audience and reported the existence of an assassination plot by unreconstructed Ricardians. As the beneficiary of Henry's murder would presumably have been the earl, the rightful successor to Richard II by strict primogeniture, this seemingly selfless act was probably motivated by March's realization that the plotters were incompetent, had no chance of succeeding, and would have been considered to have shown very bad form indeed at the outset of an expedition against the hated enemy, France. The ringleaders of the Southampton Plot, including yet another disaffected Scrope, were rounded up and executed after a hasty trial presided over by the king's brother.

The embarkation of the men and the loading of stores took three weeks, and, on 7 August 1415, King Henry and his immediate staff boarded *Le Trinite*, the largest ship in the fleet at 500 tons with a crew of 300, and hoisted a signal for all ships to concentrate off Southampton. Four days later, on Sunday, 11 August 1415, the fleet set sail for France. The destination: Harfleur.

Today, there is very little left of medieval Harfleur, and the odd section of crumbling wall and the sluggish stream of the River Lézade that remain are subsumed in the suburbs of the sixteenth-century port of Le Havre. It was a sensible choice for Henry and his army. Harfleur was situated at the north of the mouth of the River Seine and its capture would allow the king the options of striking up the Seine straight for Paris, or west and then south for Rouen and Normandy, as well as giving him a port through which to receive reinforcements. It would also allow him to blockade a major French trading route and – equally important, given that the balance of power at sea had tilted towards the French – would eliminate a nest of pirates and prevent

French galleys from getting out to sea from the shipyards at Rouen. Good choice it certainly was, and Henry hoped to capture it without too much delay, but in the event it would not be as easy a task as he thought.

The crossing from Southampton took three days and, on 14 August, the first ships hove to off what the English still called Saint-Denis Chef du Caux,* on the coast six-and-a-half miles due west of Harfleur. An amphibious operation, whether of the fifteenth or twenty-first century, is at its most vulnerable during the landing phase, but the French made no attempt to oppose Henry. They must have known from fishermen that the invasion force was on its way, and, had they had any sort of coastal watch like that in England, they could easily have identified the landing area and caused carnage among both the disembarking troops as they struggled up through the surf and the horses and cattle as they were winched over ships' sides and then swam to dry land. As it was, Henry's men went unmolested for the three days that it took to get the force ashore. It was at this time that the king issued strict orders concerning the behaviour of the troops. The usual practice of slaughtering, burning and looting was to cease: Henry was the legitimate king of France and he was not going to ill-treat his own subjects. No man of the cloth or any woman was to be molested unless they had a weapon and were obviously of aggressive intent, and churches and other sacred places were to be respected. Prostitutes were forbidden to approach the army's encampment and, if found in the lines, were to have their left arms broken before being expelled. The prohibition was presumably a security measure rather than a moral stricture.

On 18 August, an advance party under the duke of Clarence marched off to surround Harfleur, just too late to prevent a reinforcement of 400 men-at-arms from slipping in through the south-eastern gate, but in plenty of time to intercept a slow-moving convoy of gunpowder and crossbow quarrels from Rouen. Harfleur was around three miles in circumference. It was surrounded by a thick, high wall in good repair with a number of towers, and the three gates, on the north-east, south-east and south-west corners, were well protected by stout barbicans that had been reinforced

---

* The village of that name had been obliterated by a tidal wave in 1370 and rebuilt as Saint-Adresse (as it still is today). As there is no saint by the name of Adresse, this is presumably some form of French humour impenetrable to Anglo-Saxons.

by tree-trunks, driven into the ground and lashed together, with packed earth behind.* There was a deep, stone-lined moat, two spear lengths wide (twenty feet) according to one chronicler,[41] to make mining difficult, and a series of banks and ditches on all approaches. The land round about was flat and marshy, and the French soon broached the ditches and flooded much of the countryside. The garrison, now of 700 men-at-arms, was led by a competent commander, the sire de Goucourt, who had commanded the reinforcements and who had ample guns and sufficient rations to withstand a siege of at least a month, by which time he would surely be relieved from Rouen, only fifty miles or two days' forced march away.

As we have seen, cannon had made no great impact during the campaigns of Edward III and the Black Prince: they may have been used at Crécy and there were some present at the siege of Calais, but they had contributed little to the end results. Under Henry IV, however, the science of artillery had progressed, and indeed both defenders and attackers at Harfleur used guns. Eventually, guns and gunpowder would force the abandonment of the entire medieval system of defence and fortification, one which relied on high walls and moats, and, although that time was not yet, guns were to play an increasingly important part in the war from now on. Henry V had appointed the first Master of Ordnance,† whose duty it was to supervise the manufacture of cannon and the storage of guns and ammunition in the Tower of London. At this stage, most shot was still stone balls, to be replaced by iron later in the war, and cannon barrels were still made of bars of iron held together by hoops of the same material. The powder was unreliable as the type of saltpetre used was slow-burning and the practice of 'graining' – whereby the right combination of saltpetre, sulphur and charcoal was mixed, liquefied and then dried out to produce a faster-burning propellant and hence a higher muzzle velocity – was not yet standard. Guns were still dangerous to their crews and there were some spectacular self-inflicted disasters, when the gunners put in too much powder and only succeeded in bursting the barrel and killing themselves. But, if all went well, they could discharge projectiles

---

* A barbican was a fortified gatehouse with towers in front of and behind the actual gate.
† Today the Master General of Ordnance and until very recently one of the most senior appointments in the British Army.

of up to 200 pounds in weight and knock holes in walls (eventually); and they could, if correctly positioned, fire over walls and cause considerable damage to houses and people within. Guns were still heavy, awkward and of limited range, so, while useful in a siege, they had yet to fully develop as field artillery.

Once Henry had surrounded Harfleur with the army on land and the fleet blockading any approach from the sea, and had stationed men in small requisitioned boats in the rivers that criss-crossed the area, he was ready to begin his siege. But that was the last thing he wanted to do, for it would cost time, men and money, so he called upon the garrison to surrender what was, after all, legitimately part of the duchy of Normandy and therefore Henry's rightful inheritance, with a promise that, if they did so, they would not be harmed or plundered. Not surprisingly, the French declined and the siege began. The first problem was to get the English guns close enough to the walls to cause damage, and, having decided that the main point of attack would be the eastern wall and the south-eastern gate, the men-at-arms began to dig trenches to allow them to move the guns under cover from enemy crossbowmen and cannon positioned on the town walls. This was a difficult and unpleasant task given the very high water table and the flooding of much of the area, but eventually the guns were able to begin a bombardment against the south-east barbican and the adjacent walls. In order to protect the guns from counter-battery fire from the walls, an ingenious system of thick wooden planks that were reinforced with iron and hinged was devised. Mounted in front of the guns, they were raised to allow the guns to fire and then lowered to protect against retaliation. The enemy were not idle. By night, they repaired the damage as far as they could by placing tubs full of earth or sand – to be known as gabions in a later war – in any breaches and they covered the streets in earth and animal dung so as to absorb the fall of shot and thus reduce the likelihood of stone balls landing inside the town and disintegrating into showers of deadly splinters. Mindful of the risk of a full-scale escalade, de Goucourt ordered barrels of sulphur and quicklime to be placed along the walls as a blinding agent to be thrown down on attackers, and tubs of oils, pitch and other flammables to be positioned for use against belfries or other siege engines that might try to come up against the walls.

Steadily, and despite the efforts of the defenders to make good the damage, the defences began to crumble and Henry ordered fascines to be prepared. These were bundles of sticks ten feet long and bound together, to be thrown into the moat to allow men to cross and assault the walls, but, as this was a highly dangerous business, the king decided to try mining first. The Forest of Dean miners were told to dig under the moat and under the walls, and they set to with a will. It would, however, have been impossible to conceal what they were doing from the defenders, even if the ground had not been waterlogged, which made progress painfully slow, and the two attempts at mining were both thwarted by French counter-mines. Eventually, the duke of Clarence's men captured one of the enemy's ditches and turned it into a strongpoint from which an assault on the walls could be mounted. Then, on 10 September 1415, the army suffered its first major casualty – not from French guns or crossbowmen, but from dysentery. Richard Courtenay, bishop of Norwich, lasted five days and died on Sunday, 15 September, whereupon Henry sent his body back to England (his tomb is behind the high altar in Westminster Abbey).

The English had managed partially to flood Harfleur town, and that and the broaching of the ditches by the French had allowed sewage to contaminate the water supply. More would die in the days to come until soon it had become a major epidemic. The day after the bishop died, the French mounted a sally from the town, and recaptured Clarence's ditch. They were quickly driven off, but for the rest of the day taunts about the laziness of the besiegers were shouted from the ramparts. However, the barbican fell into English hands the next day, 17 September, and was set on fire in the process. Henry sent heralds to the town again to invite surrender, while ordering the army to prepare to assault the walls. All night, the English guns kept up a bombardment on the walls to prevent the defenders from repairing the breaches and to keep them awake, while the men-at-arms positioned themselves for an attack the following morning.

The attack never happened. In the town, damage to houses and to the inhabitants was considerable; the English had diverted the water supply, rations were running short and dysentery had made its appearance there too. On the morning of Wednesday, 18 September, the garrison commander agreed that, if he was not relieved by the following Sunday, 22 September, he would give up the town. King Henry accepted hostages from the nobility inside Harfleur; a truce was declared and all shelling, mining and attacks by both sides ceased. As pleas for help had gone out to both the French king and the dauphin, de Goucourt had a reasonable expectation that he would still be rescued; unfortunately for him, the king was in the grip of one of his regular bouts of madness and the dauphin was an idle and obese eighteen-year-old uninterested in the tribulations of his subjects. Not all of Henry's soldiers were happy: if the town was given up by agreement, then the possibilities of plunder would be severely limited, whereas a successful assault would, according to the customs of war of the time, permit an unbridled sack and the profits thereof.

On the morning of 22 September 1415, Raul, sire de Goucourt, and the sire d'Estouteville, who had been commander of the town before Goucourt's arrival, appeared before King Henry and handed over the keys to the city. The English army began to repair the damage that they had created – the dung barrels by the captured barbican were still smouldering two weeks later – while Henry stated his demands. Those civilians not required to run essential services within Harfleur and soldiers of no monetary value were expelled and escorted out of the army's zone of occupation, while, on 27 September, de Goucourt, d'Estouteville and 200 French knights and men-at-arms were allowed to leave, having promised to report at Calais on 11 November with the cash for their agreed ransoms, or jewels or plate in lieu. King Henry now appointed his uncle Thomas Beaufort,* earl of Dorset and Admiral of England, as warden and commander of Harfleur, the garrison to be his own retinue of 100 men-at-arms and 300 archers. By now, the health of the army was a serious worry. While battle deaths were not excessive, those from dysentery were mounting, and added to them was an outbreak of what was probably food poisoning from eating unripe fruit or contaminated oysters, undercooked shellfish and prawns, which thrive in sewage. Exact numbers are hard to come by, but according to some estimates around 2,000 English soldiers died and around the same number had to be sent back to England, too ill to continue on campaign. Among these latter were the duke of Clarence,

---

* He was the youngest of John of Gaunt's sons out of Katherine Swynford.

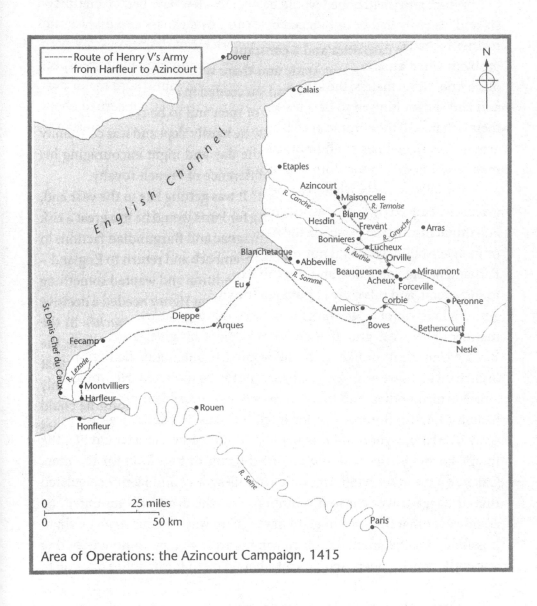

the now totally loyal Edmund Mortimer, earl of March, and John Mowbray, second duke of Norfolk and Earl Marshal of England.*

What Henry had hoped would be over in a few days had taken thirty-six and his army had been reduced by a third by sickness and disease and further by battle casualties and a constant trickle of desertion – always a problem when an army was static and there was no immediate prospect of a battle. Nevertheless, the king had succeeded in capturing a major port and had shown himself to be a leader of men and to be concerned about their welfare. All the chroniclers tell how he hardly slept and was constantly around the siege lines at all hours of the day and night encouraging his men – a far cry from the sloth and indifference of French royalty.

The question was: what to do next? It was getting late in the year and, given the reduced size of his army, going for Paris would be too great a risk and might in any case persuade the Armagnac and Burgundian factions to unite against him. He could not simply re-embark and return to England – Parliament had voted the funds for this expedition and wanted something to show for it, and this early in his reign the young Henry needed a decisive and obvious victory. He wanted to carry out a great *chevauchée* in the manner of his great-grandfather, Edward III, or his great-great-uncle, the Black Prince, but, unlike them, he wanted to maintain the fiction that French civilians were his loyal subjects, not to be molested. He would only attack armed bodies, and there were only two possible options: he could head for English Bordeaux or for English Calais. Bordeaux was 450 miles away overland, a good month's march,† and by now there would be little forage for the horses and it would be difficult to find food for the men. Calais, on the other hand, was only 170 miles away, and Henry calculated that, if baggage was cut to a minimum and the army was mounted, he could cover that distance in eight days. There was, of course, just a slight possibility that he might be able to win his great victory without adopting any of the courses open, and he sent a herald off to the dauphin offering to

---

* His brother had been executed for treason in 1405, but the family had been forgiven and lands and titles restored. The appointment stayed in the family and his direct descendant (through the female line, the male line of the Mowbrays having died out), Edward Fitzalan-Howard, eighteenth duke of Norfolk, is Earl Marshal of England today and responsible for state ceremonial.
† At the most optimistic – it would probably have taken nearer six weeks.

fight him in single combat, the winner to have the crown of France. It was a schoolboyish offer, one which the dauphin rightly refused – and, given that Henry was fitter, stronger, harder and far more experienced, he would have been daft to do otherwise.

The army prepared to set out. We can argue about the exact strengths, but it cannot have been more than 6,000 – 900 men-at-arms and 5,000 archers, according to the *Gesta* – plus heralds, priests, artisans and servants. They carried rations for eight days, and, given that the type of horse ridden by most of the men needs a minimum of ten pounds of hard feed (oats or barley) and the same weight of hay each day, then a total of around fifty-four tons of horse fodder would have had to be transported, plus spare arrows, tentage, farriers' forges and armourers' kits. Some historians have suggested that this entire load was carried on pack animals, but, as the best packhorse can only carry a maximum of 250 pounds,[42] then 484 horses would have been needed for the fodder of the warhorses alone, to say nothing of the feed needed by the packhorses themselves. It seems much more likely that baggage-wagons were used, and with horse-feed taking up thirty-six standard wagon-loads, the baggage-train, cut to the minimum though it was, would still have been around seventy or eighty wagons and have taken up a mile and a half of road. It would, however, have been a good deal easier to handle than herds of pack animals.

Henry's decision to march for Calais rather than sailing away in safety was not universally welcomed. Some in his council pointed out that the French would feel bound to oppose him and that the English would be vastly outnumbered. Henry is reported to have replied that victory in battle was decided not by numbers but by the will of God – words he had often used in his letters as Prince of Wales during the Welsh wars, when he was writing in Norman French rather than the English which he began to use as king. Whether he really believed that God took a personal interest in the outcome of battles is another matter, but it sounded good and he certainly had great confidence in himself and in his battle-hardened army, depleted though it now was. On Tuesday, 8 October, reminders of the prohibition on burning and looting were promulgated and the army marched off in the usual three battles. Two miles north of Harfleur, they skirted the fortified village of Montevilliers, still held by the French, who made a sally. It was a brief scuffle in which a few of Henry's men were killed and three captured.

No time was wasted in attempting to take the village and the army moved on. Montevilliers remained in French hands, a constant pinprick to the Harfleur garrison, until 1419, when it was taken as part of the subjugation of upper Normandy. Next day, having covered twenty miles, the army passed Fécamp and again the French garrison made a sally and again they were swiftly seen off, but not before a handful of prisoners had been taken on each side. If the intended destination of the English army was not already obvious by their marching north, then intelligence from prisoners would have confirmed the intention to get to Calais.

While the French reaction to the invasion had been dilatory in the extreme, it had become clear to the council in Paris and even to the dauphin himself that something had to be done, and summonses had been sent out for the French commanders to muster their troops at Rouen, where they would be positioned to intercept the English whether they went for Paris, Normandy, Bordeaux or Calais. Now that it was certain that the English were marching north for Calais, the French army was ordered to concentrate at Abbeville, with the aim of preventing Henry from crossing the River Somme and forcing him to surrender or starve; or, if he did cross, their hope was to block his route to Calais and force him to give battle, whereupon he and his army would be utterly destroyed, the ridiculous English claim to the French throne would be abandoned for all time, and the war would be over. The broad outline of this French plan, if not the detail, would have been known to Henry from prisoners taken, but at this stage he could do little to thwart it – he had to get to Calais.

On 11 October 1415, the English army reached Arques, four miles south-south-east of Dieppe, having covered the very respectable distance of thirty-five miles in twenty-four hours, when they were fired on by guns from the castle in the centre of the town. Heralds galloped up to the castle walls with Henry's message: stop firing and let us pass through the town or we will burn it to the ground. The army passed through Arques without opposition. The following day, another twenty miles nearer Calais, there was a stand-off at Eu, where after a brief skirmish a threat to level the town ensured safe passage through it. On 13 October, the vanguard of the English army reached Abbeville on the River Somme. Henry had hoped to cross at Blanchetaque, where Edward III had crossed during his Crécy campaign, but he found all the fords staked and guarded, all the bridges destroyed, and a sizeable detachment of the French army waiting on the northern bank. An opposed river crossing was not an option, particularly against a numerically far superior enemy, and so the only course open now was to head south-east along the left (south) bank of the river in the hope of finding a ford or a bridge further inland, where a crossing could be made unopposed. The English army could move faster than their enemy – the baggage-train, though sizeable, was smaller than that of the French, and the camp-followers, though numerous, were fewer – but not so much faster that they could bounce a crossing easily. On 14 October, Henry was twenty-eight miles from Abbeville and south of Amiens, and, on the 15th, he was held up by the French garrison in the castle of the hamlet of Boves. By now, rations were running very short and a bargain was soon struck: Henry would refrain from attacking the castle and burning the hamlet if the garrison and the villagers would provide him with a resupply of bread and wine, although he issued stern strictures to his own men about excess consumption of the latter.

Two days later, the English army was at Corbie, only another eight miles up-river, and still they could not shake off the French, who continued to shadow them from the opposite bank. Now, however, Henry might be able to steal a march on his enemy. From Amiens inland the valley of the Somme lies roughly west to east until it gets to Péronne, where it executes a sharp right turn and runs north to south. If the English army struck south-east away from the river, it would have to cover about twenty-five miles before hitting the river again at Nesle, where there was reputed to be a ford, whereas the French would have to march all the way round the bend in the river, a distance of around forty miles, to get to the same place. Nowadays, with accurately surveyed maps, aerial photographs and hand-held Global Positioning Systems, such a march would be simple, but no such aids existed in the fifteenth century: Henry had to rely on those who had served in the area before, either as *routiers* or in support of Armagnac or Burgundian factions in France's internal struggles, on local knowledge obtained by questioning civilians, and on reports brought in by mounted patrols that ranged far and wide in front of and to the flanks of the army. By this stage, a mild form of dysentery, or at least the onset of very loose bowels, had caught up with most of the army and rations had been reduced several times. It was wet and it was cold, and there was no time to erect tentage when the army stopped to snatch a few hours' rest before continuing their march. Despite all that, by the evening of 18 October, the army was within spitting distance of Nesle. Patrols confirmed that there were two fords, neither more than three feet deep ('no higher than a horse's belly') three miles east of the town, and, while the approaches were boggy and the French had felled trees across the tracks leading to them, neither was guarded.* At the same time, the French had only got as far as Péronne, fifteen miles away. That night, the English infantry prepared the routes down to the fords and the king issued his orders for the crossing. Knowing that the French army, wherever it was, consisted largely of mounted knights, the archers were ordered to cut stakes, each six feet long and sharpened at both ends, that could be driven into the ground as a barrier against cavalry. Although the chronicles say that every archer cut himself a stake, given that the archers would be massed on the wings of the army or on the flanks of the battles, it is more probable that only a proportion of men were to be so equipped – perhaps one in five or one in six.

It was at this stage that it was reported to the king that a pyx had been stolen from a nearby church. A pyx is a box, often made of precious metal, which contains the consecrated wafer that is believed to be the actual body of Christ and which is used when the priest takes communion to a bedridden or otherwise incapacitated supplicant. To steal such an object was sacrilege, and, in view of the king's orders that theft of sacred objects would attract the death penalty, unit commanders were ordered to search their men and find the culprit. The thief was found with the pyx, made of copper gilt (*cupro deaurato*) that he presumably mistook for gold, concealed in his sleeve and was duly hanged outside the church where he had committed the offence. Most modern histories say that the man was an archer, but, given the value and importance of this species of soldier, it is surely unlikely that one would be wasted in this manner. Neither Thomas Walsingham nor the Brut Chronicle mentions

---

* The crossing was probably somewhere north of where Napoleon I's Canal du Nord joins the Somme and south of Béthancourt.

the incident at all, and the *Gesta* simply says that he was an Englishman. It seems more likely that the wretched thief was an expendable asset, and possibly even a servant.

On the morning of 19 October, a force of mounted men-at-arms, followed by a contingent of archers, crossed the fords with no opposition. After dismounting and handing their horses over to holders, they formed a bridgehead on the eastern bank to prevent any interference with the crossing. At about 1300 hours, the army began to cross, the baggage and non-combatants by one ford and the soldiers by the other. One French source claims that the soldiers made a raft from window-frames taken from nearby houses, presumably to ferry across kit rather than men. By an hour before last light, perhaps around 1630 hours, the whole army was across, carrying their stakes and other impedimenta, whereupon they dispersed in the moonlight into billets in nearby villages on the right bank. French cavalry patrols that arrived as the crossing was going on wisely did not interfere, although they would have reported the location of the English army to their superiors.

The French army in the Péronne area was already enormous and growing larger by the day as more contingents trickled in. Many internal quarrels had been temporarily laid aside in the face of the greater threat from the English, but, large though the army was, there were major weaknesses, not least in the command structure. As the king, Charles VI, could not be present, being made of glass, and the dauphin was persuaded to stay in Rouen, the Constable, Charles d'Albret, and the Marshal, Jean Boucicault, were nominally in command as the senior military officers of France. While divided command is never a good idea, it might have worked were it not for the presence of the king's uncle, the duke of Bourbon, the king's brother, the duke of Orléans, and senior magnates such as the dukes of Alençon and Brittany and the duke of Burgundy's younger brothers, the duke of Brabant and the count of Nevers, along with a host of lesser nobility, none of whom considered themselves to be under the command of anyone and all of whom had to be consulted and pandered to. What all were agreed upon was that the impertinent English must be stamped upon decisively, and, on 20 October, three French heralds appeared demanding that King Henry state a time and place for a battle. The king replied that he intended to march to Calais, that he was not hiding in hedgerows, and that, if the French wanted a battle, they could easily find him. The heralds were given a handful of gold coins and sent on their way. On 21 October, the English army was past Péronne and, traversing the area over which their descendants would fight 501 years later at the first Battle of the Somme, crossed the River Ancre, a tributary of the Somme, at Miraumont. The French made no attempt to stop them, presumably because they were now unsure where exactly the English were and in any case were concentrating on finding a blocking position on the road to Calais.

On 22 October, Henry's army struggled on, heading west across the valley that would be the scene of the Newfoundland Regiment's disastrous attack on 1 July 1916, through Forceville, Acheux and Beauquesne, then north over the River Authie at Orville and the River Grouche at Lucheux, before halting at Bonnières, with the vanguard under the duke of York two miles ahead at Frévent. The duke, Edward of Langley, the son of Edward III's youngest son, was forty-two in 1415 and had a reputation for political intrigue (his brother, Richard, earl of Cambridge, had been a ringleader of the Southampton Plot earlier in the year and beheaded for it), but he was a competent and experienced soldier and was on good terms with the king, who addressed him as 'cousin'. By now, everyone was wet, hungry and exhausted, and nearly all had some form of dysentery. Some sources suggest that, rather than constantly having to undo and drop and pull up their trousers, some men took them off altogether and tied them round their waists. As riding a horse without trousers is an uncomfortable experience, this is probably dramatic licence. The rations carried from Harfleur had long been consumed, and those obtained or sequestered on the way had run out, so the men were reduced to eating horseflesh from baggage-animals no longer required once their load was exhausted, and nuts scavenged from the woods and hedges. One chronicler bemoans that for the lower ranks there was only water to drink – not as precious as it sounds in an age and a country where most water was contaminated and ale was the healthier refreshment.

On 23 October, the army was at Blangy, another twelve miles nearer Calais, and it was there that they crossed the River of Swords, the Ternoise, another tributary of the Somme, and caught sight of the enemy army. As the English soldiers struggled across the stream of the Ternoise, they saw, drawn up on a ridge a mile in front of them, line after line, battle after battle of mounted knights, armour glinting in the weak sunlight and banners fluttering in such numbers as they had never seen or imagined.

Exact numbers are hard to establish: the English chroniclers underestimate the size of the English army and exaggerate that of the French and the French reporters do the reverse, for very obvious reasons. The *Scotichronicon* puts the size of the French army at 200,000, Thomas of Walsingham says 140,000, and the author of the *Gesta*, who was there, says that the English were outnumbered by thirty to one, which would mean around 180,000 Frenchmen. All these estimates are plainly ridiculous, and, while apart from the writer of the *Gesta* the English reporters were not there, men who were there and who were spoken to by later chroniclers certainly thought that the French numbers were far greater than they actually were. While clerks and churchmen can be forgiven for being unable to assess numbers accurately, professional soldiers have to be able to make a reasonable estimate of what they might be up against, otherwise they are likely to either refuse battle when they should offer it, or offer it when they should refuse. The most credible theory to explain the overestimation by English commanders on 23 October is given by Ian Mortimer,[43] who points out that in the French army the proportion of men-at-arms to crossbowmen and archers was much greater than it was in the English forces, and that every man-at-arms had at least one page, esquire or a servant; so, if these supporters were riding their masters' spare horses, then from a distance of a mile or so they would have been indistinguishable from combatants. Whatever the true figure, it is undeniable that the English were greatly outnumbered: certainly by two to one and perhaps by three to one – not as bad as thirty to one, but a daunting prospect nonetheless.

On seeing the French forming up in what looked like battle array, Henry ordered the English to do likewise, but, after the armies had stared at each other for an hour or so, the French withdrew. The English followed them as far as the hamlet of Maisoncelle, two miles further on, while patrols reported that the French had taken up a blocking position across the Calais road at Agincourt, a mile to the north-west.* It was now obvious

---

* The village where the battle took place is and was Azincourt in French and Agincourt in English (medieval spelling had not yet been standardized). In 1415, the English only found out the name by asking a local herald, and it is easy to mishear a Z as a G.

to all that there would be a battle the next day. The only way to avoid it would be for Henry to humble himself and relinquish his claims to the French throne and to English France – which he could not possibly do without forfeiting the loyalty of his subjects, in England and in France. He had already released the prisoners taken along the way from Harfleur, and, while this was dressed up as a concession, it was really a way of getting rid of useless mouths who had to be fed and guarded, and that was as far as he was prepared to go. Henry's men had left a trail of vomit and diarrhoea all across northern France; they were starving, sick and wet; their clothes were in rags; and they were hugely outnumbered by an enemy operating in its own land. But these were vicious, hard, professional soldiers. They had trounced the Scots, the Welsh, northern rebels and the French time and time again, and they had a leader in whom they had absolute confidence and who had absolute confidence in himself. They would fight on the morrow and they would win, as they always had, and, if any man thought that they were taking on an impossible task, then he kept that opinion strictly to himself. As Sir David ap Llewellyn of Breconshire was reputed to have said, looking at the enemy ranks: 'There are enough to be killed, enough to be taken and enough to run away.' For the men-at-arms, the presence of so many French nobles – easily identified by the badges and crests on banners, shields and surcoats – meant increased prospects of riches from ransoms, while for the archers there was a more personal motive. It may not be true that any captured archer had the index and second finger of his right hand cut off to prevent him from drawing a bow again, but archers certainly believed that would be their fate if taken prisoner.*

Shakespeare has King Henry going round his men during the night in disguise, in order to properly assess morale. This is surely nonsense. In a small army which he had personally led since leaving England in August, the king would have known perfectly well what state morale was in, and he had enough confidence in his subordinate commanders to know that they would tell him the truth and not what they thought

---

* The English V sign of two fingers is said to originate from this period, as archers taunted the enemy ranks by showing that they still had the requisite digits to carry on the fight.

he wanted to hear. Indeed, when sometime during the night Sir Walter Hungerford,* a thirty-seven-year-old who combined military command with diplomatic responsibilities, the speakership of the House of Commons and chancellorship of the duchy of Lancaster, opined that what they really needed was another 10,000 good English archers, Henry replied that he was perfectly content with what he had and would not accept another man if he was offered him – clearly not true, but again, it sounded good.

In the lines of the French army, spirits were high. Unlike their English counterparts, who were sleeping in ditches and under bushes, there was no shortage of tents and warm comfortable billets in the farms and houses round about. Men threw dice to see who would have the most important prisoners, including the English king himself, and the complete silence from the English lines (in fact on the king's orders) made the commanders at one stage worry that their quarry had somehow slipped away and evaded them. Patrols confirmed that the English were still there, and it was presumed they were so quiet because they were terrified of what would happen to them in the morning.

All night long it rained, and the English army slept, or tried to sleep, in a rough battle formation. In truth, there was no risk of their being surprised by a night attack – the French high command was simply not capable of organizing it, and in any case would have regarded it as dishonourable: there was far more glory to be gained in daylight, when all could see the deeds of valour that would surely be performed. A modern army would stand to – that is, form up ready for battle in all respects – at first light, but that was not the way of medieval warfare, where breakfast (meagre in the case of the English) had to be taken, final orders given and some encouraging rhetoric promulgated. At around mid-morning of Friday 25, October 1415, St Crispin's Day, King Henry ordered his army to fall in in its three battles, across a field recently sown with winter wheat.

The army was too small to have a battle in reserve, so the three divisions lined up abreast, with the duke of York commanding the right, the king the centre, and Thomas, Baron Camoys the left. Camoys, married

---

* He had supported Henry IV's seizure of the throne and was created one of the first knights of the Order of the Bath as a reward.

to Henry Hotspur's widow, was perhaps an odd choice as a divisional commander: he was sixty-five years old in 1415 and had little experience of command in the field, and his personal retinue was only twenty-four men-at-arms and sixty-nine archers. But he was a member of the king's council, had served on numerous royal commissions, and was known as a good organizer and administrator. Sixty-five was, of course, old for field soldiering, but not as old as is often claimed. While male life expectancy in England at this time was around thirty-five years, this is a misleading statistic, made so by a very high rate of infant mortality – death in childbirth or when very young. A member of the English aristocracy, if he survived to the age of twenty-one, could, assuming he escaped the plague and was not killed in battle, expect to live until the age of sixty-nine.[44] The king had anyway no intention of getting involved in a battle of manoeuvre and Camoys' main responsibility would be to ensure that his men stood – and that they would surely do.

Assuming that casualties and desertions along the way from Harfleur had been made up by reinforcements from England, then the men-at-arms, once lined up, probably in four ranks, would have covered a frontage of 250 yards or so. The 2,500 archers on each wing, probably in ten ranks, would between them have added another 500 yards, thus the whole army from left to right would have taken up a minimum of 750 yards. Henry now ordered the archers to plant their stakes, which were in two rows (possibly more), driven into the ground at an angle so that the point was at the height of a horse's brisket and staggered so that a charging horse getting in between two stakes of the front row would run into one in the second. If the stakes were a yard apart, this would indicate a total of 1,000 stakes, implying that one in five archers carried a stake. This formation ensured that a cavalry charge would be funnelled away from the archers and towards the English centre, where it would come up against infantry in line and be seen off. The baggage-wagons were probably in Maisoncelle, with the horses picketed nearby.

The army was now in battle array. We do not know what King Henry actually said to them, although the words Shakespeare later put in his mouth must rank as one of the most evocative speeches in the English language:

From this day to the ending of the world,
But we in it shall be remembered –
We few, we happy few, we band of brothers;
For he today that sheds his blood with me
Shall be my brother; be he ne'er so vile,
This day shall gentle his condition:
And gentlemen in England now abed
Shall think themselves accursed they were not here;
And hold their manhoods cheap whiles any speaks
That fought with us upon Saint Crispin's Day.

Of course, the practical difficulties of addressing 6,000 men spread out over a distance of half a mile without a public address system are considerable, even allowing for the fact that medieval orators were accustomed to addressing and being heard by huge crowds.* The likelihood is that whatever Henry said was repeated by officers stationed along the front, as was the practice in British armies of the eighteenth and early nineteenth centuries, or that he simply cantered down the line repeating a few encouraging words – 'Good luck, and do your best' – as might any modern commander.

King Henry's plan was the tried-and-tested English tactic: find a favourable piece of ground and wait for the enemy to attack. When it was clear that the enemy was not going to attack, or not just yet, Henry ordered the banners to advance – that is, the signal to be given for the army to move forward. The decision to move was doubtless influenced by the English flanks being unprotected and thus vulnerable to a French encircling movement. It is unlikely the French would have been capable of carrying out such a manoeuvre, but they could very well have despatched cavalry to work its way round behind the English line. So the archers uprooted their stakes and the whole army began to move forward in line across the muddy open fields. When all three divisions and their flanking archers had covered around half a mile or so, they were able to anchor their flanks on two woods: the wood of Tramecourt on the right and

---

* Nearer to our own day, W. E. Gladstone regularly held crowds of 10,000 or more for several hours at a time.

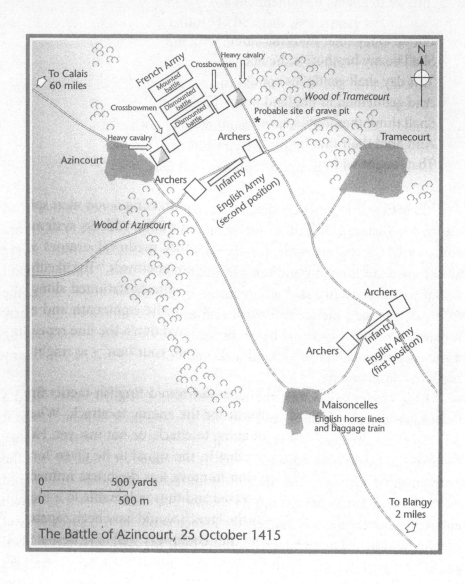

To Calais
60 miles

French Army

Mounted battle

Crossbowmen

Heavy cavalry

Dismounted battle

Crossbowmen

Dismounted battle

Wood of Tramecourt

Probable site of grave pit
*

Heavy cavalry

Archers

Tramecourt

Azincourt

Archers

Infantry

English Army
(second position)

Wood of Azincourt

N

Archers

Archers

Infantry

Archers

English Army
(first position)

Maisoncelles
English horse lines
and baggage train

0   500 yards
0   500 m

To Blangy
2 miles

The Battle of Azincourt, 25 October 1415

that of Agincourt on the left.* This move was, of course, risky, as a more competent enemy might have launched an attack to catch the English on the move. Henry was confident, however, that, given the distance from the French line, there would be ample time for his army to halt and take up the defensive, although an archer trudging through the mud with his stake over his shoulder and wondering whether his very tatty hat was keeping his bowstring dry may have felt rather less convinced.

Three hundred yards from the French line, the English army halted, realigned its formation and planted its stakes, watched by the enemy host. The size of the French army was such that there was not room for the usual formation of two battles forward and one back in reserve, and the three formations were one behind the other. They had learned something from previous defeats by the English: the front battle, of around 5,000 men-at-arms, was formed up dismounted, with the 5,000 men of the second battle behind the first and similarly on its feet, while the men of the third battle at the rear, another 5,000 or so, remained mounted. Other mounted men were stationed on each wing, perhaps 200 or so in each detachment. Missile support consisted of mercenary crossbowmen and some archers, most placed on the wings in the English fashion but some spread along the front. The standard French military establishment had two men-at-arms for every crossbowman or archer, which would indicate the presence of 7,000 crossbowmen, far more than were actually present. However, in the event, they played no part in the battle, so we need not detain ourselves overmuch in estimating their numbers.

There was certainly a French plan. The battle would open with an attack by the dismounted French vanguard, which would occupy the attention of the English infantry, whereupon the French heavy cavalry on the wings would circle round and take the archers in flank. Once the archers had been driven off, then numbers would tell and the English would be slaughtered, probably without the French even calling upon the second and third battles, although the mounted third battle might be used to pursue the fleeing remnants of Henry's army. It was a perfectly sound plan, but in hindsight it was not the best plan that the French could have made. They, after all, could afford to wait and Henry could not, so, if the

---

* Much of Tramecourt Wood is still there, but the Agincourt flank is now open.

French had simply remained on the defensive, then Henry would have had to either attack them, to his disadvantage, or starve. Even better, the French could easily have placed themselves between the two woods, instead of allowing the English to anchor their flanks by doing so.

Henry was well aware that his only hope was to make the French attack him. If he could panic them into a precipitate attack, so much the better, and the means to do just that was at hand. The overall commander of the archers was the sixty-year-old Sir Thomas Erpingham. A native of East Anglia, he had been a soldier from the age of thirteen, when he had accompanied his father to Aquitaine in the service of the Black Prince; he had campaigned with John of Gaunt in Spain and with the future King Henry IV in Lithuania, Prussia and Palestine; he had fought the Scots, the Welsh and the French: Erpingham was a true professional and there was little that he did not know about soldiering. He had directed his archers to their positions, supervised the hammering in of stakes, the stringing of bows and the placing of each archer's arrows in the ground in front of him, cantering from one flank to another as he ensured that his men knew what they had to do. Now, at a signal from the king, Sir Thomas trotted out ahead of the English line and hurled his baton in the air. It was the signal for the archers to unloose hell.

In the first thirty seconds, 25,000 arrows fell upon the French. The target area was such that no archer needed to pick a specific target; he just had to ensure that his arrow fell anywhere on the French army. The result was chaos, horror and surprise. Shot at extreme range, the heavy war arrows falling out of the sky were far too many to dodge, even if the packed ranks of men-at-arms gave any room for ducking and diving, and the only option – or so it seemed to someone on the French side, probably one of the royal dukes – was to order an immediate assault by the leading division, which began to move down the slight slope towards the English line. What should have happened now was for the French crossbowmen and archers to provide missile support until their line closed with the English, and for the cavalry then to attack the archers. It did not happen. The mounted knights on the flanks, stung by clouds of arrows to which they had no reply, bundled the crossbowmen out of the way, or rode over them, and launched a headlong charge against the English flanks. Headlong it may have been to start with, but over newly ploughed land on which rain had been falling all night, it soon slowed to a procession through the mud, with horses sinking to their fetlocks and soon barely out of a trot. Those riders that did cover the 300 yards between the armies found their horses blown and their way barred by a hedge of stakes. In the one-and-a-half minutes that the French heavy cavalry would have taken to reach the English, the archers would have discharged 75,000 arrows, not all at the horsemen, but enough to wound and kill men and madden and cripple horses.

A horse will not normally bolt, whatever the situation, and the medieval bit would have pulled up a charging elephant. But these horses were terrified and in great pain; arrows were stuck in their rumps, breasts and necks, and blood was streaming from their wounds. Heads thrown in the air, riders sawing ineffectually at their mouths, they panicked and charged wherever they could to escape the hail of arrows, and in many cases this meant bursting through their own infantry still plodding down the slope. The infantry, already seriously disorganized and disorientated by the arrow storm and exhausted by struggling through the mud in their full armour, were now even more disrupted, but they did, at last, slipping and sliding, hit the English line. Even if only half the leading French division survived to close with their enemy, they still outnumbered the English men-at-arms by two-and-a-half to one, and at first numbers told and the English began to give ground. The fighting was intense, particularly around the centre of each division where the commanders and their banners were. The duke of York was killed on the right, the king himself stood over the stunned body of his brother, the duke of Gloucester, and sustained a severe blow to the head that dented his helmet in the process, but then the archers changed roles and became light infantry.

Over the last fifty yards or so of the advance of the French, the archers had been shooting directly at them, and at that range the narrow bodkin arrowhead would go through plate armour, causing yet more death and destruction. Once the lines closed, however, the archers had done their duty and no more might have been expected of them. Unlike the French missile arm, however, these were not cowed foreign mercenaries but free-born Englishmen, and, dropping their bows and drawing their long knives, the archers stepped out from behind their protective stakes and attacked the French in flank. Normally, an armoured knight would have nothing to fear from such a lightly armed opponent, but, faced by English men-at-arms in front and the knifemen at flank and rear who stabbed though visors and severed hamstrings from behind, the French could take no more and the tide of battle quickly turned. Those in front tried to retreat but could not do so in the press of men from the second battle coming behind them, and soon knights and men-at-arms began to surrender, first in ones and twos and then in whole sub-units.

It was at this stage that the English baggage-train came under attack. When the army moved forward from Maisoncelle in the morning, the baggage followed so that the runners bringing the resupply of arrows had less distance to travel. It is uncertain who actually attacked the wagons. It was probably not the third, mounted French battle, many of whose members, seeing how the wind blew, or did not blow, had wisely left for home; it may have been the local landowner with a levy of his tenants, who would have known the paths through the woods, enabling them to get behind the English without being seen. Whoever it was, the balance could now swing back in favour of the French: the unblooded third battle might come back, the large number of surrendered knights, outnumbering their captors in many cases, might decide to reconsider their surrender and there were plenty of weapons lying about the field for them to pick up. The only way to ensure that the hundreds – perhaps thousands – of prisoners could not renege and restart the battle was to kill them, and that is what Henry ordered. The men-at-arms demurred: not only was this extremely bad form but also the prisoners represented very large sums of money in the shape of ransoms. The archers had no such inhibitions, and the butchering of the prisoners began. The attack on the baggage-train was beaten off, those French who could do so fled and the third battle made no attempt to return. The Battle of Agincourt was over.

It was a great and stunning victory, ranking with Blenheim in 1704, Waterloo in 1815 and Amiens in 1918. The French dead included Eduard, duke of Bar, Antoine, duke of Brabant, Jean, duke of Alençon, Charles d'Albret, constable of France, nine counts, ninety barons, 1,500 knights and several thousand lesser nobility, although how many were killed in battle and how many as prisoners is not known. The dukes of Orléans and Bourbon were taken prisoner, as were the counts of Richemont, Vendôme and Eu, and the marshal of France.* It was the greatest slaughter ever of the French nobility, from which it never really recovered. Today, the killing of the prisoners would be regarded as murder and a war crime, but Henry had little option. Many of the prisoners had surrendered many times and had then slipped away when no one was looking. If they were allowed to re-enter the fray, Henry's tiny army could yet be defeated. He did what he had to do, and no one at the time – not even the French – criticized him for it. On the English side, casualties were few, although probably more than were admitted to, with only the duke of York, the earl of Suffolk and two newly dubbed knights mentioned in the *Gesta*. If we assume that a French estimate of 600 English dead and wounded is too high, then the real figure is probably between 300 and 400.

There was little time to celebrate, for the army still had to get to Calais. The dead bodies were stripped of anything wearable, for the English army's clothing was falling apart, and left for the local peasants first to plunder and then to bury. Four days later, on Tuesday, 29 October, the army had covered the forty-five miles to Calais; and, on 16 November, having received the Harfleur prisoners with their ransoms, Henry and his army sailed for Dover.

---

* Orléans spent the next twenty-five years in (comfortable) captivity in England, where he won some fame as a poet.

Statue of Bertrand du Guesclin in Dinan, near his birthplace. Hardly qualifying as a hero, he was the nearest the French could get to one. Essentially a Breton mercenary, he rose from humble origins to be Constable of France, from a very small pool of candidates.

10

THE PRIDE AND THE FALL

Agincourt was the high-water mark of English military supremacy. England possessed a mobile army of professional soldiers who dismounted to fight on foot supported by longbowmen and were commanded by an experienced and capable officer class; the combination had proved unbeatable. Furthermore, with a popular and successful king, there was little incentive for internal strife or rebellion, and there was a parliament that was happy to fund English ambitions. If only Henry had lived.

As it was, Henry's crossing to Dover on 16 November 1415 took all day – the weather was appalling and the chroniclers remark on his immunity to sea-sickness. From Dover he went to Barham, then to Canterbury, on to Eltham and eventually, on 23 November, to London. The citizens of London, and indeed of the realm as a whole, had heard nothing after the siege of Harfleur; they knew that the army was heading for Calais, but that was all and rumours of disaster and defeat abounded. When on 29 October the news of the great victory of Agincourt reached London and was carried to all parts of the kingdom by heralds on fast horses, joy knew no bounds. The king's welcome by the Londoners was rapturous: he was escorted into the city from Blackheath, the streets were hung with flags and bunting, the mayor and aldermen paraded in full fig, as did the clergy and the city guilds; and on London Bridge he was greeted by a troupe of dancing virgins while the common people lined the route and cheered.

Agincourt was a great boost to English prestige and it terrified the French, who, for the time being at least, would avoid facing the English in open battle, preferring instead to lock themselves up in castles and fortified towns. It was not, however, a great strategic, as opposed to tactical, victory. Had the English army been larger, it could have struck for Paris immediately after Agincourt and won the war, but a professional army is necessarily a small army, and the huge disparity in populations meant that, to have any realistic chance of subduing the whole of France, Henry would need to find allies. In the meantime, the French had appointed Bernard of Armagnac as constable of France in succession to Charles d'Albret, who had been killed at Agincourt, while in the same year the ineffectual dauphin Louis died, to be replaced as heir apparent by his almost as ineffectual brother, Jean of Tourraine.

Henry spent most of 1416 in England while the French attempted to regain Harfleur. They managed to ambush a foraging party under the captain of Harfleur, Thomas Beaufort himself, and very nearly captured him, but were finally beaten off near the outskirts of the town. Meanwhile, peace negotiations dragged on, with both the Holy Roman Emperor and the count of Hainault attempting to mediate. The emperor, the German Sigismund, was trying to finally heal the schism in the church: the existence of two popes, each supported by different warring factions, made mediation by the Holy See impracticable. If he could broker a peace between England and France, then together they could resolve which pope was the legitimate one. Sigismund arrived in England in April 1416, to be sharply reminded on landing by Humphrey, duke of Gloucester – the brother of the king who, having recovered from his near-death experience at Agincourt, was even more xenophobic than most Englishmen – that the imperial writ did not run in England. Sigismund tried to arrange a meeting at Calais between Henry V and the new dauphin, but the new constable of France convinced his master that he could defeat the English and the meeting never happened. In the end, Sigismund realized that he could not achieve peace between England and France – the French would not offer more and Henry would not demand less. He seems to have broadly accepted the merits of Henry's claims, and in August the emperor and the king signed the Treaty of Canterbury, which, while giving England little of significance, did further isolate France.

As Sigismund was deliberating with Henry and his council in England, the French made another attempt to recapture Harfleur, by blockading the port with their fleet. On 15 August, John, duke of Bedford, another brother

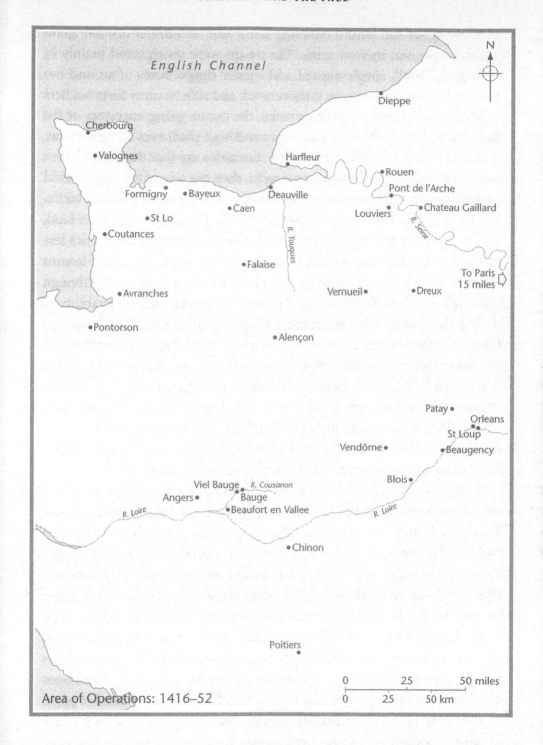

English Channel

Dieppe

Cherbourg

Valognes

Harfleur

Rouen

Pont de l'Arche

Formigny · Bayeux

Deauville

Chateau Gaillard

Caen

Louviers

St Lo

R. Seine

Coutances

R. Touques

Falaise

To Paris
15 miles

Avranches

Vernueil · · Dreux

Pontorson

Alençon

Patay ·

Orleans

St Loup

Vendôme ·

· Beaugency

Blois ·

Viel Bauge · R. Cousanon

Angers ·

Bauge

R. Loire

· Beaufort en Vallee

R. Loire

· Chinon

Poitiers

Area of Operations: 1416–52

0   25   50 miles

0   25   50 km

of the king, set sail with a relieving army said to number around 4,000 archers and 3,000 men-at-arms. The troops were transported mainly in balingers – small, single-masted and square-rigged boats of around 100 tons, equipped with oars for inshore work and able to carry forty soldiers – and probably two or three carracks, the ocean-going ancestors of the galleon, each with three or four masts and high platforms front and rear, and able to carry 200 or so men. The chronicles say that Bedford had 100 ships and, if three of them were carracks, then the size of the army would probably have been around 5,000. As this was going to be a sea battle, the ratio of archers to men-at-arms was less than it would be on land, as what was needed was men to board and fight hand to hand, with less reliance on missile support. The French had obviously forgotten the lessons of Sluys (which had admittedly been fought a long time ago): although outnumbered, had they come out to sea, the greater manoeuvrability of their galleys might have given them a fighting chance, or at least allowed them to withdraw unmolested. But, as it was, they stayed in the mouth of the Seine and allowed the English fleet to close. Once the grappling irons had pulled the ships together, the French had no chance: the English men-at-arms stormed aboard and the massacre began. The French were said to have lost around 1,500 men killed, the English less than half that. The remnants of the French fleet fled across the estuary to Honfleur, where shoals and sandbanks prevented the English from following.

In November 1416, Parliament met and agreed with the king that another expedition would be necessary to force the French to see justice. This time Henry would subdue France piece by piece, beginning with Normandy. The money was voted, taxes imposed, loans raised, and in the spring of 1417 recruiting of soldiers and impressment of ships began. Henry was well aware that after Agincourt no French army would face him in open field. If he was to bring Normandy back to its true allegiance, he would have to do it by capturing the cities, and that meant large quantities of siege engines and cannon with the requisite ammunition. Cannon-balls were still mostly of stone, but a primitive form of incendiary shell had been developed consisting of a hollow iron ball stuffed with tow soaked in pitch.

In June 1417, the earl of Huntingdon was despatched with a naval squadron to chase off some Genoese ships in French service based in Honfleur. Once he had sunk, captured or caused them to flee, the main army of around 10,000 all ranks, in the rough proportion of three archers to one man-at-arms, embarked at Southampton on 30 July and landed at the mouth of the River Touques, just north of Deauville, on 2 August. Progress was swift and Henry was aided by a resurgence of civil war between the Armagnac and Burgundian factions. The Armagnacs, supporting the dauphin, would not treat with England, but Jean the Fearless, duke of Burgundy, was ambivalent: he would not openly side with Henry but he would not attack him either, unless it looked as if his interests were threatened. From the bridgehead at Touques, the English navy ferried men, stores and siege engines along the coast and up the River Orne, and the siege of Caen began in mid-August 1417.

Long sieges did not suit the English way of waging war. England relied on mobile, rapidly moving armies that could march out of trouble if faced by far larger but ponderous enemies, and in any case being static for long periods attracted sickness. English siege commanders cut corners – they had to – and, as soon as there seemed to be the slightest chance of success, they tended to order an assault, always assuming that the garrison could not be persuaded to surrender first. After blocking all routes in and out of Caen and bombarding the city, the English army assaulted over the walls on 4 September. Then began the usual horror suffered by a civilian population in a town stormed by English soldiers, as the men, fired up by the lust of battle and the adrenalin of the attack, took revenge for the dangers they faced and the death of their comrades on anyone who was foolish enough to be on the streets. If there was nobody on the streets to rape, plunder and kill, then the houses were broken into and anything movable was appropriated and anyone resisting (and many who were not) slaughtered. The garrison had evacuated the town and taken refuge in the citadel and, once the English army had been brought under control once more, that too was invested. On 21 September, the garrison, bereft of any hope of help from Paris, surrendered.

There was always a problem with English soldiers, who, once they had stormed a town, saw plunder and rapine as their right. As, however, Henry maintained that the citizens of France were his subjects, he had no wish to make war upon them. Those citizens who resisted, on the other hand, could be considered traitors and dealt with accordingly, and that formed the basis of some sort of excuse, albeit a rather feeble one, for the treatment meted out to civilians. The fate of Caen was, however, salutary: other towns smaller or less well fortified drew the obvious inference and surrendered before they were invested. By November, a wide swathe of territory between Verneuil and Alençon had been taken; in the middle of the month, the dukes of Brittany, Anjou and Maine signed a treaty of neutrality with Henry, to last for ten months. Falaise, the well-fortified birthplace of the Conqueror, held out but fell after a three-month siege on 16 February 1418. By the end of March, Bayeux, St Lô, Coutances, Avranches and Pontorson had either surrendered or been captured, and Cherbourg, at the end of the Cotentin peninsula, capitulated after a five-month siege on 27 September. During all this time, the Armagnacs were far too busy with the Burgundians to offer any respite to their embattled and besieged compatriots, while Henry studiously avoided any provocation to the duke of Burgundy and was careful not to appear to be threatening Paris, which was held by the Armagnacs but coveted by the Burgundians.

In June 1418, Louviers fell, a siege personally supervised by the king himself, and as a cannon-ball from the defenders had gone right through the royal tent, the gun crew responsible were duly hanged. The capital of Normandy, Rouen, still held out. It was not only a political objective but also an enormously rich town which housed the main French shipyards, and, although mastery at sea was now firmly in the hands of the English, it was important to keep it so and this meant the capture or destruction of the yards. In late July, Henry took Pont-de-l'Arche, just upstream of Rouen, and established an outpost there with a huge chain stretched across the river. With the English already controlling the mouth of the Seine, this meant that Rouen was cut off from any relief by water. The town was the strongest yet tackled by the English: the walls were five miles in circumference, the gates were well fortified by barbicans in good repair, and there were towers housing cannon at regular intervals. The garrison, said to be 4,000 men-at-arms – probably a lot less but still a very powerful force – was commanded by Guy Le Boutellier, an experienced and determined soldier. Well aware of what was happening in the rest of Normandy, he had ample time to prepare the city for a siege. He had levelled the suburbs outside the wall to offer no cover for the besiegers, the ditch around the walls had been deepened and the excavated earth used to construct a bank along the inside of the walls to absorb the shock of cannon fire, and rations and water had been stockpiled. So confident was he of holding out that refugees from all over Normandy had been allowed in, and many of the civilian population had been armed with crossbows.

By now, the English were expert at siege-craft, even if they would much rather not get tied down in doing it. The king's army surrounded the city with the siege lines divided into sectors, seven on the northern side of the river and one on the south, each commanded by a senior officer. Four main redoubts were dug and connected by trenches, and the English engineers threw a pontoon bridge across the river downstream. All routes in and out were cut off and the bombardment began. Le Boutellier was confident that, even if he could not be relieved by river, an army from Paris would surely move across country to his aid. Unfortunately for him, nobody in Paris was in the slightest bit interested in his plight, or, if they were, they were unable to do anything about it. In 1417, Dauphin Jean had died, to be replaced by another, as yet unprepossessing, brother Charles. There was still no strong single central authority, and, in 1418, the Burgundians had managed to spark off a popular uprising in Paris that threw out the Armagnacs and lynched the new constable. The French chroniclers say that by the autumn the occupants of Rouen were reduced to eating horses,* and, when these were all gone, dogs and cats, followed by rats, were next.

Those who had previously sought refuge in the city were now considered useless mouths, and several hundred men, women and children, already half-starved, were expelled. King Henry would not allow them to pass through his lines, nor would he provide them with food – as he rightly said, 'I did not put them there' – although he did relent on Christmas Day 1418, when he sent one day's rations into no-man's-land. The expulsion of the non-effectives in order to make the rations stretch a little further was too late, however, and, on 31 December, a group of French knights appeared on the battlements asking for parley. Henry kept them waiting, but, on 2 January, negotiations were opened and the garrison commander agreed

---

* As horseflesh was and still is sold openly for human consumption in France, this cannot have been any great hardship, but it did reduce the number of cavalry and transport animals.

that, if no relief force appeared by 19 January, then he would surrender the city and accept the English terms – which were surprisingly generous. Although an indemnity of 300,000 crowns (£50,000) was to be paid, the garrison could march out to safety, without their weapons and having sworn not to take up arms against the English for one year, and civilians who took an oath of allegiance to Henry would not have their houses or property plundered. No relief force appeared, nor was there any likelihood of one, and so the city of Rouen passed into English hands. Henry spent two months repairing the damage and then continued the subjugation of the rest of Normandy. By the end of the year 1419, the whole of the duchy was once more in English hands.

The military conquest of Normandy was only the first step in re-establishing sovereignty there, and Henry was assiduous in setting up an administration to govern it and make it self-supporting as far as possible. Normans who would not swear allegiance had their lands confiscated and awarded to Englishmen, but those loyal to the English cause were kept on as wardens, bailiffs and justices. In general, the most senior appointments went to Englishmen, but otherwise the existing civil service, such as it was, was re-employed. Normans who took the oath could, for a payment of tenpence (£0.04), be given a certificate which was supposed to protect them from molestation by English patrols or check-points. As with Calais, Henry wanted to encourage English settlers, and several thousand, mainly of the minor gentry or the merchant classes, would migrate to Normandy in the years to come. Many of them married Norman girls and over the centuries became absorbed into the native population, and, while some of their descendants are still there today, with names rendered into French approximations, any sense of Englishness has long gone. While not all of Normandy welcomed English rule, and the taxes levied to make the duchy independent of English subsidy were much heavier than those imposed before (or perhaps were collected more efficiently), there was surprisingly little resistance. A few brigands led by dispossessed Frenchmen hid in the woods, and were duly hanged when caught, but the Norman bureaucrats stayed loyal and the English garrison left in Normandy was tiny – had the English presence been unpopular, an uprising could easily have expelled them. The fact that Normandy remained English for another thirty years would indicate that, however oppressive some aspects of English rule might have been, it was preferable to that of the French.

Then came a stroke of luck for England, and Henry got his ally. Despite the fierce enmity between the Burgundian and Armagnac factions, Jean the Fearless, duke of Burgundy, was increasingly concerned by English military successes. He had no time for the dauphin or his Orléanist supporters, but neither did he want English rule over the whole of France – that was something he coveted for himself, in due time. Negotiations between the two opposing French camps were opened, and it appeared to the Burgundians that, despite the appalling fate that they themselves had meted out to the Armagnacs in the Paris uprising, when hundreds of the latter were killed out of hand, some form of compromise agreement might be arrived at. On 10 September 1419, at Montereau on the River Yonne, forty miles south-east of Paris, the duke of Burgundy arrived to pay homage to the twenty-year-old dauphin. As he knelt, the Armagnacs, who had no intention of forgetting or forgiving, struck and Jean was hacked to pieces, his right hand being cut off first, to stop him raising the devil. It was claimed by the Burgundians that the dauphin had personally given the signal for the attack and, true or not, the murder sent shock waves throughout France, with many in Paris and the north blaming the dauphin for all the ills that the war had brought upon them. Duke Jean's heir, Philip, a mature man of twenty-five, was horrified and immediately made overtures to the only man who could help him to exact revenge – Henry V of England. In December 1419, a formal treaty of alliance between England and Burgundy was signed, whereby Philip would recognize Henry's claim to the French throne and Henry in turn would not interfere with the Burgundian territories other than as the feudal overlord.

From now on, it would be Anglo-Burgundian armies that would campaign to conquer Dauphinist France, and a combination of the threat of a now far larger military opposition, general war-weariness and disgust at the murder of Philip's father persuaded the supporters of the mad King Charles VI to make peace with Henry. The result was the Treaty of Troyes, which was signed on 20 May 1420 and granted Henry almost all that he and his forefathers had asked for. Charles may not have known what he was signing, but the treaty was ratified by the *parlement* and Henry was recognized as Charles's heir to the French throne. (Queen Isabeau, who had long presided over an alternative court in Burgundian territory, had conveniently declared her son Charles, the dauphin, the product of an adulterous affair and therefore a bastard.) Normandy was to remain an English possession until Henry became king of France, and he was to receive the homage of Brittany. The two kingdoms were not to be amalgamated but ruled separately, albeit by the same man, and Henry was required to conquer that portion of France not already pledged to him – which effectively meant south of the River Loire. In the meantime, Henry was declared the regent of France and betrothed to Katherine of Valois, the nineteen-year-old daughter of Charles VI. While this was intended as a dynastic marriage pure and simple, it seems that it developed into a genuine love match, and Katherine would eventually become a much-loved queen and queen-dowager of England.

The marriage took place within a fortnight of the treaty being signed, for Henry had no time to waste, and after a brief consummation the combined armies marched off to besiege Montereau, the scene of Duke Jean's assassination. Now any pretence on Henry's part of being an essentially kindly soul was abandoned: anyone resisting his armies was a traitor and would be dealt with accordingly. Prisoners were hanged outside the walls of Montereau, thus encouraging a swift surrender, and the army moved north to Melun, halfway between Montereau and Paris. Here the task was much harder: the town was well situated for defence – the citadel was on an island in the Seine – and the garrison commander was a particularly determined Gascon, Arnaud de Barbazon. The siege dragged on, with the English trying bombardment of the walls and, when that failed, mining. The French counter-mined and there were ferocious little battles by glimmering torchlight underground, but still the defenders held out, until at last in November there was no food left, nor a dog, cat or rat, and the town surrendered. Henry was determined to hang de Barbazon, who as a Gascon was doubly a traitor – to him as king of England and overlord of Aquitaine and to him as king of France – but the wily soldier escaped death by quoting a rule of chivalry that said, if a man fought with a king, he was therefore his equal, and de Barbazon claimed to have fought Henry in one of the scuffles in the tunnels. There was no such objection to Henry's hanging of Scots soldiers in the Melun garrison. Their king, James I, while in fact a prisoner in the Tower, was officially a guest and ally of Henry, so any Scots in arms against England were traitors.

In September 1420, Henry made his ceremonial entrance into Paris to general acclaim: the citizens might not have liked the English, but, if the price of peace and stability was turning out to cheer the traditional enemy, then so be it. Henry spent Christmas 1420 in the Louvre and then left a garrison in Paris to guard against any revanchist tendencies before setting off for England with Katherine. She was crowned queen of England by the archbishop of Canterbury in Westminster on 21 February 1421, and then the royal couple set off on a progress throughout England, partly to show the people their new queen and partly to enforce the collection of more taxes to support the war. Monies raised in Normandy and France were not yet sufficient to make the continuance of the struggle self-supporting, and, while individuals from great nobles to humble archers had done very well out of the war, the English treasury had not. Although there were grumbles, Parliament nonetheless agreed the necessary subsidies.

While the royal progress was going on, news arrived of the first English defeat for many a year, at the Battle of Baugé on 22 March 1421. The king's brother, the duke of Clarence, was campaigning along the River Loire and intended to invest Angers, but he found that town too strong for his force of, perhaps, 1,500 men-at-arms and 4,500 archers and withdrew to Beaufort-en-Vallée sixteen miles east of Angers. Archers out foraging took some Scottish prisoners who were on the same errand, and, when they were interrogated, they reported that the Franco-Scottish army of around 6,000 men was in the area of Viel Baugé, eight miles to the east-north-east of Beaufort. The chronicles are hazy about exactly what happened, but it appears that Clarence disregarded the advice of his senior commanders, forgot everything the English had learned from decades of campaigning in France and, instead of waiting until his archers returned from foraging, set off with his mounted men-at-arms – probably around 800 or so – in the hope of surprising the French. He seems to have charged uphill on marshy ground against considerably greater numbers, and the result was predictable: he was forced back against the River Couasnon and charged in turn by the Scots under the earl of Buchan. Clarence himself was killed, as were a number of his officers, including Sir Gilbert d'Umfraville, who had advised against the foray, while others were taken prisoner. Only the arrival of the archers under the earl of Salisbury prevented a defeat from becoming a massacre; Clarence's body was rescued and eventually sent back to England and buried in what is now

Canterbury Cathedral near the tomb of his father, Henry IV. Clarence must have known that what he was doing was foolish in the extreme, but, unlike his other brothers, he had not been at Agincourt and dreary sieges held little appeal. He may have thought that here was a chance to win glory for and by himself in a real battle, and that his mere arrival on the field would so frighten and disorganize the French that he could gain an easy victory even against far greater numbers. Had the enemy been entirely French, that might have been the case, but the Scots were experienced mercenary soldiers and quite happy to learn from the English and meet a mounted charge with a battle line of determined infantry. The result of the battle gave some much needed cheer to the Dauphinists but had little or no strategic consequences. What it did do, however, was to make Jean of Brittany have second thoughts about his own position; and despite the debt he owed to English arms – without which he would not have become the duke – he began to make plans to change sides.

In June 1421, King Henry returned to France with another 6,000 troops. He took Dreaux forty miles west of Paris, then went south, taking Vendôme, and then east to Beaugency. Having reduced those towns, he next considered Orléans, but, concluding that a siege of that heavily fortified town with a strong Armagnac garrison would take too long, he bypassed it to the north. In October 1421, he laid siege to Meaux, eighteen miles east of Paris, hoping that it could be taken before the winter set in. Alas, that was not to be, and, as the weather got wetter and colder, dysentery and an outbreak of smallpox hit the army. Even the king fell ill and specialist physicians had to be summoned from England to tend him. He appeared to recover, and the siege went on, the only good news being the announcement of the birth of a healthy son to the king and Queen Katherine at Windsor on 6 December. Henry spent Christmas in Paris with Charles VI and his now reconciled queen Isabeau before rejoining his army in the field. Then finally, on 9 March 1422, the garrison of Meaux abandoned the town and withdrew into a well-defended locality in the suburbs known as the market, where they held out until 10 May. Henry was so exasperated that he had the garrison commander beheaded and his body exhibited upside down on his own gallows.

The English army marched on, responding to a cry for help from the Burgundian town of Cosne, 112 miles south on the Loire, which was being besieged by the Armagnacs, when quite suddenly Henry found

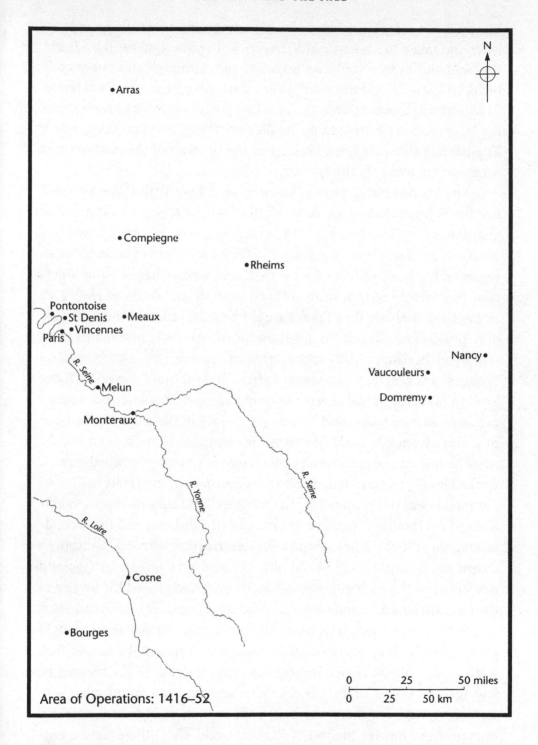

• Arras

• Compiègne

• Rheims

Pontontoise
• St Denis   • Meaux
    • Vincennes
Paris

R. Seine

Nancy •

Vaucouleurs •

Domremy •

• Melun

Monteraux

R. Yonne

R. Seine

R. Loire

• Cosne

• Bourges

Area of Operations: 1416–52

| 0 | 25 | 50 miles |
| 0 | 25 | 50 km |

he could not ride. He developed a high fever and was transferred to a litter and taken to his castle at Vincennes. The finest medical brains in England and France could do nothing, and, although still completely lucid, he knew the end was near. After summoning his council and laying down the way in which he wished his two kingdoms to be governed and his infant son to be brought up, he died on 31 August 1422. The greatest Englishman that ever lived (at least in the opinion of this author) was no more. He was only thirty-four.

On his deathbed, Henry V nominated his thirty-three-year-old brother John of Lancaster, duke of Bedford, as regent of France and guardian of his eight-month-old infant son, now Henry VI, and his youngest brother, thirty-two-year-old Humphrey, duke of Gloucester, as regent of England. At first all went well, and, when Charles VI of Valois died two months later, it seemed that a smooth succession of Henry VI of England as Henri II of France would be achieved, and the baby was duly proclaimed as such. Anglo-Burgundian armies continued to press south and the dauphin, whose court moved between Poitiers, Chinon and Bourges, was generally considered to be of little account – even by those loyal to his cause. Bedford was not only a competent soldier but also an excellent administrator, and he was well aware of the need to win what in a much later age would be called the campaign of hearts and minds. After he had purged the French civil service of Orléanist sympathizers, it worked loyally for him, and, despite the provisions of the Treaty of Troyes, Normandy was still run as a separate territory. Militarily, Bedford was ably assisted by Thomas Montague, fourth earl of Salisbury, and his second-in-command Richard Beauchamp, thirteenth earl of Warwick. Salisbury's father had been involved in the plot to murder Henry IV in 1399 and was killed by the mob as a result, but Thomas had proved his loyalty to the Lancastrians over and over again; he was an artillery expert and was said to have been Henry V's favourite general. Warwick had been brought up a Ricardian, but, when Richard II had turned against the family, they were saved only by Henry Bolingbroke's assumption of the throne; he had served in most of the Lancastrian wars and been on pilgrimage to Jerusalem. Between them, the pair, both in their early forties, directed operations to recover the rest of France. Under them there were a host of thoroughly competent commanders, men who were by no means all of noble blood but had earned their rank and position by professional ability in the field. All did well out of the wars, most became immensely rich, and many acquired French titles and lands which, by and large, they administered fairly and well.

At the height of English power, the whole of Normandy, the valley of the Seine, the Île de France (Paris and its environs), Picardy, much of Maine and Anjou, Aquitaine, Calais and its surroundings, and part of Champagne were under English rule. But however benign that rule was to begin with – and Bedford did his best to keep it so – there were problems. The English parliament was becoming reluctant to raise the money to fund the war, thus taxes in English France, particularly in Normandy, had to rise. There was a sales tax (effectively VAT), a hearth tax (council tax), the *pattis* (road tolls) and an ever-increasing tax on alcohol. On top of the officially levied taxes, there were the depredations of *routiers*, highwaymen and gangs of brigands, and the unofficial enterprises of many English garrisons, which ran what were effectively protection rackets. Feelings among the peasantry, initially thankful for an English victory that would bring peace and stability, began to turn. Nevertheless, Bedford intended to mount a major campaign in 1424 to subdue the rest of Maine and Anjou and then push south to Bourges and end the war once and for all. Before the operation could be launched, however, there was the distraction of Verneuil, an English-controlled town sixty miles west of Paris on the borders of Normandy. A Scots army had persuaded the town to surrender without a fight by convincing the garrison commander that there had been a battle and that the English army had suffered a major defeat.* Bedford duly set off to retake the town with a force of around 1,500 men-at-arms and 4,500 archers. Arriving before Verneuil, he formed up in the usual English way: himself commanding the right-hand division of dismounted men-at-arms and Salisbury the left, archers on each flank and a reserve of mounted archers behind. He then waited for the French – a force of around twice his number, composed of Scots and French infantry, Italian mercenary cavalry and crossbowmen.

The Scots were too canny to attack an English body of men formed up, however small it might be, and from first light until mid-afternoon

---

* The Scots turned up outside the walls with what appeared to be large numbers of English prisoners tied to their horses' tails. In fact, they were English-speaking Scots.

the two armies looked at each other. Eventually, Bedford gave the order to advance at a slow pace. The lines crashed into each other and the hacking and slashing began. At first it looked as if the Scots might win: their cavalry outflanked the archers and attacked the baggage-train, and some of Salisbury's archers ran away; but experience and leadership told, and, when Salisbury swung his division round and attacked the Scots in flank, the balance swung in favour of the English and the Scots were driven back and the slaughter began. The English were accustomed to fighting the French and thought little of it, but to be attacked by Scots was a very different matter, and many Englishmen had a genuine hatred of their northern neighbours. Few prisoners were taken and the Franco-Scottish dead may have numbered as many as 2,000. In the aftermath of the battle, a captain of archers by the name of Young, who had panicked when the Italian cavalry swept around them and run away, taking some of his men with him, was duly hanged.

Now matters in England began to distract Bedford from the planned campaign. His brother Humphrey had got himself involved with Jacqueline, countess of Hainault, who was now estranged from her thoroughly unpleasant husband, and had taken a contingent of troops to Flanders to enforce her rights. The expedition was a disaster, which might not have mattered too much except that it infuriated the duke of Burgundy, who had ambitions of his own for Flanders, so Bedford had to return to England to get a grip of his brother and then use all his diplomatic skills to preserve the alliance – a task in which he was hardly helped by Burgundy making (unreciprocated) amorous advances towards the earl of Salisbury's young wife, a grand-daughter of Geoffrey Chaucer. Returning to France, Bedford now began a methodical reduction of Armagnac towns on the Loire. It was not without setbacks, including a defeat for the duke of Burgundy, the loss and recapture of Pontorson in 1426, and a revolt in Maine in 1427 sparked by excessive taxation and English arrogance, but by 1428 all had been resolved and a major offensive could begin. By mid-August, the combined Anglo-Burgundian armies under Salisbury had captured forty towns and fortified places en route to and in the area of Orléans, the jewel of the Loire. And, on 12 October 1428, they laid siege to that town, the capture of which would give England control of the Loire and would trap the dauphin between Aquitaine to the south-west, Burgundy to the east and English France to the north.

Then there occurred one of the most extraordinary episodes of an extraordinary age. The adventures of the Maid of Orléans, Jeanne d'Arc, Jehanne La Pucelle, the Witch of Orléans, to give only some of her names, had been largely consigned to myth, legend and French folk memory until 1920, when, in the aftermath of the First World War – in which France had found herself on the winning side but with her heart and soul ripped out and desperately seeking something of glory and pride in her distant past – Joan became Saint Joan. Jeanne was probably born in 1412, the fourth child of five, in the village of Domrémy (now Domrémy-la-Pucelle) on the borders of the Holy Roman Empire twenty-five miles south-west of Nancy. She was certainly not a simple peasant. Her father was a minor official responsible for the collection of taxes, the maintenance of law and order, and the general administration of the surrounding area, and he owned, rather than rented, a fifty-acre farm with a substantial stone-built house. The transcript of her answers to questions at her eventual trial would suggest that she had an education of some sort, but whether any of her letters were actually written by her or dictated to a clerk is uncertain. All those questioned at a subsequent investigation twenty-five years after her death are adamant that she was given a good grounding in the Catholic faith and that she was unusually assiduous in attending church.

Sometime around the age of twelve, Jeanne began to hear voices, which she claimed were from various saints and then from God himself. It is not entirely uncommon for girls going through puberty to experience emotional turmoil, but Jeanne was convinced that she really was the recipient of divine instruction and sometime in 1428 tried to obtain an interview with the captain of the nearest French garrison, Robert de Baudricourt at Vaucouleurs, ten miles to the north. After several failed attempts, she was eventually seen by Baudricourt, who, after a number of meetings, became convinced that she did indeed hear the voice of God and that she could help in expelling the English. Baudricourt gave her an escort and sent her off to Chinon to see the dauphin, who also thought that there might be something in what she was saying and sent her on to Poitiers in March 1429 to be examined by a team of churchmen, an interrogation that went on for eleven days. By now, Jeanne was claiming that God had instructed her to go to Orléans, where she would lift the siege. It was around this time that she took to wearing men's clothing, a fact that was subsequently held against her, but which may initially have been a simple ploy to avoid molestation on the road, and later was part of her persona as a soldier.

While one's first reaction today might be to write Jeanne off as a mentally disturbed teenager, there must have been far more to her than that. Medieval man may have been superstitious but he was not stupid, and to convince a hard-baked cynical soldier like Robert de Baudricourt, the dauphin (admittedly described at this time as 'a graceless degenerate'[45]) and a host of suspicious churchmen inherently reluctant to grant the right of audience with the Almighty to anyone but themselves would have required extraordinary powers of persuasion. In the modern age, people who hear voices are generally considered to be mentally unbalanced and may be confined in psychiatric hospitals, so, assuming that, whatever the voices Jeanne heard were, they were unlikely to be those of God, the question arises whether she was mad or whether she invented the voices to lend force to her arguments for a military revival. While there are some signs of religious mania in what we know of her character, she does not appear to have exhibited any other symptoms of insanity – but then modern murderers who claim to have killed on the instructions of a supernatural voice are not necessarily obviously mad either. The conclusion must be either that her affliction was confined to the voices, or that she was inventing them. What motivated a country girl at the fringes of what would become France to set out to revive, or ignite, French patriotism, we cannot know at this distance, but patriot she surely was.

Meanwhile, the English had surrounded Orléans, and within a few days had driven the French away from the Les Tourelles, a towered fort that guarded the southern end of the bridge across the Loire. Then, on 27 October 1428, when Salisbury was observing the town from the towers, a lucky cannon shot from the walls took away half his face. He lived in agony for a week and died on 3 November. Command passed to William de la Pole, earl of Suffolk, another example of social mobility in medieval England. Suffolk's great-grandfather, also a William, was but a merchant, albeit a wealthy one, when he became banker to Edward III, then anxious to escape the clutches of Italian money-lenders. So successful was he that Edward made his son a knight, and later the first earl of Suffolk. The current William, like many younger sons, sought a career as a soldier and went to

France with Henry V in 1415. When his father, the second earl, was killed at Harfleur, where he himself was wounded, and his elder brother killed at Agincourt, he became the fourth earl at the age of nineteen. Suffolk's later career – his involvement in Henry VI's government when English fortunes in France had long been in decline and his extra-legal beheading as a so-called traitor in 1450 – has given him a bad press, but he was a perfectly capable and experienced military commander, albeit not of the calibre or reputation of Salisbury, whose widow he married in 1430.

The siege dragged on into winter and rations were running short for both besieged and besieger when, on 12 February 1429, an English supply convoy with a military escort of around 1,500 men commanded by the forty-eight-year-old Sir John Fastolf was intercepted by a Franco-Scottish force of perhaps 4,000 or 5,000.* In what became known as the Battle of the Herrings – the convoy included rations to last the army over Lent† – Sir John ordered the wagons into a circle and put his men within it. Attack after attack was broken up by the archers, and the French were driven off. The skirmish illustrated once again the inadvisability of attacking an English army with a strong component of archers standing in a defensive position of its own choosing.

Fastolf's reinforcements allowed Suffolk to tighten the cordon around Orléans, but that was soon nullified when the duke of Burgundy quarrelled with Bedford over the eventual control of the town, flounced out in a fit of pique and left the siege along with his men. Suffolk was able to control the west side and the south bank but could only patrol around the eastern approaches. Then, on 22 March 1429, a letter was delivered to the English camp signed by Jeanne and addressed to 'You king of England, and you duke of Bedford who call yourself regent of the kingdom of France. Surrender to the maid who is sent here from God, the king of heaven, the keys to all

---

* The model for Shakespeare's Falstaff, Fastolf was born of minor gentry in Norfolk and rose to eminence by his performance as a soldier, a progress not hindered by his marrying a rich wife.

† In accordance with a thirteenth-century papal instruction, Christians were required to refrain from eating meat on Fridays and throughout Lent, hence the herrings. The Second Vatican Council of 1962–5 made the Friday requirement advisory rather than mandatory, and prior to that soldiers in the modern British Army (and presumably in others too) had a dispensation excusing them when in the field.

the good cities that you have taken and violated in France'.[46] As nobody had any idea who this maid was, the letter was ignored, but copies survive. On 29 April, Jeanne herself arrived at Orléans, probably in a convoy of boats bringing supplies (the English had omitted to place chains across the Loire) which were unloaded on the north bank and taken in by the Burgundy gate, which was unguarded by the English. Jeanne seems to have had no problem convincing the garrison commander, the illegitimate son of the murdered duke of Orléans,* that she was the answer to his prayers, and, clad in armour and carrying a standard that had been blessed in the church of Saint-Saviour in Blois, on 4 May, she accompanied a French sally to occupy the fort of Saint-Loup, two miles east of Orléans on the north bank. There was nobody in the fort, but this could be attributed to God's work and was a much-needed morale boost for the French. Thursday, 5 May was Ascension Day, when Christians were not supposed to fight, but, on 6 May, the French, egged on by Jeanne, came out of the Burgundy gate, crossed the river, and attacked the fort of Saint-Jean le Blanc on the south side of the river and the fort of the Augustins just south of the bridge. This latter gave them a jumping-off line for an attack on Les Tourelles, which they duly attacked and captured next day. During this action, Jeanne was wounded in the shoulder by an arrow (as the voices of various saints had predicted), but she crossed the bridge and entered the town. The next day, Sunday, 8 May, the English withdrew and the siege of Orléans was over. The French were convinced, then and now, that it was all due to the Maid.

It was, of course, nothing of the sort. The English withdrew because they had bitten off far more than they could chew, they were running out of rations, the Burgundian contingent had gone, money and reinforcements were slow in coming from England, and Bedford needed the army elsewhere. To suggest that Jeanne was a military commander who planned the movement of troops and led them into battle, as some historians do (mainly French but some British ones too), is surely not believable. While the potential for leadership may be inborn, the execution of it requires training and practice, and it is not remotely credible that a farmer's daughter, however intelligent, with no involvement or previous

---

* The legitimate son, now the duke, was of course still composing poetry in the Tower of London.

experience of war, could possibly have acquired the skills needed to direct the activities of large bodies of troops. It was not Jeanne d'Arc who drove the English out of France but money, population, defecting allies and political in-fighting at home. There can be little doubt, however, that Jeanne was an inspiration to the French troops, who had become accustomed to being beaten by smaller but far more professional English armies. The French resurgence would have happened anyway, once the dauphin's supporters stopped fighting among themselves and concentrated on raising the funds to prosecute the war – and Valois France, which had not been fought over time and again, was potentially far richer than English France.

French forces under the duke of Alençon – a fervent believer in Jeanne – now began to try to recover English positions along the Loire, and, on 18 June 1429, 2,000 archers under John Talbot, the forty-two-year-old first earl of Shrewsbury – another younger son who had made his name as a professional soldier – and a contingent of 1,000 Parisian militiamen in English pay under Sir John Fastolf were surprised at Patay by an Armagnac army of perhaps 7,000. Talbot was forming up his archers when the French attacked in flank, dispersing them. The Paris militia broke and ran, Talbot was captured, and only Fastolf with some archers got away. It was an embarrassment to the English for which Jeanne got all the credit, whereas in reality it was caused by Talbot's overconfidence. Now many Frenchmen were convinced that God, so long on the side of the English, had switched allegiance.

Mad King Charles VI having died in 1422, Jeanne's next ploy was to suggest to the dauphin that he should be crowned in Rheims, the traditional coronation site of French kings, and by carefully avoiding English armies and garrisons – and in spite of the fact that much of the necessary regalia was in Paris – the dauphin was duly crowned as Charles VII by the archbishop of Rheims in July 1429. Militarily, this might have made no difference whatsoever, but it had an enormous propaganda effect and persuaded the duke of Burgundy to sign a truce with the French. When the Armagnac army moved towards Paris, egged on by Jeanne, many towns opened their gates to them and they got as far as Saint-Denis before Bedford drove them back and Charles ordered the army to disperse for the winter. Jeanne was furious and constantly urged the resumption of the war. She managed to persuade some of Alençon's men to accompany her and a few minor towns were taken and then lost again.

Jeanne's usefulness to Charles VII had, however, now run its course. She had inspired French armies to great things, she had been the motivating spirit for the march to Rheims and the coronation, and French soldiers had got almost to Paris with her name on their lips. But she was becoming an embarrassment; more and more she was excluded from council meetings and her supposedly God-given advice ignored. When in May 1430 Burgundian troops were laying siege to Compiègne, despite the supposed truce, she was captured during a French retreat back into the town from an unsuccessful sortie. It has been suggested that the French commander of the Compiègne garrison deliberately closed the gate in her face and allowed her to be captured.

Jeanne was transferred between various Burgundian prisons – and made several attempts to escape – before the English bought her for 10,000 francs (£1,600) and put her on trial in Rouen, the heart of English Normandy. The English had to destroy Jeanne's reputation, and, while most Englishmen seemed to believe that she was a witch, it was not for that that she was put on trial, but on the far more serious charge of heresy. There was some tolerance of witchcraft in England and in France, but not of heresy, which, if not abjured, carried the death penalty by burning. It was vital that Jeanne be found guilty, for by association the inference could be drawn that Charles VII was a heretic too; and vital, too, that the churchmen who tried her were French and not English. The first trial, before a French bishop, a French Dominican monk and a number of clerical assessors, opened in January 1431 and ended on 24 May. Jeanne conducted herself well, was careful not to incriminate Charles VII, refused to relate any conversations they had had and, when faced with a difficult question, fell back on invoking the will of God. She denied all charges but finally signed a disavowal of her voices and agreed to stop wearing men's clothing. To the fury of the English, she was sentenced not to death but to life imprisonment. Four days later, however, the English demanded the court take note that Jeanne had relapsed by once more cutting her hair short and wearing men's clothing, and, on 30 May 1431, she was burned at the stake in the Place du Vieux Marché in Rouen. Her last prophecy, which was probably invented in hindsight, was said to be that within seven years the English would suffer a greater loss than that of Orléans and that they would eventually be driven out of France.

With the witch burned and the Valois resurgence only just held, the English had to do something to restore prestige and emphasize Bedford's claim that he was the rightful regent for the rightful king. So, in December of the same year, 1431, an English bishop crowned the ten-year-old Henry VI of England as Henri II of France in Notre Dame Cathedral in Paris. It was not lost on the populace that the crowning was carried out by an Englishman and that it was not in Rheims. There was now a military stalemate and once again both sides turned to negotiation, overseen by representatives of the pope, who was now, following the ending of the schism in 1417, in Rome. In 1435, the interested parties gathered at Arras and the horse-trading began. It went on for weeks but neither side would budge, and the only result of significance was that the duke of Burgundy formally withdrew from the Treaty of Troyes and renounced his allegiance to Henry as king of France. This was seen by the English as a disgraceful act of betrayal – as indeed it was – and from now on Burgundy would either stay neutral or, if he fought at all, would do so on the side of the French. Burgundy's relations with Bedford had been difficult for some years, exacerbated by the death of Bedford's childless wife, a sister of the duke's, and his somewhat rapid remarriage. It may be, too, that Burgundy realized that, once the magnates of Valois France stopped their internecine quarrelling, a far smaller and less rich England could not hold the vast tracts of France to which she laid claim.

The negotiations abandoned, the campaigning went on and, in 1435, the French managed to recapture Harfleur and Dieppe. The loss of Harfleur was particularly serious for it meant that river traffic to and from Rouen would have to run the blockade of French ships, and the loss of Paris the following year was not only a propaganda blow but also added weight to those who believed Jeanne d'Arc's prophecy of five years previously. A far greater blow than the loss of Harfleur, however, was the death of the duke of Bedford in Rouen on 14 September 1435, at the age of only forty-six. We do not know how he died – the Brut Chronicle simply says that he took sick – but he was hugely overworked and could have fallen prey to any of a number of possible diseases. With him went the last realistic hope of securing an English France: a consummate diplomat who was genuinely popular, particularly in Normandy, he understood and respected French culture, was a sound strategist, and managed to maintain reasonably civilized relationships with most factions, including those of his enemies.

Even had Bedford lived, the problem for the English was that their forces were vastly overstretched, trying to hold a frontier of 350 miles with Valois France south of the Loire, and another 170 or so miles along the eastern border of Aquitaine. Without allies and without sufficient funds to pay mercenaries, there were simply not enough English soldiers to provide the frontier garrisons to guard against inroads. Mobile English expeditionary forces seeking out French armies and defeating them was one thing; holding the territory thus taken was a very different matter. Further negotiations in 1439 failed, this time over the position of English settlers in Normandy whom England would not dispossess to restore their lands to the original owners, and, in 1441, Pontoise, the last English stronghold in the Île de France, twenty miles north-west of Paris, fell. In 1444, a truce was agreed and the marriage of Henry VI and Henri II to the fourteen-year-old Margaret of Anjou, whose aunt was the wife of Charles VII, was arranged. As it turned out, she was a far stronger character than her husband, who would eventually fall prey to the Valois madness inherited from his mother, but even at this stage Henry was much more inclined to peace at (almost) any price than his great father would ever have been.

Henry VI as a child had been under the control of his uncles, but as he grew older he began to take more and more power into his own hands, as indeed he was entitled to do. A wise king, however, would consult with his council and the great men of the realm, and, even if he need not always follow their advice, he should at least seek it. The problem was that Henry was kind, generous, pious and abstemious; he hated bloodshed of any sort and only very reluctantly agreed to executions, frequently pardoning criminals from murderers to petty thieves; he desperately wanted peace with France and would go to great lengths to get it. While all these qualities would have been excellent in a country parson, they were not the qualities of a king, and both the in-fighting that went on in the English court as rival blocs jockeyed for power and the king's own clumsy attempts to make peace under the Francophile urgings of his wife inevitably had an impact on the war.

At some stage during the dialogue prior to Henry VI's marriage, Suffolk, now a duke and the chief negotiator, promised to restore Maine to

Charles VII, a pledge he made with Henry's knowledge but without telling the rest of his advisers. The result was the king's government following one policy – sovereignty over all of France – and the king following another. When the news got out, the London mob was furious, blaming Suffolk, and of course the precedent was now set: if the English would give up Maine without a fight, what about the other territories? It took another three years for the French to get Maine, as the English garrisons held on regardless of what their king might have promised, but finally they had to be surrendered. Normandy at least was thought to be secure: the population was genuinely loyal to their duke, the king of England, and a whole generation had grown up knowing nothing but English rule. The military garrison was tiny, however, and made even tinier by long delays in paying the soldiers, which encouraged desertions, and, when Charles VII sent his army into Normandy in the summer of 1449, there was little to stop them swiftly capturing the cities and towns, including Rouen, where they captured Talbot (taken prisoner at Patay in 1429, he had been exchanged for a French nobleman in 1433). Now only the Cotentin peninsula was held, and that was under immediate threat.

The French military revival came as an unpleasant shock in England. At long last, Charles VII had decided to be a king and had rooted out the incompetent and corrupt administrators and replaced them with hard-faced accountants who were able to raise the taxes that had hitherto gone uncollected. With much of this money he created a new, professional army. At long last, the French were beginning to learn the lessons of defeat by the English: instead of going to war with an army of well-bred nobles leading a half-trained rabble, there would be battalions of paid men-at-arms, archers, crossbowmen and light infantry, who would not be disbanded at the end of every campaign but retained as a permanent force. In addition, he spent money on developing and greatly enlarging the artillery arm. Now tiny bodies of English professionals would no longer find it so easy to beat far larger French armies: the era of English total military supremacy was coming to an end. English soldiers were still better trained, better led and better equipped, but the margin was steadily decreasing and there were not nearly enough of them.

Something had to be done to redress the situation in Normandy and, in October 1449, Sir Thomas Kyriell was ordered to assemble an army at

Portsmouth to sail to France. Kyriell, a Kentish man of fifty-three, a knight of the Garter and a knight banneret, had started his military career as a man-at-arms under Sir Gilbert d'Umfraville and had won ennoblement and promotion by military prowess. There was no doubt of his abilities as a soldier and a commander, but there was always a cloud hanging over him. He had been suspected of corruption and of fraudulent conversion of his soldiers' pay, although this was never proved, and his personal conduct left much to be desired. In Portsmouth, he allowed his soldiers to run amok – they even lynched the bishop of Chichester, who was bringing their pay – and the time it took to restore discipline, combined with an unfavourable wind, meant that he did not reach Cherbourg until mid-March 1450, with around 1,500 archers and 500 men-at-arms. Instead of marching straight for English-held Bayeux, as he had been ordered to do, Kyriell decided instead to lay siege to Valognes, a town of little strategic significance about ten miles south-east of Cherbourg, the only possible justification for this breach of instructions being that the garrison of Valognes might conceivably have been able to cut off Kyriell's supply route from the sea and his line of retreat. The delay allowed the French to bring up more troops, so, when Kyriell eventually marched for Bayeux, reinforced by another 1,500 archers from the Cotentin garrisons, he found a French army of about the same size commanded by the count of Clermont advancing down the road towards him. Kyriell did everything that he should have done. He formed his men-at-arms into line along a ridge near the village of Formigny, about ten miles north-west of Bayeux, where he had a stream to protect his rear. He put his archers on the flanks with some in the centre, and ordered them to plant their stakes and dig anti-cavalry holes in front. It was a classic English tactical position and Kyriell waited for the French to attack, confident that he could slaughter the lot.

Clermont knew better than to attack the English on their own ground and instead brought up two light cannon, intending to blow the archers away. The guns opened fire and the archers did indeed leave their position, but only to charge the guns, capture them and drag them back to the English line. This would have been the time to unleash the arrow storm, but instead Kyriell did nothing, perhaps through overconfidence, and that gave the French time to reconsider. At this stage, the constable of France, Richemont, arrived from St Lô with his division of 1,200 men and

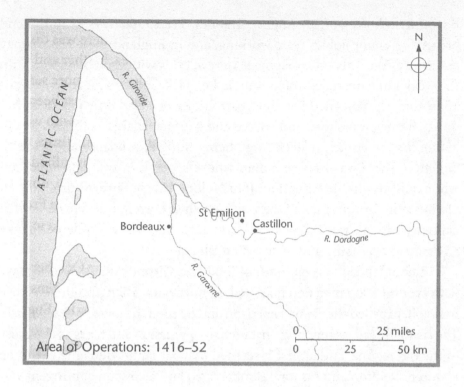

Area of Operations: 1416–52

immediately threw them into a flank attack from the south on the archers. With enemy in front and enemy to the left, Kyriell could only form his men into a rough semi-circle and hope for the best. The French closed and engaged the English in savage hand-to-hand fighting and numbers began to tell; the English were forced back against the brook and the killing began. Kyriell was captured and many of his men butchered, with only a handful managing to escape to Bayeux. It was the first major English defeat for nearly forty years. In June of the same year, Caen fell, followed by Falaise in July, and finally, on 12 August 1450, Cherbourg surrendered and Normandy, except for the offshore islands, was gone. A relief force commanded by Sir John Fastolf never left England.

Now only Aquitaine was left, and, sure enough, in late 1450, the French invaded. Initially, there was resistance; Aquitaine had been English since the twelfth century and most Guiennois had no wish to change that, but, in the absence of a sizeable English army, garrisons began to fall. The following year, another French army attacked, and, on 30 June 1451, Bordeaux fell,

Bayonne following on 20 August. The new French tactics of cannon and bribery of minor nobles were working, and in England there was dismay and confusion. There the magnates were at odds with each other and with the weak king; the rebellion in Kent led by Jack Cade – a far more serious affair than the so-called Peasants' Revolt of 1381 – had only just been put down, money was short, and charge and counter-charge as to who was to blame for the French debacle were being flung around, sometimes with violence. There was only one man whose reputation was unsullied and who could restore the situation: John Talbot, earl of Shrewsbury, now an old but still vigorous man of sixty-six, who had been released from French captivity with his ransom paid. In September 1452, he was ordered to take an army to Aquitaine and restore English rule.

Talbot landed at the mouth of the River Gironde on 17 October 1452 with around 2,500 men and marched on Bordeaux. There the citizens rose in revolt, expelled the French garrison and opened the gates to the English. The rising spread, as much against French oppression and taxes as in loyalty to the old regime, and at first it seemed that the status quo ante might be restored. Reinforcements for Talbot arrived and a Gascon contingent was raised. But Charles VII spent the winter concentrating a new army, and, in the spring of 1453, he launched it into Aquitaine. On 17 July 1453, Talbot marched to the relief of the town of Castillon with around 8,000 men and attacked the French artillery redoubt, a deep ditch with a bank behind it on which were mounted cannon – no longer the old bar-and-hoop type but with barrels cast in bronze or brass and a few even in iron.

The recent invention of the powder-mill meant that the gunpowder used was far more reliable and allowed a much higher muzzle velocity than that available in the earlier years of the war. And, as the guns were sited to produce cross-fire, the result was a murderous hail of iron and stone at a very short range. Even then, the fighting went on for nearly an hour as Talbot's men tried desperately to cross the ditch, climb the bank and get at the cannon, but, when a Breton force of around 800 infantry suddenly arrived and attacked Talbot's right flank, the end was only a matter of time. Talbot was an easy target: he was the only mounted man, he was not wearing armour (one of the conditions for his release from captivity), and he had an obvious tabard with his coat of arms. A cannon-ball felled his horse, and he was killed by a French infantryman with an axe. Large numbers of English were killed and the pursuit went on as far as Saint-Émilion, thirty miles away. Although nobody would have forecast it at the time, it was the last battle of the Hundred Years War. There were no more troops to send from an England riven with internal strife, and, on 19 October 1453, Bordeaux surrendered. Now there was only Calais, and the great adventure was over.

EPILOGUE

Nobody in England thought that the withdrawal of 1453 was the end of the struggle to retain English France; the French had huge problems trying to control Aquitaine, and, in 1475, Edward IV took an army to France but allowed himself to be bought off by the French Louis XI. From the 1450s, however, with Henry VI alternating between madness and weak and ineffective rule, the focus of English military energy turned inwards, and English armies, hardened and brutalized by the fighting in France, slaughtered each other in a vicious civil war that went on for thirty-three years. The dynastic struggles for the throne between descendants of Lionel of Antwerp, third son of Edward III, and those of John of Gaunt, fourth son of Edward III, were finally settled at the Battle of Bosworth in 1485, when Henry Tudor, with only a very tenuous blood claim to the Lancastrian inheritance, defeated and killed Richard III, a direct descendant of Lionel.* It would not be until nearly 300 years later that Sir Walter Scott would name this period the Wars of the Roses.

With the Tudor dynasty firmly in place, war with France resumed. Henry VII of England supported French rebels in what was termed the 'mad war' – actually a civil war – from 1488 to 1491. His son Henry VIII

---

* Henry Tudor, who reigned as Henry VII, was the son of Margaret Beaufort, who was a great-granddaughter of John of Gaunt out of his third wife, Katherine Swynford. In the male line Henry's only claim to status was from his grandfather's marriage to Queen Katherine of Valois, widow of Henry V. Richard III had a much stronger blood claim, but did not help his cause by (almost certainly) having Edward IV's young son, who would have been Edward V, and his brother murdered in the Tower.

sent a probing expedition to Aquitaine in 1512 and, when that met with inglorious defeat, followed it up the following year with an army of 25,000 men that invaded from Calais. Despite a stunning English victory at Thérouanne – called the 'Battle of the Spurs' because of the number of spurred French knights killed – a peace treaty in 1514 gave England little, and raids from Calais into Picardy in 1522 and 1523 produced no lasting gain. An alliance with the Holy Roman Emperor Charles V in 1542 led to the capture of Bolougne by English troops in 1544, and, even after Charles made a separate peace with France, Henry VIII's and later Edward VI's soldiers withstood repeated French attempts to capture the town, until it was returned to France as part of a peace settlement in 1550. Then, in 1557, Mary Tudor brought England into the war between France and Spain on the side of her Spanish husband Philip II, and, in the following year, a well-planned French attack on the weak garrison of Calais lost England's last outpost in Europe.

The Hundred Years War had changed English society and attitudes profoundly. At its start, English nobles thought of themselves as Europeans; they had lands on both sides of the Channel, they spoke a form of French, they travelled to and fro, they married into cross-Channel families, and they owed religious allegiance to the pope. By the end, they thought of themselves as English, they spoke English, they owned little outside England, and they were increasingly suspicious of any theological direction from abroad. English hooliganism abroad and xenophobia within may not have started with the Hundred Years War, but they were certainly confirmed and hardened by it. The war did make many individuals very rich, but it also very nearly bankrupted the national treasury. The effort of sending the last expedition of 2,500 men under Talbot in 1452 to relieve Bordeaux was the equivalent of despatching an expeditionary force of 50,000 today; in 2012, we had very great difficulty in maintaining a mere 10,000 men in Afghanistan.*

Militarily, the advances in England were enormous. The old amateur feudal system was swept away and replaced by a regular, professional army. As professional armies are expensive, they would always be small, but they

---

* The population of England and Wales in 1450 was around 3 million; today it is over 60 million.

consistently defeated far larger but badly led French armies whose activities were uncoordinated and undisciplined. Only when the French, very late in the day, began to copy the English system did the vast differences in population and national wealth begin to take effect. The experiences of such a long period of sporadic campaigns were to lay the foundations for the English, and later the British, way of waging war. Professionalism would stay. In the civil war of the mid-seventeenth century, both royalists and parliamentarians initially attempted to conscript; it did not work, was regarded as an unacceptable imposition on free-born Englishmen and was abandoned. It took great debate and much deliberation before conscription was imposed halfway through the First World War and it was stopped once peace was declared; and, although imposed again for the Second World War and for some fifteen years after, it was always intended as a short-term and temporary stop-gap. Britain would wage her wars with career servicemen wherever possible, and most British soldiers looked, and still look, with disdain at European pressed men. Indeed, a further reason for the success of English arms in France in the Hundred Years War was the steady supply of good junior and middle piece officers, not, as was the case in the French army, promoted for their breeding or their influence, but for their professional ability: England was and still is a class-ridden society, but that class system was and is mobile and men did and do move up (and down) according to their merits. England had a host of military heroes, France only the very overrated du Guesclin and the mystic child Jeanne d'Arc.

After the withdrawal from France, England, and later Britain, developed into a world power at sea, which was natural enough for an island nation. As Admiral of the Fleet John Jervis, Earl St Vincent, said in 1803 when asked about the possibility of a French invasion, 'I do not say they cannot come – I do say they cannot come by sea' – a remark repeated by the heads of the Royal Navy in 1914 and in 1940. An essential for the success of a necessarily small army is the use of technology as a force multiplier, and this was rarely forgotten by English and then British generals: from the longbow to the Baker rifle to the machine-gun to the tank, any advantage that would substitute machines or weapons for men was seized upon. A major lesson from the Hundred Years War was that a small nation with a professional army may be able to win its battles, but it takes many more men to hold ground than to win it in the first place. In her future wars, Britain would only operate on land as part of a coalition.*

France, very far from being a united country when Edward III stated his claim in 1337, was almost so by the end of the war. In the face of constant invasion from across the Channel, the occupants of Artois, Burgundy, the Île de France and even, albeit reluctantly, Brittany began to think of themselves as Frenchmen first, with provincial loyalties being replaced by a wider affinity, and there can be little doubt that the war accelerated nation-building there. It also created a reservoir of hatred of the 'goddams', the English who ravaged their lands. There cannot have been a town of any size in northern France that was not plundered, burned, attacked and despoiled by English soldiers, many of them over and over again, and, when the soldiers were not fighting over their fields and in their streets, the *routiers* were extracting loot and the English garrisons protection money.

In subsequent years, fighting the French seemed the natural occupation of English and then British armies. Elizabeth I sent troops to France to help the persecuted Huguenots. And, while for much of the Thirty Years War (1618–48) England was mainly concerned with her own internal troubles leading up to the English Civil War, she was always ready to prick the French when an opportunity arose, and one of the causes of the civil war was a perceived French influence over Charles I through his French wife Henrietta. Among the reasons for the Glorious Revolution of 1688, followed almost immediately by English participation in the War of the League of Augsburg (1688–97), was the pro-French foreign policy of James II. The War of the Spanish Succession (1701–14) saw British troops under the great John Churchill, duke of Marlborough, inflict massive defeats on the French and their allies. An uncharacteristic alliance with France during the War of the Quadruple Alliance (1718–20) only came about because Spain was seen as the greater threat, but the War of the Austrian Succession (1741–8) saw a reversion to the usual line-up. The Seven Years War (1756–63) brought

---

* This lesson seems, however, to have been forgotten in the recent Iraq campaign. British forces performed brilliantly in the war-fighting phase, taking Saddam Hussein's second city of Basra in a classic example of the cost-effective use of force in 2003, only to be forced into a humiliating scuttle in 2009 largely because there were insufficient boots on the ground to seal the borders from infiltration.

vast British overseas territorial gains at the expense of France, although French support for the rebellious American colonists from 1775 to 1783 was a major factor in the establishment of the United States.

Then, in 1793, began the longest period of sustained warfare in modern British history. The French Revolutionary and Napoleonic Wars lasted until 1815 with only two short breaks in 1802/3, when the English claim to the French throne was dropped, and from April 1814 until March 1815, culminating in the Battle of Waterloo in June of that year. That war was always referred to as the 'Great War' until supplanted by an even greater slaughter from 1914 to 1918. Even as recently as the twentieth century we have fought each other. The Royal Navy crippled the French Mediterranean Fleet at Mers el Kebir in July 1940 (after which the French attempted unsuccessfully to bomb Gibraltar) and then went on to attack the French port of Dakar in September of the same year. In June and July 1941, British and Indian troops fought a vicious campaign against Vichy French soldiers in Syria, and again in Madagascar from May to November 1942, while the Anglo-American Operation Torch landings in 1942 in French North Africa were stoutly resisted until the defenders realized the hopelessness of their situation.

Despite warm personal relations that exist between many Britons and French men and women, France as a nation has never liked us, and does not now. The feeling is mutual, and one suspects that the widespread British antipathy to the European Union might be a lot less intense were France not a major player in it. Some years ago, this author, having commanded the British contingent at a French Armistice Day parade in Limoges, was invited to lunch with the French general who had taken the salute, a delightful and cultured man who employed a superb cook and kept a very fine wine-cellar. After the consumption of much excellent claret and a considerable quantity of fine cognac, the general put his arm around me, looked me straight in the eye, and said: 'N'oubliez jamais: vous êtes l'ennemi héréditaire.'

Could things have been different? Perhaps, if Henry V had not died when he did, he might have been accepted by the French as king, with his French wife; or if England had not tried to achieve quite so much and had contented herself with recovering Aquitaine, unquestionably English by legal and moral right, and fought to have it in full sovereignty, then we might perhaps still have a foothold in Europe today. Certainly, there was no excuse for the Tudor laxness that lost us Calais in 1558. It is much more likely, however, that at some stage the sovereignty of English France would have been given to a younger son and that the crowns would have once more diverged. As it was, an English child king and internal strife at home after the death of Henry V left little appetite for further European adventures until it was far too late, and, despite her going to war with France many times in the succeeding centuries, England's future lay in the seas and in empire, whereas that of France was as a land power. For all that, the Hundred Years War was a great adventure, and a great and righteous cause.

NOTES

1 All verses from R. T. Davies (ed.), *Medieval English Lyrics*, Faber & Faber, London, 1963.
2 Seward, Desmond, *The Hundred Years War*, Constable, London, 1978.
3 Maxwell, Sir Herbert (tr. and ed.), *The Chronicle of Lanercost, 1272–1346*, J. MacLehose, Glasgow, 1913.
4 Thompson, E. M. (tr.), *Chronicon Galfridi Le Baker de Swynbroke* (facsimile reprint), General Books, Milton Keynes, 2010.
5 Sumption, Jonathan, *Trial by Battle, The Hundred Years War I*, Faber & Faber, London, 1990.
6 Brie, Friedrich (ed.), *The Brut; or the Chronicles of England*, K. Paul, London, 1880.
7 Bartlett, Robert, *England under the Norman and Angevin Kings 1075–1225*, Clarendon Press, Oxford, 2000.
8 Soar, Hugh D. H., *The Crooked Stick: A history of the longbow*, Westholme, Yardley, Penn., 2009.
9 Hewitt, H. J., *The Organisation of War under Edward III*, Manchester UP, Manchester, 1966.
10 Ibid.
11 Powicke, Michael, *Military Obligation in Medieval England*, Oxford UP, Oxford, 1962.
12 For the detailed organization of indentured retinues, see N. B. Lewis, *The Organisation of Indentured Retinues in Fourteenth Century England*, Transactions of the Royal Historical Society, vol. 27, issue 1, Cambridge UP, Cambridge, 2009.
13 Ayton, Andrew and Preston, Philip, *The Battle of Crécy, 1346*, Boydell, Woodbridge, 2005.
14 Hewitt, op. cit.
15 For a detailed account of the Battle of Morlaix, see Kelly DeVries, *Infantry Warfare in the Fourteenth Century*, Boydell, Woodbridge, 1996.
16 I have found the most convincing assessment of the size and composition of the 1346 army to be that of Andrew Ayton, 'The English army at Crécy', in Andrew

Ayton and Philip Preston (eds.), *The Battle of Crécy, 1346*, Boydell, Woodbridge, 2005.

17 Sumption, Jonathan, *Trial by Battle, The Hundred Years War I*, Faber & Faber, London, 1990.

18 For an account of how ransom worked, see Michael Prestwich, *Armies and Warfare in the Middle Ages*, Yale UP, New Haven, 1996 and Christopher Allmand, *The Hundred Years War*, Cambridge UP, Cambridge, 1988.

19 Wrottesley, George, *Crecy and Calais*, Harrison & Sons, London, 1898.

20 Sumption, op. cit.

21 The arguments for and against the 'traditional' site are well and meticulously examined by Sir Philip Preston in 'The traditional battlefield of Crécy', in Andrew Ayton and Philip Preston (eds.), *The Battle of Crécy, 1346*, Boydell, Woodbridge, 2005.

22 Maxwell, Sir Herbert (tr. and ed.), *The Chronicle of Lanercost, 1272–1346*, J. MacLehose, Glasgow, 1913.

23 McKisack, May, *The Fourteenth Century*, Oxford UP, Oxford, 1959.

24 Geoffrey le Baker, *Chronicle*, quoted in A. R. Myers (ed.), *English Historical Documents*, vol. 4, Oxford UP, Oxford, 1969.

25 James, G. P. R., *A History of the Life of Edward the Black Prince* (2 vols.), Orne, Green & Longmans, London, 1839.

26 Barber, Richard, *Life and Campaigns of The Black Prince*, Boydell, Woodbridge, 1979.

27 Martin, G. H. (tr. and ed.), *Knighton's Chronicle 1337–1396*, Oxford UP, Oxford, 1995.

28 Geoffrey le Baker, *Chronicle*, quoted in A. R. Myers (ed.), *English Historical Documents*, vol. 4, Oxford UP, Oxford, 1969.

29 De Smet J. J. (tr.), *Corpus Chronicorum Flandrensium*, Brussels, 1856, quoted in Clifford J. Rogers (ed.), *Essays on Medieval Military History*, Ashgate, Farnham, 2010.

30 Martin, G. H. (tr. and ed.), *Knighton's Chronicle 1337–1396*, Oxford UP, Oxford, 1995.

31 Ibid.

32 Sumption, Jonathan, *Trial by Fire, The Hundred Years War II*, Faber & Faber, London, 1999.

33 Prestwich, Michael, *The Three Edwards: War and state in England 1272–1377*, Weidenfeld & Nicolson, London, 1980.

34 Brereton, Geoffrey (tr. and ed.), *Froissart: Chronicles*, Penguin, London, 1978.

35 Preest, David and Clark, James G. (tr. and ed.), *The Chronica Maiora of Thomas Walsingham (1376–1422)*, Boydell, Woodbridge, 2005.

36 Preest, David and Clark, James G. (tr. and ed.), *The Chronica Maiora of Thomas Walsingham (1376–1422)*, Boydell, Woodbridge, 2005.

37 See Boardman, A. W., *Hotspur: Henry Percy, Medieval Rebel*, Sutton, Stroud, 2003.

38 Bradmore described the process in a Latin treatise *Philomena*, which survives (British Library, Sloane Manuscript 2272). He died in London in 1412.

39 Details of retinues from Anne Curry, *The Battle of Agincourt, Sources and Interpretations*, Boydell, Woodbridge, 2000.

40 Taylor, Frank and Roskell, John S. (tr.), *Gesta Henrici Quinti*, Oxford UP, Oxford, 1975.

41 Ibid.

42 War Office, *Animal Management*, HMSO, London, 1933.

43 Mortimer, Ian, *1415: Henry V's year of glory*, Bodley Head, London, 2009.

44 Lancaster, H. O., *Expectations of Life: A study in the demography, statistics and history of world mortality*, Springer Verlag, New York, 1990.

45 Quoted in Seward, Desmond, *The Hundred Years War*, Constable, London, 1978.

46 Pernoud, Régine and Clin, Marie-Véronique (tr. Adams, J. duQuesnay), *Joan of Arc: Her story*, Phoenix, London, 2000.

SELECT BIBLIOGRAPHY

Allmand, Christopher, *The Hundred Years War*, Cambridge UP, Cambridge, 1988

Ayton, Andrew, *Knights and Warhorses*, Boydell, Woodbridge, 1994

Ayton, Andrew and Preston, Philip (eds.), *The Battle of Crécy, 1346*, Boydell, Woodbridge, 2005

Barber, Richard, *Life and Campaigns of The Black Prince*, Boydell, Woodbridge, 1979

Barber, Richard, *The Pastons*, Boydell, Woodbridge, 1993

Barker, Juliet, *Agincourt*, Little, Brown, London, 2005

Barker, Juliet, *Conquest*, Little, Brown, London, 2009

Barnie, John, *War in Medieval Society*, Weidenfeld & Nicolson, London, 1974

Barratt, John, *War for the Throne*, Pen & Sword, Barnsley, 2010

Beffeyte, Renaud and Contamine, Philippe, *L'art de la guerre au Moyen Age* (3rd edn), Éditions Ouest-France, Rennes, 2010

Bennett, Matthew, 'The development of tactics during the Hundred Years War', in Curry, A. and Hughes, M., *Arms, Armies and Fortifications in the Hundred Years War*, Boydell, Woodbridge, 1994

Bennett, Matthew et al, *Fighting Techniques of the Medieval World*, Spellmount, Staplehurst, 2005

Blair, Claude (ed.), *Pollard's History of Firearms*, Mamlyn, Feltham, 1983

Boardman, A. W., *Hotspur: Henry Percy, Medieval Rebel*, Sutton, Stroud, 2003

Brereton, Geoffrey (tr. and ed.), *Froissart: Chronicles*, Penguin, London, 1978

Brie, Friedrich (ed.), *The Brut; or the Chronicles of England*, K. Paul, London, 1880

Burne, A. H., *The Crécy War: A military history of the Hundred Years War from 1337 to the Peace of Brétigny 1360*, Eyre & Spottiswoode, London, 1955

Burne, A. H., *The Agincourt War: A military history of the latter part of the Hundred Years War from 1369 to 1453*, Eyre & Spottiswoode, London, 1956

Cole, Robert, *A Traveller's History of France* (5th edition), Windrush, Moreton-in-Marsh, 1998

Colvin, H. M. (ed.), *The History of the King's Works*, vol. 1: *The Middle Ages*, HMSO, London, 1963

Cooper, Stephen, *Sir John Hawkwood*, Pen & Sword, Barnsley, 2008

Creighton, Oliver and Higham, Robert, *Medieval Town Walls*, Tempus, Stroud, 2005

Cross, Peter, *The Knight in Medieval England*, Sutton, Stroud, 1993

Curry, Anne, *The Battle of Agincourt: Sources and interpretations*, Boydell, Woodbridge, 2000

Curry, Anne (ed.), *Agincourt 1415*, Tempus, Stroud, 2000

DeVries, Kelly, *Infantry Warfare in the Fourteenth Century*, Boydell, Woodbridge, 1996

DeVries, Kelly, *Joan of Arc*, Sutton, Stroud, 1999

Dockray, Keith, *Henry V*, Tempus, Stroud, 2004

Emerson, Barbara, *The Black Prince*, Weidenfeld & Nicolson, London, 1976

Featherstone, Donald, *The Bowmen of England*, Clarkson N. Potter Inc., New York, 1968

Fiorato, Veronica, Boylston, Anthea and Knusel, Christopher (eds.), *Blood Red Roses* (2nd edn), Oxbow, Oxford, 2007

Fowler, Kenneth (ed.), *The Hundred Years War*, MacMillan, London, 1971

Fryde, E. B., *William de la Pole*, Hambledon, London, 1988

Girault, Pierre-Gilles, *Jeanne d'Arc*, Gisserot, Paris, 2004

Goodman, Anthony, *The Wars of the Roses*, Tempus, Stroud, 2006

Gravett, Christopher, *Knight*, Osprey, Oxford, 2008

Harrison, Brian and Matthew, Colin (eds.), *The Oxford Dictionary of National Biography* (60 vols.), Oxford UP, Oxford, 2004

Hallam, Elizabeth (ed.), *Chronicles of the Age of Chivalry*, Weidenfeld & Nicolson, London, 1987

Hanley, Catherine, *War and Combat 1150–1270*, D. S. Brewer, Cambridge, 2003

Haswell, Jock, *The Ardent Queen*, Peter Davies, London, 1996

Hewitt, H. J., *The Organisation of War under Edward III*, Manchester UP, Manchester, 1966

Hicks, Michael, *Who's Who in Late Medieval England*, Shepheard-Walwyn, London, 1991

Horne, Alistair, *Friend or Foe*, Weidenfeld & Nicolson, London, 2004

Hyland, Ann, *The Warhorse 1250–1600*, Sutton, Stroud, 1998

James, G. P. R., *A History of the Life of Edward the Black Prince* (2 vols.), Orne, Green & Longmans, London, 1839

Jestice, Phyllis G., *The Timeline of Medieval Warfare*, Amber, London, 2008

Jolliffe, J. E. A., *The Constitutional History of Medieval England*, Black, London, 1937

Jones, Michael (ed.), *Camden Miscellany*, vol. 24, Royal Historical Society, London, 1972

Kenyon, John R., *Medieval Fortifications*, Leicester UP, London, 1990

Lacroix, Paul, *Military and Religious Life in the Middle Ages*, Frederick Ungar, New York, 1964

Lambert, Michael, *Medieval Heresy* (2nd edn), Blackwell, Oxford, 1992

Lloyd, Alan, *The Hundred Years War*, Granada, London, 1977

Martin, G. H. (tr. and ed.), *Knighton's Chronicle 1337–1396*, Oxford UP, Oxford, 1995

Maxfield, Stephen, *The Battlefield of Shrewsbury*, WPG, Welshpool, 2003

Maxwell, Sir Herbert (tr. and ed.), *The Chronicle of Lanercost, 1272–1346*, J. MacLehose, Glasgow, 1913

McKisack, May, *The Fourteenth Century*, Oxford UP, Oxford, 1959

Miller, James, *Swords for Hire*, Birlinn, Edinburgh, 2007

Mortimer, Ian, *1415: Henry V's year of glory*, Bodley Head, London, 2009

Mortimer, Ian, *The Fears of Henry IV*, Jonathan Cape, London, 2007

Mortimer, Ian, *Medieval Intrigue*, Continuum, London, 2010

Mortimer, Ian, *The Perfect King*, Jonathan Cape, London, 2006

Mortimer, Ian, *The Time Traveller's Guide to Medieval England*, Bodley Head, London, 2008

Packe, Michael, *King Edward III*, Ark, London, 1985

Pernoud, Régine and Clin, Marie-Véronique (tr. Adams, J. duQuesnay), *Joan of Arc: Her story*, Phoenix, London, 2000

Powicke, Michael, *Military Obligation in Medieval England*, Oxford UP, Oxford, 1962

Preest, David and Clark, James G. (tr. and ed.), *The Chronica Maiora of Thomas Walsingham (1376–1422)*, Boydell, Woodbridge, 2005

Prestwich, Michael, *Armies and Warfare in the Middle Ages*, Yale UP, New Haven, 1996

Prestwich, Michael, *The Three Edwards: War and State in England 1272–1377*, Weidenfeld & Nicolson, London, 1980

Reid, Peter, *By Fire and Sword*, Constable, London, 2007

Rogers, Clifford J., *Essays on Medieval Military History*, Ashgate, Farnham, 2010

Rogers, Clifford J., *War Cruel and Sharp*, Boydell, Woodbridge, 2000

Saul, Nigel, *A Companion to Medieval England 1066–1485*, Tempus, Stroud, 2005

Saul, Nigel, *Richard II*, Yale UP, New Haven, 1997

Seward, Desmond, *The Hundred Years War*, Constable, London, 1978

Soar, Hugh D. H., *The Crooked Stick: A history of the longbow*, Westholme, Yardley, Penn., 2009

Sumption, Jonathan, *Divided Houses, The Hundred Years War III*, Faber & Faber, London, 2009

Sumption, Jonathan, *Trial by Battle, The Hundred Years War I*, Faber & Faber, London, 1990

Sumption, Jonathan, *Trial by Fire, The Hundred Years War II*, Faber & Faber, London, 1999

Sweetinburgh, Sheila, *The Role of the Hospital in Medieval England*, Four Courts Press, Dublin, 2004

Taylor, Frank and Roskell, John S. (tr.), *Gesta Henrici Quinti*, Oxford UP, Oxford, 1975

Taylor, Larissa Juliet, *The Virgin Warrior*, Yale UP, New Haven, 2009

Teutsch, Christian, *Victory at Poitiers*, Pen & Sword, London, 2010

Thompson, E. M. (tr.), *Chronicon Galfridi Le Baker de Swynbroke* (facsimile reprint), General Books, Milton Keynes, 2010

Urban, William, *Medieval Mercenaries*, Greenhill, London, 2006

Vale, Malcolm, *War and Chivalry*, Duckworth, London, 1981

Warner, Philip, *Sieges of the Middle Ages*, Barnes & Noble, New York, 1968

Watts, John, *The Making of Polities: Europe 1300–1500*, Cambridge UP, Cambridge, 2009

Weir, Alison, *Isabella*, Jonathan Cape, London, 2005

Wenzler, Claude, *Genealogy of the Kings of France and their Wives*, Éditions Ouest-France, Rennes, 2010

Wilkinson, Frederick, *Edged Weapons*, Guinness, London, 1970

Wrottesley, George, *Crecy and Calais*, Harrison & Sons, London, 1898

Wylie, James Hamilton, *The History of England under Henry the Fourth* (3 vols.), Longmans, Green & Co., London, 1884

Ziegler, Philip, *The Black Death*, Harper Collins, London, 1969

NOTE ON THE AUTHOR

Gordon Corrigan was commissioned from the Royal Military Academy Sandhurst in 1962. He was awarded the MBE (military) in 1996 and retired from the Royal Gurkha Rifles in 1998. He is a member of the British Commission for Military History, a Fellow of the Royal Asiatic Society and a Liveryman of the Worshipful Company of Farriers. He is the author of a number of books of military history including *Sepoys in the Trenches*; *Mud, Blood and Poppycock*; *Blood, Sweat and Arrogance*; and *The Second World War*.

ACKNOWLEDGEMENTS

The staffs of the National Portrait Gallery, the British Library, the National Archives at Kew and the Prince Consort's Library at Aldershot have all been unfailingly helpful to my often arcane requests for books and documents, most long out of print. The Dean and Chapter of Canterbury Cathedral were kind enough to permit me access to King Henry IV's tomb at a time when, apart from myself, that great monument to a glorious past (and with luck a reasonably good future too) was entirely empty. Even the most cynical could not have failed to feel a deep sense of spirituality. Mathew Bennett was kind enough to cast the critical eye of a medieval and military expert over the manuscript. At Atlantic books Angus Mackinnon, my indefatigable editor, Ben Dupré my copy editor and James Nightingale, Caroline Knight, Margaret Stead, Lauren Finger, Mark Handsley and Martin Lubikowski have all played a huge part in the piloting of the book from keyboard to bookshop, and I thank them for all that they have done.

INDEX